Marx after
the Kyoto School

East Asian Comparative Ethics, Politics and Philosophy of Law

Series Editor: Sungmoon Kim, Associate Professor of Political Theory at City University of Hong Kong

East Asian Comparative Ethics, Politics and Philosophy of Law. This series Path-breaking and field-defining works in East Asian comparative philosophy with a special interest in works of normative and applied ethics, political theory and philosophy of law.

Confucianism, Law, and Democracy in Contemporary Korea, edited by Sugmoon Kim

Traditional Korean Philosophy: Problems and Debates edited by Youngsun Back and Philip J. Ivanhoe

Contemporary Korean Political Thought and Park Chung-hee, Jung In Kang

Korean Confucianism: The Philosophy and Politics of Toegye and Yulgok, Hyoungchan Kim

Skill and Mastery: Philosophical Stories from the Zhuangzi, Edited by Karyn Lai and Wai Wai Chiu

Marx After the Kyoto School: Utopia and the Pure Land, Bradley Kaye

Marx after the Kyoto School

Utopia and the Pure Land

Bradley Kaye

ROWMAN & LITTLEFIELD
Lanham • Boulder • New York • London

Published by Rowman & Littlefield
An imprint of The Rowman & Littlefield Publishing Group, Inc.
4501 Forbes Boulevard, Suite 200, Lanham, Maryland 20706
www.rowman.com

86-90 Paul Street, London EC2A 4NE

Copyright © Bradley Kaye 2022. Copyright in individual chapters is held by the respective chapter authors.

All rights reserved. No part of this book may be reproduced in any form or by any electronic or mechanical means, including information storage and retrieval systems, without written permission from the publisher, except by a reviewer who may quote passages in a review.

British Library Cataloguing in Publication Information available

Library of Congress Cataloging-in-Publication Data

Names: Kaye, Bradley, author.
Title: Marx after the Kyoto school : Utopia and the Pure Land / Bradley Kaye.
Description: Lanham : Rowman & Littlefield, 2021. | Series: Ceacop East Asian comparative ethics, politics and philosophy of law | Includes bibliographical references and index.
Identifiers: LCCN 2021040406 (print) | LCCN 2021040407 (ebook) | ISBN 9781538154076 (cloth) | ISBN 9781538154090 (paperback) | ISBN 9781538154083 (ebook)
Subjects: LCSH: Buddhism and politics. | Buddhism and state. | Communism—Religious aspects—Buddhism. | Nishida, Kitarō, 1870-1945—Criticism and interpretation. | Marx, Karl, 1818-1883—Criticism and interpretation. | Communism and philosophy—Japan.
Classification: LCC BQ4570.S7 K39 2021 (print) | LCC BQ4570.S7 (ebook) | DDC 294.3/372—dc23
LC record available at https://lccn.loc.gov/2021040406
LC ebook record available at https://lccn.loc.gov/2021040407

Contents

Introduction: The Struggle Is Real   vii

1. Buddhist Marxism: A Communist Hermeneutics   1
2. Samsara, Pervasion, and Conditioned Coproduction   39
2a. Dialectics: Ideology, Reproduction, and the Falling Rate of Profit   73
3. What Is Communism? Mu!   101
4. Kokka Minzoku (State Nation) ~ Minzoku Kokka (Nation State)   161
5. Nishida Kitarō and the Later Marx: Ground Rent, Utopia, and the Pure Land   183

Acknowledgments   227
Bibliography   229
Index   239

Introduction
The Struggle Is Real

THEORY/PRAXIS AS NEGATION OF MESSIANIC POLITICAL THEOLOGY

First, I must clarify my intentions. This is not a book about Karl Marx. Nor is it a book about the Kyoto School. I am not offering a "faithful" reading of either. The book is, in the words of the Buddha, both and neither. Marx and Nishida differ on several points, each with their own style and brilliance; however, there is a way in which, throughout this book, I attempt to insert my own thinking into a hypothetical "round table"[1] discussions as Michel Foucault called it. In imagining a possible conversation between Marx and Nishida, I can fill in the gaps in this imaginary missed connection with my own hermeneutics of interpretation. My main thesis is simple—to interpret Marx through Buddhist thought rather than spiritual practices that lend themselves to messianic political theology. Implicit in this is more of an exegesis rather than a hermeneutical style of interpretation. If you look at the root of the word "Hermeneutical," it relies on the mythos of "hermes," the messenger of the Gods in ancient Greek cosmology, and my goal is to not rely on the return back to a central text as if it were sacrosanct; however, the common and academic usage of the term "hermeneutics" has been so watered down that the technical etymology of the term itself has been lost. My writing is an attempt at an exegesis, a deviance from the common and correct, verifiable interpretation of "Marx"; my hope is to open up new interpretations, while relying closely on the texts, but not in the sense that there is or ever was a singular correct interpretation of "Marxism" as such. Even reflecting on the absurdity of reducing "communism" down to one single definitive form of itself is the kind of self-identical metaphysics that I am trying to disrupt in this book. This firmly sets Marxist thought as a negation of any and all forms of messianic political theology, be they Judeo-Christian, Confucianist, or the bizarre forms of State-Shintoism that Japanese fascism found so amenable toward its goals. While Marx has been criticized for utilizing a kind of universalist view of culture that a kind of fashionable cultural relativism finds abhorrent, his views may seem symptomatic of a kind of modernist developmentalism that post- or decolonial theorists find repugnant; this does not mean that he was completely wrong, if anything, the post/de colonial "theory" has been driven by an academic barricading of philosophy that has totally absconded from any sort of praxis whatsoever. When Marx writes, in an off-the-cuff remark in the first volume of *Capital*, he is saying that every contact leaves a trace:

> Plato's Republic, in so far as the division of labor is treated in it as the formative principle of the state, is merely an Athenian idealization of the Egyptian caste system, Egypt having served as the model of an industrial country to others of his contemporaries, e.g., Isocrates. It retained its importance for the Greeks even at the time of the Roman Empire.[2]

While there is not enough room to go through each of these in full detail, the problem I try to address is one of "theory/praxis" because wherever Marxism has been enacted into a political praxis, we wind up with personality cults. This is not a problem with praxis only, it is a problem with a lack of imaginative reinventions of "Marxist" political philosophy. When Marx is interpreted, if his work is interpreted at all let alone read or carefully read, his work is typically read through Hegel. Or, through a pantheon of Western Marxist theorists[3] and yet, for all of the push toward postcolonial, decolonial, and various "anti-Eurocentric" forms of political theorizing, there is very little published in the West regarding the vast influence of Marx upon modern Asian thought. It is strange, because thinking "Marx" through western eyes seems to always result in the most bizarre messianic figures taking the helm of state apparatuses. Problems seem to emerge when Marxists take hold of power, and there is a political theology that fosters messianism from a historical a priori perspective. Leaders are forced to work against the grain of thousands of years of religious consciousness building that goes against the revolutionary changes in property relations necessary to produce actually existing communism. This includes Mao Tse Tung, who sanctioned a pamphlet entitled "Ghosts of Confucius, Fond Dream of the New Tsars," who writes:

> Confucius was a reactionary thinker who stubbornly upheld the slave system. He lived in the latter part of the Spring and Autumn Period (770–475 BC) when the slave system was being replaced by the feudal system...Confucius and his

followers failed to stem the historical tide that took China from slave to feudal society.[4]

The problem that Mao faced is the same problem everywhere including Japan under State-Shintoism, the problem of messianic political theology as a latent bias. In Mao's China, it was the problem of what he called "worshipping" Confucius as a result of the centuries-old legacy of legalism, the belief that laws should be understood as punitive measures to instill virtuous behaviors into citizens. China's centuries-long legacy of torture (see Ling Ch'i, the 10,000 cuts torture for parricide or regicide) is a by-product of centuries of legalist forms of political theory, and it is a deeper psychic bond with power that the praxis of a liberatory movement meets its aporia—nationalism produces its most loyal subjects among those who have sacrificed the most for its ends.

Most spiritual practices produce this sense of self-negating moral asceticism in the service of loyalty toward a messianic figure, except perhaps the metaphysics of interdependent origination (some call this interdependent arising) in the deeper philosophical veins of Buddhist metaphysics, which is the belief that every cause is caused by more than one cause; therefore, there is no central point with which to finalize a conclusive all-encompassing causality to everything. In other words, if there is a "God" in the clearest sense, it is a communist idea insofar as God is closer to a Spinozist pantheism—a community of interconnected causes and effects spanning all of existence, beyond national, ethnic, racial, even class boundaries and cannot be focused onto some sort of spiritual entity. God is not anything supernatural. More like the trace of history and memory, one should not infer any sort of spiritual allegory from events in reality other than the material conditions of the forces of interdependent arising, *Pratītya samutpāda*, which is sometimes translated as conditioned coproduction. When we utilize that translation, it lends itself to an interpretation of interconnectedness through production, akin to what Marx says in relation to conditions of production as interpreted as if these were the motions of heavenly bodies:

> While it is not our intention here to consider the way in which the immanent laws of capitalist production manifest themselves in the external movement of the individual capitals, assert themselves as the coercive laws of competition, and therefore enter into the consciousness of the individual capitalist as motives which drive him forward, this much is clear: a scientific analysis of competition is possible only if we can grasp the inner nature of capital, just as the apparent motions of the heavenly bodies are intelligible only to someone who is acquainted with their real motions, *which are not perceptible to the senses.*[5]

I would like readers of this book to consider that perhaps Maoists missed a golden opportunity to fully engage with the ways that there are affinities with eco-communism and some of the philosophical trajectories of early neo-Confucianism. For example, consider this beautiful and well-known piece of philosophy from a student of Confucius. Obviously, Confucianism carries over from China to Japan in many various forms and so as to avoid being labeled as a "reductionist," it is good measure to make the reader aware that I myself am also aware of the dangers of conflating something called "China" with something called "Japan," even though if the reader sticks with this book long enough, the chapter on the state makes it clear that a reading of Ground Rent through Pure Land Buddhism as a utopian physics of power enables us to discover that the entire game of state-identity politics is an "illusion we have forgotten is such,"[6] to borrow from Friedrich Nietzsche, whose writings inspired Michel Foucault to claim that Nietzsche's philosophy and life ethos were "the only path toward what we expected from communism."[7]

MENCIUS' NIU MOUNTAIN AS ECO-COMMUNISM

One of Confucius' best students was Mencius (372–289 BCE). In the following quote you can see, perhaps, some of the neo-Confucian themes regarding nature and perhaps "second nature" when taken too far. The political themes in the following quote from Mencius' *Trees of Niu Mountain* expose the ways that the state can become a repressive apparatus that enables the abuse of nature. Only when our minds are imbalanced does this affect the policies of the state. It also smacks of classical hyperbole and its emphasis on e-qualia—which I will look at in the last portion of the third chapter in this book where I hypothesize that Marx has been wrongly cast into a "classicist economism" of monetary harmony, when in fact his theses on utopia is closer to a moneyless post-wage labor "kyōdōshughi" or cooperativism as forwarded by Miki Kiyoshi, which has little or nothing to do with an equality of wages. In these passages here, you can see an ancient interpretation of this interdependent origination thesis in Confucianist schools of thought known as "Mohism"—which forwards a thesis that compassion and virtue need not rely on institutional forms of behavioral conditioning, and negative reinforcement through punitive measures to coerce people away from wickedness into virtue. While reading this you might consider whether or not Mao's views on Confucius, and religion in general, were perhaps too narrowly attached to a "legalist" interpretation of power—which are unfortunately reproduced in virtually all forms of communism that view the telos of revolution as the seizure of state apparatuses. The result being the reproduction of violence inherent to the structures of power that the revolution sought to dismantle from the start.

Mencius said, "The trees of the Niu Mountain were once beautiful. But can the mountain be regarded any longer as beautiful since, being in the borders of a big state, the trees have been hewed down with axes and hatchets?

Still with the rest given them by the days and nights and the nourishment provided them by the rains and the dew, they were not without buds and sprouts springing forth. But then the cattle and the sheep pastured upon them once and again. That is why the mountain looks so bald. When people see that it is so bald, they think that there was never any timber on the mountain. Is this the true nature of the mountain?

Is there not [also] a heart of humanity and righteousness originally existing in man? The way in which he loses his originally good mind is like the way in which the trees are hewed down with axes and hatchets. As trees are cut down day after day, can a mountain retain its beauty? To be sure, the days and nights do the healing, and there is the nourishing air of the calm morning which keeps him normal in his likes and dislikes. But the effect is slight, and is disturbed and destroyed by what he does during the day.

When there is repeated disturbance, the restorative influence of the night will not be sufficient to preserve it, man becomes not much different from the beast. People see that he acts like an animal, and think that he never had the original endowment (for goodness). But is that his true character? Therefore with proper nourishment and care, everything grows, whereas without proper nourishment and care, everything decays.

Confucius said, "Hold it fast and you preserve it. Let it go and you lose it. It comes in and goes out at no definite time and without anyone knowing its direction." He was talking about the human mind."

PURE LAND AS ALWAYS ALREADY INTERCONNECTEDNESS

What happens to the labor power in Southeast Asia has an enormous ripple effect on the rest of the world as global markets are more interconnected today than ever before—therefore, the move toward communism on a global level presents us with the most urgent exigency of our time, which requires a new exegesis on Marx via modern Japanese thought as understood through the Kyoto School.

In other words, we must read the texts left by Marx through a non-Christian metaphysics—that is, Buddhist, Vedic, or Zen/Mahayana/Theravada philosophy and the ideas of Samsara, Karma and Dharma, Dukkha, and there are some sympathetic voices in the Kyoto School, Tosaka Jun and Miki Kiyoshi, whose work has benefited my readings. I also try to work with the oeuvre left by Nishida in ways unlike most other scholars who approach his work. He was blasted as a bourgeois intellectual by some of his students, and yet, there are ways that his work has only begun to gain traction among scholars who work in Marxist political theory/praxis.

There are two sub-theses to forward by zigging from classical Buddhism to the writings of Marx, and zagging into translations and serious deep dives into Kyoto philosophy, and yet the thesis forwarded from this "zigzagging" is simple. I wish to unearth the concealed influence of classical Asian philosophy on the philosophy of Karl Marx, mostly focusing on ancient Buddhist and Taoist thought, but primarily through what is called "Pure Land" Buddhism which I see as amenable to Marx's theories of "Ground Rent" and can be helpful to those who are engaged with struggles over resources, ecology, and the politics of land use.

The first thesis is simple: after reading this book, readers will better understand the influence of Asian philosophy on Marx himself, and how this can enrich our understanding of the struggles of "Marxist" political theory and praxis.

The second thesis takes the stance that these concealed influences in Karl Marx's oeuvre made it much easier for the Kyoto School philosophers to find his works amenable to theirs. The other point of departure in this book deals with the ways that Marx can be read in the wake of the Kyoto School philosophy, and in doing this, their works open up new vistas of "tetsugaku" or "wise thought" with which to approach these contemporary struggles.

For me to successfully accomplish this, the reader must understand that this work conveys a method aligned with what Gilles Deleuze once wrote in the introduction to *Difference and Repetition* "A book of philosophy should be in part a very peculiar species of detective novel, in part a kind of science fiction."[8] A detective searching for clues to a problem, the coherence of which is received from elsewhere. Science fiction in the sense that the advent of a coherence which is not our own, with the full understanding that this writing is completely untimely, bringing a light at a time when light is not demanded, the lantern-bearing hermit who arrives at noon to whom people reply: "How else can one write but of those things which one does not know, or knows badly?" It is precisely there that I imagine myself having something to say, not as an expert, but as a writer, philosopher, and hopefully "tetsugaku" or, wise thinker, but not in any veridical sense of "getting our papers straight" and correctively aligning East and West thoughts to the same thought hemisphere.

In philosophy there is a strange desire to search for evidence that may conclusively answer profound questions such as "What is the correct interpretation of Nishida's philosophy?" As Nishida himself once said, "Let others do as they will. I am who I am."[9] My approach is inspired by this and another line from Nishida: "It is because of Marx that I cannot rest."[10]

ENCLOSING THE LAND IN THE MEIJI RESTORATION

If the enclosing of land through its seizure by the state is an effect of a fascist desire to immobilize movement among its subjects and to trend toward the stasis of grounding, to stabilize the ground, then most scholars believe that fascist desire began in Japan during the Meiji Restoration beginning in 1868.

Japan had an emperor who was only an adolescent, and this made it easier for colonial powers to persuade the government of Japan into political and economic partnerships that were advantageous to western colonial interests. Brought on by colonial intimidation tactics from the American military, the Meiji Restoration, as it is called, enacted a series of political and social reforms that were intended to have a modernizing effect upon Japanese society.

The leadership in Japan hoped to give their people a chance to compete with the rapidly advancing western powers, and at the time this may have seemed like their only option, because harsh intimidation tactics were used by the American military to pressure the Japanese leaders. American Commodore Perry was sent around the globe by President Millard Fillmore with the purpose of opening new markets for American Capital. Commodore Perry utilized "gunboat diplomacy" which consisted of threatening the Japanese leadership into opening its economy into trade relations with the United States.

In a series of visits to Japan where the Commodore brought larger military cadres designed to show stronger military might on the US side of the negotiations, the Japanese eventually ceded their closed relations and opened up to American trade. Incidentally, the Shogun was ill during the first of these meetings (much like Nishida falling ill during the Pearl Harbor attacks), and there was great panic about the threat that the US military presence may pose to the Japanese capital. In the second negotiations, there was a sense on the Japanese side that perhaps the documents that Commodore Perry signed and brought back to the United States were illegitimate because the Shogun himself had not signed them.

In fact, the person who signed them was the Dagaku-no-kami, named Hayashi Akira whose political post was equivalent to the secretary of education. This last meeting occurred while the Commodore brought ten ships and 1,600 men in 1854. In an intentional display of American military hubris, Commodore Perry's flag was flown from Annapolis to Tokyo for display during the surrender ceremonies which officially ended World War II. Needless to say, the bad blood between the United States and Japan has a long history. Shortly after the opening of Japan to Western trade, the Meiji Restoration began. Emperor Meiji began his reign in early 1867, at the age of only fourteen, and little over a decade after Commodore Perry's last visit. Emperor

Meiji grew up having been born in 1852 as someone who today would be called a nativist to American trade in Japan.

Emperor Meiji (1852–1912) was born in a time when his subjectivity was nativist to American economic spheres of influence in Japan. The major reforms, the Meiji Restoration, involved rapid military development, the end of the Tokugawa reign of the Shogun, which began in the seventeenth century as a way to bring social order after centuries of warfare in Japan. Capital is the definite social relation of production pertaining to a particular historical social formation, a specific historical shape of the social production process.

The Shogun was stripped of property, which was given to the new Meiji government, as well as all dissidents who resisted the new imperial government. State-Shintoism became the new official state religion and there was rapid industrialization, rapid growth in the economy, production of many commodities expanded. This was only possible through the seizure of public lands (the commons) and putting those lands under private/governmental control (what Marx details this process occurring in England during the "Enclosures Acts")—in Japan this process of enclosure took place in the form of the Japanese Land Tax Reform of 1873. In only the sixth year of the Meiji government, this policy restructured the tax policies to create private land ownership in Japan for the first time.

All of these policies are what Marx refers to throughout his work as "primitive accumulation." I will develop what Marx meant by that in the chapter on the state. "Enclosures" in England are relevant parallels. With the emergence of capitalism there is almost always immediately in its aftermath, or at its origin, primitive accumulation and enclosures of the commons into "private property"—even the US constitution is a method of primitive accumulation and enclosures—as payment back for the private investors who put up money to back the Revolutionary War. "Private property" rights were put into the constitution (in place of the unsustainable "pursuit of happiness") and land was doled out in the aftermath of the war through what was called the Holland Land Grants and the "treaty of Red Tree"; so forth, these are also similar to the ways that benevolent structures are placed around a culture first in order to pacify through cultural persuasion prior to establishing political and economic hegemony.

There was expansion in the development of military products as well, most of which were purchased through trade with the United States and in one of the worst policies, there was the development of a new militarism, which created the first paid, professionally trained, full-time standing army in the history of Japan.

The day Japan attacked Pearl Harbor, Nishida became ill and had to be hospitalized. There he studied all sorts of mathematics, physics, and he said he "rediscovered Leibniz" in a way that was much richer than in his youth when he did not have the breadth and depth of knowledge that he had later on in life. As Japan was growing ill so was Nishida, which is apt because of his emphasis on the connection to nature and the world, no human being can exist without a connection to earth, world, and not merely environment or setting, but literally relying on plants, animals, for nutrition, the air to breathe, the sunshine, the mountains, the water, all life relies on a natural ground. So, élan vital or the "life force" that Bergson describes is not truncated and detached from the earth. It springs forth from the world, not from above as if by the metaphysics of a transcendental cosmology.

Nishida is in many ways a philosopher of immanence, life originates and is sustained by forced within the physics of the cosmos—and yet, he is also not completely a thinker of a vulgar economic determinism, or a reductionist materialism in the sense of some straight and narrow Marxists readings might give him, he does have ample criticisms of Marx, but this is not to throw away Marx's work, but to augment and supplement it with new perspectives. If the Meiji Restoration marked the emergence of State-Shintoism and set forth an inertia toward Japanese fascism, this new political conjunction of fascist desire banked upon rapidly accelerated growth in material conditions, technology, and enhanced military capabilities.

New technology does not fall from the sky as if spontaneously invented by the spirit of a lone genius. Invention is the result of enhancing other machines, conjoining new emerging science, and the investments for those are usually derived from state funds, that is, the force of the state is behind the remodeling of new technologies. Science is in a covenant with truth; however, this covenant is a contract with governance (i.e., it always already corresponds to the governmentality of those who provide the material support for that science, technology, and poiesis to develop).

Even aesthetically, there was a conjunction of territorializing processes in Japan during and since the Meiji Restoration that produced a new subjectivity, a new socius characterized by new relations of production. Japan did what Marx observed to be happening in England during the Enclosures Acts and became the project of most states in the nineteenth century. Marx details this process in the portion of the first volume of *Capital* devoted to primitive accumulation. Where before the enclosures most land was cultivated in common and was understood as open common property, the closing of land by private or state ownership resulted in a dispossessing of labor power from the land into a situation where labor had to rely on markets to supply material necessities, and in order for laborers to obtain those necessities, one had to earn a wage or own capital. This transition did not always occur peaceably, and yet the hegemony of the enclosures eventually won a seismic victory for the bourgeoisie and the state. It should be mentioned that these are not necessarily two separate entities.

As I will detail in later chapters, particularly chapter 4: "Kokka Minzoku (State Nation) ~ Minzoku Kokka (Nation-State)"—if we take a truly critical approach to the state and its effect on capitalism, we shall see that these are not two separate entities. State is capital. Capital is the state. The state is congealed capital, the "hard core" of capital as Louis Althusser called it, is the police, military, and the thuggery with which capital will relentlessly use violence to maintain the hegemony won during the enclosures. Even though the names and faces within these class relations are contingent, the content of who embodies these relations may change, yet the form has stayed relatively the same.

As markets opened up and trade ships sailed back and forth, European culture became infatuated with ancient Japanese culture. The exotic fads of kimonos, fans, and various motifs also drew attention from European painters to the extent that the French journalist and art critic Philippe Burty, in an 1876 article, called this enthusiastic trend japonisme.[11]

Marx may have even been responding to what he saw as this trend when in his only mention of Japan in all of the first volume of *Capital*. His remarks speak to the ways that "liberals" may not see the eurocentrism behind spreading the gift of capitalism around the world. Marx is saying that there were, and still are, real workers living in pre-capitalist, feudal conditions. We catch a glimpse of Marx as critical of the very developmentalism that his critics claim he propagated. In the agrarian modes of production seen in medieval Europe as well as Japan, there may be conditions where communal exchanges can occur, that a "liberal"-reformist transition through the Meiji Restoration was not necessary to prepare the way for communism. I will not go into detail on this, but Marx writes thusly:

> Japan, with its purely feudal organization of landed property and its developed small-scale agriculture, gives a much truer picture of the European Middle Ages than all our history books, dictated as they are, for the most part, by bourgeois prejudices. It is far too easy to be "liberal" at the expense of the Middle Ages.[12]

In this seminal essay, "Literary, Much too Literary" in 1925, Ryunosuke Akutagawa complains that language has lost its poetry. With the commodification of the literary arts, language has become "confused," and words are being "misused" (85). The poetry of literature has given way to mere journalism or superficial stabs at originality; artists now "produced" (seisan) rather than created. Language has become corrupted by the forces of production in the present—forces that affected a break in the transmission of poetic resources from the past. The desire to dispense with the communicative function of language, a desire that would become so central to the writers in this study, was understood by Akutagawa as a stand against formulaic writing that had become indistinguishable from journalism. From Akutagawa's standpoint, it appeared as though the development of modern Japanese letters had exhausted its potential.

Now facing exhaustion, it could only be revived by fanning the slight flicker that remained. Akutagawa could see that Japanese prose was constructed, not given: "Our prose, like Rome, was not built in one day." Akutagawa is like other writers in this study whose movement back to the native tradition is, in fact, an act of modernist creativity built on a cosmopolitan literary sensibility. He was rekindling a universal poetic spirit for the sake of the native voice:

> This is a spirit belonging to our ancestors—not only to Japan's, but to all ancestors—it is the burning of a flame invented by geniuses and passed on to geniuses, a flame not yet extinguished, neither in prose nor in criticism.

Akutagawa called on the genius of the ancestors to revive the transmission of a tradition he believed to be at its end. My question is, who has the privilege of calling on those "traditions" and is it even correct to hold a tradition as "private property" most especially the Marxist traditions in philosophy and something eclipsed in the mad rush toward "development" as if the economic realm holds the master key to every other problem of human development.

Perhaps a sense that in the aftermath of the Meiji Restoration traditional Japanese culture would be eclipsed by western economic interests. If the modernizing process had not effaced precapitalist Japanese ways of life, the citadel of Japanese culture would eventually disappear, and like most of the world today, we have been cast in this postmodern amalgamation of influences that can only leave those of us concerned with the future of life on this planet in a nihilistic malaise.

With the incursion of western economics into Japanese life, intellectual life in Japan was also exposed to western philosophical influences as well. Nishida and his students would have a unique opportunity to study and engage with a wider range of texts from the western tradition than any generation in Japan prior to opening up cultural tributaries. There are numerous books written detailing the ways that Hegel, Kant, James, Heidegger, and the Greeks had an immense influence upon Kyoto School philosophy, most of which are carefully cataloged research tools. Then, if an interested scholar digs into the journal articles on these subjects, the list suddenly numbers into the hundreds, if not thousands.

PHILOSOPHERS HAVE ONLY INTERPRETED THE WORLD, IN VARIOUS WAYS, THE POINT IS TO CHANGE IT

The very first problem one encounters when attempting to compare philosophers from Kyoto, Japan with philosophers from the continental European traditions is the use of the term "philosophy" and how it varies between traditions. In the West, the word commonly used to denote "philosophy" is derivative of the Greek terms: Philo and Sophia, fraternal love of wisdom. A friendly, dialectical game between intellectual sparring partners most commonly understood to be popularized by Socrates and his intellectual progeny of Plato and Aristotle. In Japan, the word "philosophy" is often translated from "tetsugaku" which literally breaks down into "wise thought," and it most likely has its etymology connected to mindfulness practices from various Zen and meditational practices, rather than a dialectical sparring match, ala Nietzsche's understanding of Socrates as the "first fencing master for the noble circles of Athens."[13]

The problem of defining "philosophy" in terms of the comparative potential between Marx and Kyoto philosophers is complicated because Marx had such an unusual perspective on philosophy and his philosophical project. He claimed his role as a philosopher to be that of revolutionary practice, rather than objective unbiased observer. He wrote in his now famous eleventh and final thesis on Feuerbach: "Philosophers have only interpreted the world, in various ways, the point is to change it." Surely, some members of the Kyoto School have undertaken this aspect of Marx's philosophy with more seriousness and rigor than others, in particular Miki Kiyoshi and Tosaka Jun, and some have already shown that there are elements of this laden throughout the later writings of Nishida.

The debate about what constitutes real "Zen" thought, let alone the lesser-known subtleties of the discourses within the Kyoto School, has been overcoded by the legacies of colonialism that the pairing of philosophies from Japan with "Marx" may seem as though there is a thinly veiled ideological agenda as part of an Orientalist condescension. I do not intend to pit an ephemeral Marx against or above a diverse team of thinkers who were often caught in very instructive disagreements with one another called the "Kyoto School."

I think it is important to start with the understanding that these debates occurred within the Kyoto School itself, and that often, I am not looking at these questions as an outsider who imposes something called "Marxism" onto a foreign entity, but that the emergence of Nishida's philosophy was a result of his working through of many parallel problems alongside the textual basis left by Marx himself. Nishida was also responding to many of his students at the time who were drawn into Marxism in the later period of the 1920s and through the rest of their lives. While most if not all of the important thinkers in the Kyoto School were in some way influenced by Buddhist thought, philosophers such as Miki Kiyoshi were not indebted to a particular version of Buddhism into which their thought processes on Marx would have to be reduced into, and vice versa. Therefore, "Marxism" can learn just as much from these Kyoto philosophers as the Kyoto philosophers had their own unique way of thinking. It is just as fascinating to think that the brilliance of these writers has yet to be fully absorbed into continental thought, not that this volume will get to the bottom of these comparisons, but that there is a rich and diverse set of texts that have yet to be fully embraced by Western philosophers, even though the primary intellectuals within the Kyoto School were all very well trained in European thought.

It makes sense to find discursive interlocutors between Marx and Nishida, because Nishida himself claimed that the inspiration for his first major philosophical work, *An Inquiry into the Good (Zen no kenkyū)*, came from "transcendental philosophy starting with Fichte,"[14] meaning Fichte, Schelling, and Hegel. In other words, the exact German idealists who formed the intellectual responses of Marx. By extension, since Nishida is universally considered the most important modern Japanese philosopher, whether philosophers in Japan agreed with Nishida or not, they had to respond to his work in some thoughtful way, it makes sense that there is parallel ground between the philosophy that his work responded to initially, and the work of Marx. It should not be difficult to see how some of his students might take the work of Marx as a point of affinity with their work.

In this introduction, I try to present what I see as some of the useful background stories from Buddhist mythology about the life of Siddhartha Gautama, the historical Buddha, and "Marxist thought," but there is no need to rely on this as the anchor point of the Kyoto School. For example, Miki Kiyoshi kept copies of Dōgen's Shōbōgenzō, and Shinran's work on Jōdo Shinshū at his bedside, but these were quite possibly texts that Miki liberated from dogmatic traditionalist readings, previously confined within religious institutionalism. Since Miki did not have any formal background in "Buddhist" ceremonial decorum, his readings should not be confused with a colloquial philistine's one-off, but a deeply freeing sense of openness unbiased by any ecclesiology of "Zen" bureaucracy.

In Miki's thinking through of a revolutionary view of religion, there is a sense that religion need not be merely an "opiate of the masses, the cry of an oppressed people," as the young Marx penned, but an open multifaceted discourse that can function to further the interests of the bourgeois class, or in the case of many variations on Buddhism, there can be ways that revolutionary consciousness can develop through religious thinking. He forwards the argument that it is possible to differentiate religion's essence (honshitsu) from religious phenomena (genshō), whereas the religious institutions that regulate experiences through ritualistic interpretations of religion should be deconstructed, the pure phenomena of religious experience (junsuina shūkyō) should be liberated.

It is important to realize that these conversations were happening within the academic life of Japanese philosophers prior to the Kyoto School, and there were efforts to clarify these ideas while leaving room for the subjective ambiguity that makes philosophical discussion fun. Yet, by drawing from Marx, we soon see that the universalization of capital on the world stage threatens to homogenize subjectivity into regional categories around nation states. Today, philosophy cannot center around difference as "analogous" in the sense that we see similarities among things that are different in form. As John Maraldo expresses a sentiment that I patently agree with: "Just as there are reasons to revere Nishida as a Zen philosopher, there are also considerable reasons to disconnect the philosopher from Zen."[15] Nevertheless we need only to recall comments like this one written by Nishida to his student Nishitani Keiji: "Certainly it is fine if you say that Zen elements are present in my thought, but if ordinary uninformed people call my thought 'Zen,' I would strongly object, because they do not understand Zen or my thought."[16]

U-TOPOS AND THE PURE LAND

Theodor Adorno informs us that dreams of utopia are universal:

> All humans deep down, whether they admit it or not, know that it could be possible for things to be different. Not only could they live without hunger and probably without anxiety, but they could also live as free human beings.[17]

However, in the modern era, the utopian imagination that once nurtured these dreams contains the mental images created for it by ideological state apparatuses that block consciousness of imaginative possibilities. Within the limitations of this kind of blocked consciousness, utopian images come to be viewed as naive or foolish. People universally say today what was once reserved only for Philistines in more harsh times, "oh that's just utopian"—in religion, Buddhism included, the Pure Land has stood for an image of a better afterlife and is rarely thought through as the actual construction of an actual topos (or, basho) here on earth.

Either way "pure land" and utopia have constituted a metaphor of consolation. As the Buddha once said, "the world is upside down." Adorno and Ernst

Bloch turn this assessment of utopia on its head. Far from indicating a robust engagement with the real world, he says, the anti-utopian focus on the present reflects the fact that the capacity to imagine the future has so drastically deteriorated that the best future we can think of "consists largely only in a repetition of the continually same 'today'."[18] Images of utopia, if taken seriously as real possibilities, allowed for the imaginative possibilities of negation of the real as something that is necessary for the transformation of the world as it is.

Intentions that cater to a sense of realism in the people often lead to actions that produce the most suffering in the world; hence, the first step along the way out is detachment.

By detaching from the way things are is to form an awareness that things can change. From there, it is only a matter of time before a modicum of imaginative labor power is liberated to create the world differently. Hence, Nishida claims that the intellectual intuition of ideal forms are most commonly found in the realm of art and religion.[19]

There are many reasons to distrust utopianism in the twenty-first century, as previous attempts to "immanentize the eschaton," or bring the heavens to earth, as Eric Voegelin called it, have ended in totalitarian nightmares. A healthy skepticism of utopian rhetoric is probably a good thing; however, this is not the same as actual utopianism. A political coup that utilizes a term like "National Socialism" to stir up the working class against their own interests, to put one another into death camps, because the proletariat may have had sympathies with a real socialist form of progress. To appropriate from the rhetoric of socialism in order to exterminate people is one thing, but the actual process of creating a utopian experience on earth is entirely another process altogether. We have to deal with this "epiphenomenon" from prior generations. The echo effect of secondary traces, the reification of past "truths," that "what is subsequent appears within a past that never ends,"[20] and the paradox that "when we speak of today's consciousness, yesterday's consciousness has clearly disappeared"[21] except for the meontological problem that "what has already become nothing must be thought to be acting"[22] that which is mere memory, and is divorced from time, also have a resonance upon consciousness occurring now.

ORIGINS OF PURE LAND PHILOSOPHY: HŌNEN AND SHINRAN

In Asia, philosophy is not neutral and various parts of Asia make different uses of the term philosophy. Even though thinkers understood to be Asian philosophers, such as Confucius, Lao Tzu, Dōgen, and Sun Tzu never heard of the term "philosophy," many utilize the word in reference to their writings.

In China, philosophy (zhexue) applies to thinkers as different as Confucius, Zhu Xi, Nishida Kitarō, and Kojin Karatani. Whereas in Japan, most universities make an important distinction between the intellectual activity in Asia until the twentieth century, referring to it as intellectual history (shisōshi) and twentieth-century thought as philosophy.[23]

Pure Land Buddhism had its formative period during the Heinan (794–1185) and Kamakura (1185–1333) eras, with Hōnen (1133–1212) being the first major figure within the Pure Land tradition. Shinran (1173–1263) was his most important pupil. The term "pure land" is a Chinese adaptation of an Indian Buddhist notion that the ground or topos of a Buddha, or in fact of any sacred being, is sanctified or "purified" by that Buddha's presence. In Sanskrit, the term is Buddha-ksetra, in reference to the "field" or "space" occupied by a Buddha.[24]

Hōnen's understanding of the Pure Land is as a site within which the law is suspended. In describing the pathway to the Pure Land, he had this to say,

> there is a Mahayana path, and a Hinayana path to perfection. Within the Mahayana itself there are two ways: the Buddha vehicle and the "bodhisattva" vehicle . . . Rebirth in this realm depends on whether or not one accepts the authority of the Buddha's vow of universal acceptance . . . Thus, people these days who desire to leave behind the realm of birth-and-death should abandon the path to perfection that is difficult to realize and look towards the Pure Land as easier to reach.[25]

The practice of birth into the Pure Land was none other than *nenbutsu*, and at the time, this consisted of complex rituals, dances, chanting, sacred rites, in preparation for the Pure Land with the emphasis on cleansing the soul for the moment of death when the gate of rebirth opens up. Hōnen's incredibly influential thesis was that our entire lives are preparation for the Pure Land, not just the moment before death. One must live a good life all the way through, and in doing so, the pure land can be made immanent in this world.

Although it is uncertain when Miki Kiyoshi wrote his unfinished Shinran essay, found after his death among his papers, it is clear that pure land Buddhism had an influence upon his interpretation of Marx. Some have considered Miki a bad "Marxist" by turning to religion in the way that he did; however, his motivation is clear. There are ways that Marxists overlooked the impact of religion on the powerless worker. If the workers have been driven from the land and labor is totally enclosed by the cash nexus of the wage-labor system, then religion becomes the sigh of the oppressed creature, the heart of a heartless world, and the soul of soulless conditions. It is the opium of the people, because it offers a numbing effect that distracts from exploitation and alienation and provides pleasant illusions that allow workers to carry on in exploiting and alienating conditions, the point is not to only interpret, but to change those conditions.

NOTES

1. Michel Foucault. *Nietzsche, Freud, Marx.* 1967.
2. *Capital Volume 1.* Pg. 488–489.
3. Antonio Gramsci, Theodor Adorno and Max Horkheimer, Walter Benjamin, Georgy Lukacs, Herbert Marcuse, although less so now, and perhaps Gilles Deleuze, Michel Foucault, and a pantheon of French Political Theorists associated with Lacanianism and Althusserianism, and then there are the Italian Marxists, Mario Tronti, Antonio Negri, and so forth.
4. Mass Criticism Group of Peking and the Tsinghuo Universities. *Ghosts of Confucius, Fond Dream of the New Tsar.* Foreign Language Press: Peking, 1974. Pg. 3, 40.
5. Karl Marx. *Capital Volume 1.* Pg. 433.
6. On Truth and Lying in an Extra-Moral Sense by Friedrich Nietzsche, this manuscript was left unpublished by Nietzsche and discovered in his desk drawer after he entered the decade long period of incommunicable silence, the abyss staring into him as he stared into the abyss.
7. Michel Foucault. *Power, Interview with Michel Foucault.* Pg. 249.
8. Gilles Deleuze. *Difference and Repetition.* Translated by Paul Patton. Columbia University Press: New York. Preface. Pg. xx.
9. Nishitani Keiji. *Nishida Kitaro.* Cambridge Press, 1991. Pg. 30.
10. Ibid.
11. Jason Wirth. *Truly Nothing: The Kyoto School and Art.* Japanese and Continental Philosophy: Conversations with the Kyoto School. Pg. 287, Indiana Press: Bloomington.
12. *Capital Volume 1.* Pg. 878, footnote 3.
13. Friedrich Nietzsche. *Twilight of the Idols.* The Problem of Socrates, #8.
14. Nishida Kitarō, preface to an Inquiry into the Good. Pg. xxx.
15. John Maraldo. Nishida's Philosophy in Europe and North America. *Japanese Philosophy in the Making 1, Crossing Paths with Nishida.* Pg. 113.
16. Michiko Yusa. Pg. xx.
17. Theodor Adorno and Ernst Bloch. "Something's Missing: A Discussion Between Ernst Bloch and Theodor Adorno on the Contradiction of Utopian Longing." In *The Utopian Function of Art and Literature.* MIT Press: Cambridge, 1989. Pg. 1–17.
18. Adorno and Bloch. Pg. 2.
19. Zen no Kenkyu. Chapter 4 "Intellectual Intuition." Pg. 30.
20. Nishida Kitarō. "Expressive Activity." In *Ontology of Production: Three Essays by Nishida Kitarō.* Translated by William Haver. Duke University Press. Pg. 48.
21. Ibid.

22. Ibid.

23. Tetsuo Najita, "Method and Analysis in the Conceptual Portrayal of Tokugawa Intellectual History." In *Japanese Thought in the Tokugawa Period 1600–1868: Methods and Metaphors*. Edited by Tetsuo Najita and Irwin Scheiner. Chicago University Press: Chicago, 1978. Pg. 3–38.

24. Heisig, Kasulus, Maraldo. *Japanese Philosophy: A Sourcebook*. Pg. 236.

25. Hōnen. *The Philosophy of Nenbutsu*.

Chapter 1

Buddhist Marxism
A Communist Hermeneutics

> "The materialist conception of history has a lot of them nowadays, to whom it serves as an excuse for *not* studying history. Just as Marx used to say, commenting on the French 'Marxists' of the late 1870s, 'All I know is that I am not a Marxist.'"
>
> Letter from Frederick Engels to C.
Schmidt. London, August 5, 1890

From here I want to play the role of philosophical science fiction writer and offer a communist exegesis of capitalism through Buddhism. "Buddhist Marxism" is inspired by the famous theses on Feuerbach—philosophers—have interpreted the world, the point is to change it.[1]

The thesis in this book is that Marx intended for one sort of change to be the unleashing of multitudes of interpretations. Rather than "change vs. interpretation" the process of interpretation promotes intellectual change and consciousness raising. Hence, a Buddhist-Marxist hermeneutic can offer a radical awakening at the level of consciousness; in my case, I am not focusing on a messenger passing from heaven to earth as if there is a veridical truth to be discovered as an objective fact, or an interpretive narrative that rotates around a center. Hence, in some regards, Marxist usages of the term "revolution" as a turning around a central point is an antiquated idea from classical metaphysics, which relies on a natural correspondence between word and thing. In an exegesis, there is a sense that is best summarized in this excerpt from the poem *The Second Coming* by William Butler Yeats:

Turning and turning in the widening gyre
The falcon cannot hear the falconer;
Things fall apart; the centre cannot hold;

Mere anarchy is loosed upon the world,
The blood-dimmed tide is loosed, and everywhere
The ceremony of innocence is drowned;
The best lack all conviction, while the worst
Are full of passionate intensity.[2]

It is interesting, however, in the context of my work here, to think about the connections that Marx may have had with what the Buddha called "sitting yoga" or meditation. This will be useful to relay a modicum of awareness of Buddhist practices to Karl Marx in this discursive give and take. It is also important to note that Marx became aware of the practice of meditation, perhaps in the early 1860s, and most certainly prior to the publication of the first volume of *Capital* in the autumn of 1867. There may be a subtext of Buddhist thought in this first volume that has yet to be fully unraveled, as those who study yoga know that the yoga of karma is the yoga of work and action. If we look closely at what Marx says, it is clear that he perhaps stumbled upon the basic yoga of "work" in the sense that our actions and labor in this world create the world into which our reincarnated selves return. Therefore, if our work is alienating and destructive in this life, we create a world in ruins into which we must return.

Karl Marx was not a Buddhist in any conventional sense and, as far as can be ascertained, never personally encountered any form of "ethnic" Buddhism on his travels around Europe. His connection with Buddhist philosophy, however, stemmed from his life-long friendship and association with Karl Koppen—one of the recognized and early European academic experts upon the subjects of Early Buddhism and Tibetan Buddhism. As Marx had known Koppen from having attended the University of Berlin and in 1837 they became good friends. Both of them were in the Young Hegelians. It is logical to assume that this is where he (Marx) first encountered a Western academic interpretation of Buddhist philosophy and religion.

Certainly, Marx mentions Buddhism in his *The German Ideology* (completed in early 1846) and again in his 1857 article for the *New York Tribune* titled "Sepoy Revolt in India." In 1861, while visiting Berlin in the hope of retrieving his Prussian citizenship (previously withdrawn because of his "revolutionary" activity), Marx met with Karl Koppen, and after a drinking session, Koppen presented Marx with his two-volume study of Buddhism.

A full five years go by, and to what extent Marx absorbed Buddhism is unknown, but in 1866, Marx wrote a letter to his niece Antoinette Philips. He states that he is exercising his mind and has been "keeping his mind in a state of nothingness," in accordance with the Buddhist teachings.

What is certain from this information is that Karl Marx knew about Buddhism and understood some of the basic non-theistic teachings including the everyday practice of "sitting yoga" along with meditation as mindfulness while the body is in action. Whether or not this is something that can be extrapolated beyond a few brief allusions from Marx is another question altogether. Look carefully at what Karl Marx says in his letter to Antoinette Philips about his experience with the Buddhist meditative technique:

> As it is, "I care for nobody, and nobody cares for me." But the air is wonderfully pure and reinvigorating, and you have here at the same time sea air and mountain air. I have become myself a sort of walking stick, running up and down the whole day, and keeping my mind in that state of nothingness which Buddhism considers the climax of human bliss. Of course, you have not forgotten the pretty little diction: "When the devil was sick, the devil a monk would be; when the devil was well, the devil a monk was he."[3]

This seems that Karl Marx understood very little about the Buddhist meditative technique even though he did perhaps playfully utilize the techniques in his own life. He reveals his knowledge that meditation can be performed standing, walking, lying down, and sitting. Marx appeared going about his day at the seaside, exercising a self-discipline that maintained the "non-arising" of thoughts in his mind while busying through tasks is less than a stellar example of mindfulness. As well as the physical rest away from the city and his incessant intellectual activity, this letter seems to suggest that as part of his exercise and rest regimen, controlling the intensity of the function of his intellect was a key component. Beyond this, there is very little to know.

BUDDHISMS: PHILOSOPHIES OR RELIGIONS?

This is an interesting question though, in talking about basho and the dialectics of place, one has to wonder in which temporal and spatial "place" does a religion begin? Is it Lumbini Gardens in what is today called Nepal? Was it at the moment of the birth of Siddhartha? Was it at the moment of Siddhartha seeing the Four Sights that would make him renounce his life of luxury in the beautiful palace in which he grew up? Is it during his awakening under the lengthy meditation underneath the Bodhi Tree? After which event he began to refer to himself as "Buddha" or "the one who is awake?" When does this process begin? When Buddha tells us about the four noble truths and the eightfold path? Or, when he takes the rotten pork that accidentally poisons him to death, whereby he tells his friend Cunda that his purpose as "Buddha" has been fulfilled because he may now reach nirvana? Is there a specific place in time, or is it more akin to a "worldview" where a myriad of factors brings the story into focus?

In considering affinities between the thought of Karl Marx and the myriad discourses of Buddhist thought, one might be wise to revisit the thought processes of Inoue Enryō (1858–1919), who began his 1893 essay, *Buddhism and Philosophy*, by asking a methodological question: "One of the questions facing us is whether or not Buddhism is a philosophy or a religion . . . it is one part religion, one part philosophy."[4] Following is the simple Venn diagram with A = Buddhism as religion, B = Buddhism as philosophy, and C = Buddhism as both religion and philosophy.

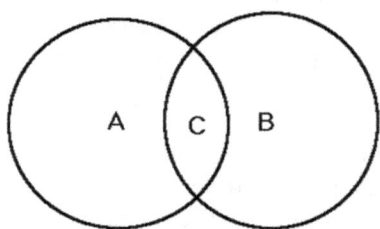

One might conceive of the philosophy of Marx in a similar Venn diagram but with slightly differing categories: A = Marxism as a political theory, B = Marxism as a revolutionary "philosophy of praxis," C = the synthesis of the two into a revolutionary theory of praxis.

Buddhism breaks down into two main categories under which there are several sub-categories: otherwise called Theravada and Mahayana. Theravada originates within India and stems back, most likely to Siddhartha himself who was born into a royal family in India in the sixth century BC, although Mahayana develops later through the great vehicle of the bodhisattva vow, today these two traditions tend to consist of strong followings that practice concurrently and throughout most of Asia.

Siddhartha grew up in Brahmanism. His beliefs and practices should be understood as a simplification and popularization of many Brahmanist concepts. Much like Jesus fulfilling scriptural ideas from the Book of Isaiah, most of these portrayals of Jesus were written after the fact by the disciples 70–90 AD, a full half century after he died. As Alain Badiou shows, in *St. Paul: The Foundation of Universalism*, the real emergence of a uniquely "Christian" philosophy emerges from Paul. We must understand Buddhism in exactly this way. The same goes (in some cases) for Marx with Lenin, Mao, Stalin, Althusser, Gramsci, and so forth. There is the oeuvre of the philosopher who starts the discourse and the hermeneutical adjustments that occur afterward. This is a hermeneutical combination, a "clash of interpretations" as Ricoeur called it.

Buddhism arrived in China with the transmission of the dharma to Bodhidharma in the fifth to sixth century AD, and you have to understand that when Buddhism carries over into China, it appropriates from prior existing philosophical traditions indigenous to China. Therefore, Mahayana Buddhism, and later Ch'an Buddhism (also referred to as Zen), has to accommodate itself to Confucianism and Taoism. Those belief systems originated sometime prior to or shortly after the Warring States Period, and both had their share of discursive appropriators. Neo-Confucianism solidified the place of Confucian thought in Chinese society, as Confucius was not necessarily able to solidify his own legend without the help of "Paul-like" characters in the history of philosophy, Mencius, and other neo-Confucians.

Mahayana emphasizes meditational styles that differ from Theravada. Indian meditation as a practice, in its earliest conceptions and in the way that Buddha appropriated his formation of the four yogas into the sitting yoga, was a way of escaping samsara. In all extents and purposes, moksha was nirvana in the historical Buddha's understanding; the point was release from the cycle of rebirth, which would give rise to the body returning and along with it, all the desires, lusts, appetites, and greediness that coincide with having a bodily form will return again and again until the process of nirvana is completed. Meditation in the tradition of Theravada typically tried to use meditation as a way of avoiding external influence to temper desires.

BUDDHA WAS NOT BORN A "BUDDHIST" AND MARX WAS NOT BORN A "MARXIST"

Buddha was not born the "Buddha."[5] He was born Siddhartha Gautama, a prince born into the nobility of the ancient warrior Sakiya dynasty, which claimed descent from the so-called solar race, the surya vamsa, and from the bloodline of King Iksvaku.[6] Throughout this book, wherever possible, I try to show the belief systems that Siddhartha appropriated from in creating his new spiritual practice, which I am also trying to appropriate into a "political spirituality"[7] useful for those who still engage with the work of Karl Marx. Ancient scriptures in the Vedic traditions tell of solar and lunar dynasties, and the passage of time through eras of awakening and enlightenment, decline, destruction, and darkness. Key symbols that would later become reified in the image of the yin and yang. Caravans and nomadic tribes not only transported commodities through the land mass of Euro-Asia, traders and conquerors carried ideas as well. With the messianic figure cloaked in a ring of light, a protective aura upon a king gives hope to those in need of redemption (a word that literally means "to buy back"), and the erlösung salvationist tropes that would eventually make their way to the European peninsula, to which barriers were erected in the form of Judeo-Christian-Islamic metaphysics as covenant with the state, and the feudal Lords.

The Bhagavad-Gita (translated from Sanskrit as the "Song of God") tells the myth behind King Iksvatu as the "solar king,"[8] the son of Manu, that is, the primordial legislator of the Indo-Aryan races, creator of the Laws of Manu, which produced the caste system. Clearly, this is the system of governance that Siddhartha would eventually rebel against. This section of the Bhagavad-Gita tells the story of how Krishna passed on the enlightenment of Jnana Yoga through the ages and will pass it on to Arjuna. Jnana is the yoga of self-knowledge, and as is understood through the text, the revealing of self-knowledge is the unveiling of God as "appearing in age after age."[9]

Legend has it that Siddhartha grew up in the material conditions where every luxury imaginable was available to him—delicious food, decadent life in a palace accompanied by beautiful courtesans. The stories about his early years make for the kind of fantasy that most poor people in capitalism are told to dream about, typically through ideologically driven forms of social reproduction that shape consciousness and desires. Siddhartha had immaculate wealth at his fingertips and never wanted for anything he could not obtain.

According to the Sukhamala Sutta, Siddhartha describes his childhood to the monks who gathered to hear him speak: "Monks, I lived in refinement, utmost refinement, total refinement. My father even had lotus-ponds made in our palace: one where red-lotuses bloomed, one where white-lotuses bloomed, one where blue-lotuses bloomed, all for my sake."[10] As if to brag about owning clothing that identified him as connected with a metropolitan center, he went on to say: "My clothing was from Varanasi, as were my tunic, my lower garments and my outer cloak."[11] Siddhartha Gautama, before his awakening, was fully immersed in the life of luxury.

King Suddhodana wanted nothing more than for his son Siddhartha to one day succeed to the throne and run his kingdom. One day, King Suddhodana called eight brahmins into his palace. They were ordered to predict Siddhartha's future destiny and to share these visions with the king. Most of the conclusions from these wise and noble brahmins claimed Siddhartha would stay in the palace with his family, leaving the young prince on the path to succeed his father on the throne. Most of the brahmins revealed that Siddhartha was a brilliant young man. Some of the ways these stories filter through Mahayana narratives give the impression of residual Confucianism because you can see parallels in the ways spiritual excellence serves as a rationalization for the impotence of revolutionary political agency exerted through the state. If he chose the political path, he would become the greatest king in the history of the world. Siddhartha would have been revered by those who lived in his kingdom and his reign would echo throughout history as the greatest king in the history of India.

One lone brahmin dissented and believed Siddhartha would not choose to be the greatest king in the history of the world; claiming instead that he would take the other path down the road of spiritual awakening. He would develop into the humble servant of the people and create practices that would awaken all beings from the slumbers of delusion and suffering. Kaundinya was the name of this wise man and legend; he is considered the first monk of the Buddhist faith (called a "bhikkhu") and he is known as the first believer to obtain arahat, which is a term to describe someone who has attained nirvana, but for themselves. There is a nuanced, yet major difference between the arahat and the bodhisattva.

Arahat crossed over into enlightenment and no longer returned to help others. Bodhisattva takes the Bodhisattva Vow to eternally return until the world is awakened with the caveat that they will reject their own nirvana until everyone is awakened. Bodhisattva is the "great vehicle" originating in the Mahayana tradition. The good end being the utopian vision of salvation in nirvana/pure land for everyone.

As the story goes, his father attempted to force Siddhartha to choose the family business and become the heir to the throne. The father plays a role similar to the devil in relation to Jesus over the mountains prior to the Beatitudes where there is a tempter who tries to force the choice of the one who becomes awakened. Knowing that his son was growing up and could not be held captive in the palace forever, the process of concealing the suffering of the world from the boy was becoming an impractical and laborious task. The father, trying as he could to do what he thought was best for his son, could not clear a path free of suffering for him. He wanted to make his son's life easier and keep him in the palace forever, where he would be safe, protected, and living with every advantage that his wealth could purchase. The king may have even felt a little remorseful contempt that his son might not appreciate the riches that his family accumulated over the course of several lifetimes. Thinking about the possibility that his son had the freedom to choose to walk away from his empire and family business terrified Siddhartha's father.

Until one day the family was on a journey through their kingdom in a glorious ornate carriage and the king realized that they were coming upon a peasant village up ahead and ordered his servants up the road to clear out any indication that there was suffering in the world. Even the most rudimentary knowledge of the teachings of the Buddha reveals that this is his oft cited, and more often misunderstood First Noble Truth: There is suffering (dukkha). It is not the point of the first noble truth to detach completely from the suffering in the world as if to advocate for a form of escapism. The point is to detach with full compassion for those who are suffering, in awareness, hence the major difference between arahat and bodhisattva. The arahat detaches from suffering in order to find nirvana for oneself, whereas the bodhisattva goes through the four noble truths with compassionate intentions to assist others in the path to nirvana—a theme that I will discuss later on in further detail.

By the time the carriage was travelling through yet another village, the king sent out the servants to do the same thing again, and then again, and then again. Each time the carriage passed through a village, Siddhartha never suspected his father had concealed the truth from him. Nothing seemed odd. Even though there were no people, no villagers milling about with their daily chores, their routines and the villages seemed normal.

Everything ran smoothly. The villagers were going about their daily chores. They tended their fields and nothing seemed out of place. Life among the peasants appeared as perfect as it was in his cloistered palace. Clean, neat, orderly everyone presented themselves as happy. Siddhartha never suspected that the people were putting on an act.

Unbeknownst to the young man Siddhartha, the villagers were all playing a part as directed by the king. The young man was the only one not in on the act, since his life had been a simulacrum since his birth—role-playing a ready-made script. He did not know any other way. Marx might have put it in terms like this: Siddhartha's consciousness had been produced by the material conditions in his life up to that point. As with all of us, the mind is material consciousness shaped by our position within the class system. Could Siddhartha upend the vicious circle of his own material reproduction? Surprisingly, yes!

A sort of question of false consciousness arises from this story. If one takes the teachings of Karl Marx seriously, the story is about Siddhartha overturning his false consciousness. Why had it never occurred to Siddhartha that everything was contingent? That his material conditions were produced by social relations rather than intrinsic natural laws? This realization could only happen when the "Four Sights" (old age, sickness, death, and the yogi) appeared to him, and more central to the story, these had to appear after the king tried to conceal these facts of life from his subjects—perhaps the moral of the story is that the first "awakening" in Buddha's life occurred when suffering presented itself, only after the ideological hegemony of the state could no longer conceal it from him—an ideological screening out of the real that occurred through the conceptual personae of paternalism. Siddhartha's father tried to steer the direction of his free will and failed. Hence, the figure of the father serves the function of showing the failure in a compassionate paternalism that shields rather than exposes the hero to suffering (dukkha). A key first stage in moving into liberation is acknowledging that there is suffering in the world, not acting "as if" there is and feigning care.

THE FOUR SIGHTS: SIDDHARTHA OBSERVES "MATERIAL CONDITIONS" OF DUKKHA

What happened next would shift the course of the rest of his life, and forever change world history. Siddhartha would soon learn the contingency of class, an awareness that would abruptly tear apart his life of unreflecting joy. Since he was born and raised wealthy, he had no point of reference with which to understand that the rest of the world was not wealthy like he had been all his life, and more importantly, there were some facts of life against which wealth could not form a barrier.

Until there appeared an old man by the side of the road. It was the first presentation of an irrepressible form of suffering he had ever encountered in his life. Old age. The appearance of the inevitable aspects of "suffering" shocked the young man. What are now called the Four Sights tore a hole in his universe. All the servants had tried their best to conceal this from the young Siddhartha as the kind had ordered them, but as with all things created by humans, there is a limitation to the political powers necessary to censor out the suffering of the world. Try as they could, the state can only do so much to screen out the poverty of the world from those in wealth. Modern examples of this might be things like natural disasters, global pandemics, diseases, and just the facts of life like old age. The eternal existential problems of being human.

The best summary of these debates occurs in a pamphlet published by Frederick Engels at various times in the 1880s and under the editorship of Paul Lafargue, Marx's son-in-law whose work *The Right to Lazyness* might be seen as a communist sitting yoga manifesto, even though Marx once said, "If that is Marxism, then I am not a Marxist." Engels' pamphlet, *Socialism: Utopian and Scientific* can be swiftly summarized, and it is as follows: Utopian Socialists believe that

> socialism is the expression of absolute truth, reason, and justice, and has only to be discovered to conquer all the world by virtue of its own power. And as absolute truth is independent of time, space, and of historical development of man, it is a mere accident when and where it is discovered.[12]

Hence, most of the unfounded criticisms of what circulates as if it were "Marxism" start from the perspective that Engels criticizes—a transcendental universalism of the "utopian socialist" where a socialist naturalism is always already there in anticipation of the "good news of socialism" to be evangelized around the world. What happens in this absurd understanding of utopian socialism is that nothing could come but a kind of eclectic, average Socialism . . . a mish-mash allowing the most manifold shades of opinion; a mish-mash of such critical statements, economic theories, pictures of future society by the founders of different sects, as to excite a minimum of opposition.

Hence, there is a discursive openness symptomatic of democratic forms of spectacle that are easily appropriable into a social homeostasis. Nevertheless, the dialectical nature of nature itself forms the basis of the turn toward "scientific socialism" and as Engels posits: "Nature is the proof of dialectics . . . nature works dialectically and not metaphysically; that she does not move in the eternal oneness of a perpetually recurring circle but goes through a real historical evolution." And, this process of social evolution is termed dialectical materialism and historical materialism by Engels (not Marx, who never used either of those terms by the way), is how we can better understand the narrative mythos of samsara, which is not necessarily the love of fate as the eternal circulation of karma as the identical repetition of market forces.

Engels wanted his readers to understand that if the dialectics of nature were left to their own devices, the tendency among capitalist formations of "anarchical social production," his term for laissez-faire capitalism, is an extreme inequality of wealth. The materialist conception of history is not merely a discursive exchange of ideas through propositional logic and the exposure of latent contradictions in the terms of the capitalist social contract. Materialist views of socialism "are to be discovered in the stubborn facts of the existing system of production," and one might add, these are lived experiences among the proletariat and the excess of displaced labor power that Marx and Engels referred to as the "industrial reserve army," those who are displaced by machine labor. As Engels points out, "the fundamental form of production is that spontaneous division of labor which creeps in gradually and not upon any preconceived plan." Laissez-faire capitalism has no plan, even though the forces of the market manipulate human behavior, consciousness, and the utilization of labor power, it would be a mistake to suggest that there is an intelligence behind these naturally forming hierarchies. There is no single locus of control that commands the market. Rather, what occurs gradually through the development of factory production and the extension of the production of commodities with the introduction of the capitalist mode of production is that the "old bonds were loosened, the old exclusive limits were broken through, the producers were more and more turned into independent, isolated producers of commodities." Capitalism is wonderful at tearing away all repressive social norms, as in the case of Marx and Engels famous line from the *Communist Manifesto*: "all that is solid melts into air." Thus, the social anarchy of production that casts the workers into precariousness, competition, and chaos is mirrored in the species-being of those who upend old, seemingly repressive social ontologies. As the material basis of the modes of production are held firmly intact while a mish-mash of discourses and identity politics becomes the ideological horizon of a so-called revolutionary politics.

As the perfecting of machinery makes physical labor power superfluous, this is "by the anarchy of social production, turned into a compulsory law that forces the individual industrial capitalist always to improve his machinery always to increase its productive force." Out of sheer necessity of the law of competing capitals, if one firm slows down and has zero growth, the other firms in that industry will swoop in and steal those untapped markets left by the other firm, and "capitalist production has begotten another 'vicious circle,'" as Engels points out, and thus, what is commonly talked about as if it were "samsara" is actually just another form of this "vicious circle" of competing capitals, historical market forces moving as if this reflexive inertia is natural, rather than the ideological homeostasis of class-conflict set on autopilot minus the conflict.

The process of production without any definite plan, or what capitalists call "freedom," Engels describes in somewhat reflexive terms as capitulating to the production of a definite plan by the invading socialists (i.e., the displaced "industrial reserve army" and the exploited proletarian class). The big crisis occurs when the bourgeoisie are incapable of managing the modern productive forces, because the crisis is so immense that another society must be created. Engels describes this as "the capitalist mode of production more and more completely transforms the great majority of the population into proletarians, it creates the power which, under penalty of its own destruction, is forced to accomplish this revolution" in terms that Marx uses elsewhere, the bourgeoisie are accumulating wealth and transferring it away from workers, and if left to its own devices the anarchy of spontaneously occurring market forces will create the conditions for its own gravediggers. Engels makes a mistake by thinking that the proletarian class must rise up and lay claim to the modes of production and turn them over to the state. Thus, establishing a planner state where scientific socialism can install workers in positions of power to guide the production projects that maximize growth and allocate resources effectively for maximum societal flourishing.

We now know that this tactic is extremely problematic precisely because it forms the foundation of fascism. The notable example is state-Shintoism during the Meiji Restoration in Japan, which is why the Kyoto School is so important to this work. Kyoto philosophy is post-Meiji and therefore a reaction to the impetus to turn power over to the state, even though most of the work on Nishida tends to interpret his work as if it were a "pro-nation-state" ideology.

The young Siddhartha saw the sickly, the elderly, and poor, and realized that bodies break down, they grow old, and there are also forms of suffering that are completely unnecessary due to material conditions of poverty. This discovery inspired him to devote the rest of his life entirely toward the cultivation of pathways out of suffering. "Dukkha" as he would later call it in his Four Noble Truths were the Four Sights (aging, sickness, death, and a wandering ascetic) with the process of detachment symbolized by the quiet meditating yogi who worked on breaking free of the process of rebirth known as samsara. He did not find these answers immediately, the journey to his own awakening took about six years before the famous scene under the Bodhi Tree when he discovered the Middle Path his journey of self-negation came to a dead end. He then spent decades teaching until his death.

SAMSARA

"Having realized the endlessness of samsara, all grasping (tanha) has ceased."[13] Samsara is understood to be the cyclical nature of rebirth of all life, matter, and being, the return to the world after death. Siddhartha, upon achieving the condition of sublime bliss while seated in the lotus position underneath the Bodhi Tree, made this declaration. Buddha found his deepest insight on the pathway out of rebirth. Detachment within the Theravada traditions gives a powerful escape from the ways of the world. It should be noted that in realizing the endlessness of samsara, all grasping (tanha) are unclenched.

Finding sublime bliss ("ānanda") the Buddha ("the one who is awake") emerged from the chrysalis of Siddhartha. Dying to self, a new self was born. Buddha's transformation out of endless samsara occurred within this world. Therefore, we can deduce through this interpretation of the Bodhi Tree story and the subsequent awareness that awakening into the "pure land" must occur here, now, as immanence (i.e., within) rather than transcendence (i.e., beyond). There are no guarantees that the pure land awaits us in the next life. Within the working of the "active polytheist imagination," as Gayatri Spivak's analysis of Hindu polytheism, is shaped by its negotiations with "unanticipatable yet perennial possibility of the metamorphosis of the transcendental as supernatural in the natural."[14]

Anything at any moment might be cathected by the transcendent divine and announce itself as a descended transcendence (avatār), and everything without exception is open to cathexis. However, in this sort of analysis from Gayatri Spivak, which is clearly infused with

Derridean's "negative theology," there is clearly a telos of messianism derived from Judaism. The Messiah as "yet-to-come" is a view that has infected all Western religious perspectives (what I refer to as the Jewish-Christian-Islamic vicious circle); and the "yet-to-come" of the messianic presence of God is exactly the problem that creates conditions for the eternal recurrence of fascism in the form of political theology as state ideology.

In committing himself to sit beneath the Bodhi Tree, the Buddha had his great awakening, an enlightenment that occurred literally and figuratively at the dawn of the forty-ninth day, after persevering through great temptations. After taking a small bowl of rice for nourishment, he pushed through the test of his endurance and stayed seated in lotus position with legs crossed and hands outstretched upon his knees.

Mara, the devilish figure of temptation with her beguiling ways, tested his will in various ways. First he tested with severe inclement weather. She sent a tremendous gale of freezing wind and pounding rain swirling through the trees for several days. Free from that taint of evil thinking, he obtained the first level of meditative absorption, a state composed of thought-conceptions (vitakka) and discursive thinking (vicāra). He persevered through physical and mental nonattachment in the rapture of inner-bliss (ānanda). The second wave of temptations consisted of lustful images. Beautiful voluptuous women danced around the Siddhartha whispering fantasies in his ear, revealing their bodies in front of him, caressing him, trying to seduce him for several days. To this, he maintained his mental acuity and experienced the mental joy, as a result of unwavering concentration—the peaceful calm of inner-stillness known as (samādhi), realizing a wisdom characterized by perfect inner-equanimity.

The last temptation Mara sent to Siddhartha was nihilistic hopelessness. The slightest hint of the futility in his efforts, she whispered in his ear: "Why go on at all? Nobody will listen. Nobody will care. Give up!" Of course, he realized while coursing in the deep that these were thought-constructions from within his own mind. Mara, the temptress that he himself had to overcome was within himself. Obtaining his deepest level of stillness he obtained the third level of deepest absorption (jhāna) which combines equanimity, unwavering mindfulness, and contentment. This lengthy process extended for forty-nine days.[15]

The Buddha then has his deepest and most profound insights. His previous ways were based on an extreme form of moral asceticism based on practices of self-negation and grounded in self-berating thought processes. The path that would lead him nowhere might be comparable to the fictional character in the Kafka story the Hunger Artist—starving himself for public display to set an example for others.[16] Buddha's path of extreme self-denial, a dialectical pendulum swing from his childhood in the lap of luxury, had led him to discover the facts of possessing a body: man cannot live without food, period. Material reproduction of basic needs like food are crucial for becoming-awake. Buddha once said while he was dying that the two greatest meals in his life were the nine grains of rice given to him over the course of the forty-nine days under the Bodhi Tree.

That small bowl of rice sustained him through the trials on the path to become-awake, and many people miss the "liberatory" aspects of becoming-awake. The moral allegory, the moral lesson from this story is that freedom occurs through a process of moral asceticism. By taking less, you free yourself from desires that were previously controlled by external sources. By practicing moral asceticism and minimal consumption, you pattern your behavior and through self-discipline a subject can accomplish self-mastery, which ultimately cultivates in self-autonomy.

Buddhist narratives are full of these kinds of moral allegories. Another key example is the way that the Buddha allegedly died. Legend has it that he slowly died from food poisoning while remaining conscious until the very last moments of his death. Buddha revealed that his two greatest meals were the few grains of rice that sustained him through the forty-nine nights under the Bodhi Tree. The other one was the mistake made by his friend Cunda who accidentally fed him undercooked boar's meat. Motivated with compassionate intentions, the Buddha soothed Cunda's shame telling his closest adviser ānanda how thankful he was for the meal. While it seems like an odd sentiment to have, the meal allowed him the opportunity to enter parinirvana, a stage right before dying where there is an experience of release from samsara, karmic rebirth, and culminates in the dissolution of the skandhas (the senses that are the doorways into the body, through which the self is formed). Interpreted as a sign of his unyielding faith in the principles of *pratitya-samutpāda* (conditioned coproduction), the Buddha insisted that the meal had nothing to do with his illness. Thus, he believed the two greatest meals were the ones that began his journey into the Middle Way and the one that allowed him to enter into nirvana ensuring safe passage out of the wheel of samsara.

Upon Becoming-Awake under the Bodhi Tree, Buddha set out on a new path. It would later be referred to as The Middle Way. Indicating a shift toward equanimity, balance, non-judgment, rather than battle against himself, he found strength within and began a practice on the basis of moderate asceticism and moderate sensual enjoyment. This is perhaps the position where many laypeople may see common ground between "Buddhism" as The Middle Way and the "Marxist"-Aristotleanism of virtue ethics that *grounds* the restlessness that marks the earlier stages in Buddha's life and the extreme polarities that may have marked many failed communist states. Trying to pin "good" moderate virtues and moral asceticism onto everyone in terms of resource allocation and draconian rationing, this is precisely not the purpose of this book. By turning to the Kyoto School in the next few chapters, my thesis tries to bring the oeuvre of texts left by Marx into conversation with modern Japanese philosophers.

Classical views on the Buddha's experiences are that they teach a liberatory kind of *grundwerke*. A work of immanent-grounding from within the telos is the deepest level of absorption or "jhāna" accomplishing an unwavering equanimity within oneself. As a social ontology, the *grundwerke* of capitalism is differential rather than integral. The being of beings in capitalism presents us with many forces that pull our resources away from ourselves. We are thrown into a process of propertylessness, and since, for Marx, consciousness is a product of material conditions, as material conditions consist of the expropriation of resources away from us, we can conclude that our selfhood is also expropriated away from ourselves as well. Hence, this is the last stage of alienation in the early notebooks from the Young Marx—self-alienation, a material, as well as perhaps spiritual sense of losing oneself, losing the soul of who you were, as well as losing power over property, in the sense of an ontology of the self, and also property that might aid and assist in the material reproduction of basic needs like food, clothing, shelter, and security.

"Tanha" as unclenching, liberation consists of removing the self from "samsara," and the cycles of rebirth on the basis of appetitive motivations. There is no individual nirvana (arahat) without a collective returning detachment as a sort of Bodhisattva Vow, or else the only beings left would be those completely stuck in samsara. As consistent with the thesis forwarded throughout this book, the second interpretation makes the most sense in reading Buddhist teachings alongside the Marxist oeuvre.

Samsara within early Vedic belief systems served as a way of understanding the cycle of rebirth within this realm of concrete existence. Samsara often carries a negative connotation as it sets up existence as if it were a kind of devious trap. This endless cycle or round of existence[17] is precisely what we must escape. Buddha's awakening, as the story goes, eliminated the many defilement that crept into his existence. He resolved himself to become pure and rid himself of the least bit of defilement, some versions of the story claim that he was chaste for the rest of his life, but these are extreme examples. What the mythos of messianism in these stories reveals is a recurring libidinal tug of war while struggling to negate the eight worldly elements that cause defilement.

In discussing these worldly elements that some Buddhists claim cause moral defilement, there are no clear definitions of these, and it remains very vague what are the correct or incorrect interpretations of what is and is not defilement. Co-rectified is the deconstructed etymology of "co" as together, in agreement, and "rect" as uprightness. To agree upon what the right version of upright morality is is to veer into virtue ethics, something that my formulation of Marxist thought with this does not include because these ideas from virtue ethics are readily appropriable by political theology.

Who decides what is "co-rrect"/upright and what is incorrect? States and governments decide, typically with force. In making a political and economic category out of the "kleshas," my aim is to avoid presenting the eightfold path as merely a resource for self-help gurus because discussion of "kleshas" often quickly deteriorates into a subjectivist mish-mash of ideologies that feel right, even though these discussions do not utilize the kleshas in any technical sense if at all.

Whereas the three absorptions are clear as day, thought-conceptions and discursive thinking are clearly representational of surface chattering in the mind. Our minds cast a trance upon our deeper selves through the habituation of conditioned responses, which are then easily appropriable by culture industry that creates fashionable trances over the minds of millions through behavioral and operant conditioning. One example of the subconscious mechanisms of disciplinary control is the pupillary response in the eyes of someone watching television. Studies have shown that when the onscreen camera angle changes, the pupils dilate and audiences are more likely to stay tuned to a program. For maximum effect, the camera must change perspective every seven to ten seconds to ignite an automatic response in the pupil.

Stepping out into nature can attune you to a more peaceful, less disruptive set of thought-conceptions. As you move deeper, you gain blissful awareness of a deeper love than the surface levels of superficiality (ānanda)—a love that bonds us all on a natural, universal level, as singular entities from the same material ground. Lastly, the deepest absorption of jhāna is an unwavering contentment with self, because you then realize that the self is temporary, we only have this body for a limited time. Why worry? Be happy, but on a much deeper level than those who remain on the plane of immanence of "vitakka and vicāra," without control of thought-concepts (mind-movies as I sometimes call them) and discursive thinking in a dualistic sense at war with oneself and others. In a way, we are all oneself in different bodies—plant, animal, mineral, and all being of beings. It may have taken numerous returns to accrue karmic momentum to allow the universe to have cosmic awareness of itself in the form of the human mind and its intelligence.

A virtue ethics interpretation of these stories emerged over the years because virtue ethics was the only philosophical system available at that time with the eight worldly elements being cast as gain, fame, praise, happiness, and each of their opposites, poverty, ignorance in obscurity, humiliation, sadness as a cyclical round of existence matching the seasonal changes in nature, each with vices that accord with imbalance in the self. Each virtue can become a vice if the behavior is taken to its extreme. Mahayana refers to these vices as kleshas. Mental states that give rise to defilements. These kleshas are too numerous to list here. Some monks have listed approximately 1,500 different kleshas. The major ones that lead to defilement are jealousy, anxiety, fear, anger, and depression. The three poisons as they are called are the three root kleshas that form the roots of samsaric existence. The cycle of samsara derives from ignorance, attachment, and aversion. Grounding behaviors in these intentions means that the cycle of rebirth will continue. The self will return. In a way, Buddhist thought is a precursor to psychoanalysis.

Understanding mastery of the kleshas as release from samsara is crucial to understanding the connections with corporeality, because embodiment is often misconstrued as an aporia in Marxist thought. Some consider kleshas passed on through reincarnation. If habitual behaviors can be transmitted unreflectively from one generation to the next, this awareness deepens our insights into what it means to be a human being, the sole being that can reflect upon its own history in an individual sense of producing a personal life story, as well as constructing collective narratives that provide a sense of embodied selfhood.

I have maintained the thesis that reincarnation must be understood in purely materialist terms, because if something is reborn it must possess a corporeal form of embodiment into which it inhabits. Nevertheless, the belief in the "atman" maintains that if the soul is reborn, it inhabits another form of embodiment, even as the soul is inscribed with the karma/kleshas of previous lives. Moral inertia from past lives is carried over into this incarnation and perhaps into the next as well, even though there are no guarantees that another incarnation will occur. All we have are the collective kleshas with us now. Reincarnation must be understood in historical materialist terms as history weighs like a nightmare upon the living, one of the more famous lines penned by Karl Marx that is often taken out of context. To think historical materialism as kleshas (what Freud might call "cathexes," or what is fashionable to call "collective trauma" or intergenerational transference) passed on from previous lives, there are people who do think that meditation cleanses the karma inscribed upon the self from past lives.

There is circularity to time indicated by Nishida Kitarō when he says, there are no round trips in time, in other words, the only way out is through what is now, and yet we must also deal with the past as the inertia from the past is here now. Marx insinuates this when he writes in *Capital*:

> We suffer not only from the development of capitalist production, but also from the incompleteness of that development. Alongside the modern evils, we are oppressed by a whole series of inherited evils, arising from the passive survival

of archaic and outmoded modes of production, with their accompanying train of anachronistic social and political relations. We suffer not only from the living, but from the dead. *Le mort saisit le vif!*[18]

FOUR STAGES OF LIFE IN HINDUISM

Buddha says, upon reaching his enlightenment:

> Oh, householder (gahakara). Having broken the crossbeams and destroyed the peak of the roof of that house, I have attained nirvana, and am freed from all conditions. I have attained the transcendental state of the destruction of the intoxicants in which all grasping is destroyed![19]

Siddhartha was raised in Hinduism and was an appropriator who synthesized complex beliefs into simpler forms so that all people might have the opportunity to overcome dukkha. For those with a passing knowledge of the Hindu stages of life when Buddha refers to the householder, he means the Ashrama or the "householder" stage in life. This is the second stage after Bramachraya or "student" and before Vanaprastha or "retirement" after which is Sanyassa or "resignation" in preparation for moksha, the release from the cycle of rebirth—which we have already discussed as samsara. Depending on which sources you study, moksha may vary slightly from nirvana, yet the overall understanding is that there is a release from rebirth and the clenching of desire must occur only through completely shedding the corporeal form.[20] Buddha's use of the term "gahakara" described a move from householder into retirement as he moved into the Middle Way. A step along the path out of work, responsibility, child-rearing into a detached life, and this process can only be fully realized after being in the busy-ness of the householder stage where the responsibilities of being a pillar of the community fall on the shoulders of the virtuous if the society still has the ability to circulate virtuous people into positions of power and responsibility. Moving into the retirement phase is considered a liberating move where the burden of responsibility has been passed to the next generation.

The emphasis on moving past child-rearing is crucial, as few people know his son was named "Rahula" meaning little devil, or little anchor. Kids are little burdens, and the blessing is that they keep you grounded, however, as Engels revealed in his study of the formation of the family, the best way to keep someone anchored to private property is to pin down the worker by virtue of responsibility to a child.

To shed relationships is often a problematic part of Buddhist thought. A major aporia in philosophy is a bizarre fatalism, which is where a "do as thou will" attitude becomes kind of a problem when the world is imploding in almost constant exigencies. Both Marx and Buddha were not "general philosophers" and both carry serious limitations in their work. The marxism and Buddhism, with lower case letters, not as big historical movements, understand that any belief system must be revised, refined, developed, and advanced so as to perhaps detach from detachment in order to make progress. A revolution is a turn, a move, a circulation on the round of existence.

The kleshas were passed on through past lives to this "house" and his mind is merely the current householder of this particular body, from which the past desires, attachments, lusts, appetites, habits, and aversions that lead one into defilement have been transferred. Before enlightenment, no individual can know how many lifetimes have occurred in which the "I" looking out from behind those eyes has experienced suffering, suffering that has been inscribed upon the current house. Buddha continues by saying those who practice will not build a house, because the samsaric recurrence of being that identifies with itself on the basis of immediate sense-perception has been broken. The chain of being that traps the subject in the immediacy of the Five Aggregates (the five senses of perception, the five doorways into the body) has been broken.

If you think about rebirth and apply historical materialist analysis to the concept, as Marx tried to describe the development process of the determinate mode of production, Marx indicates the intertwining of different times in the determining process of capitalist production. Althusser describes this as a type of "dislocation" or (décalage) a torsion of different temporalities produced by different levels of the structure.[21] The inertia of previous generations has an effect on what occurs now, the previous generations are you. If your ancestors polluted the river that you now drink from, then their behaviors have an effect upon you, you have inherited their missteps. One might see glimpses of samsara as a materialist concept in the way Marx wrote that history weighs like a nightmare upon the living, and elsewhere that history repeats differently, first as tragedy then as farce. There are cyclical aspects to historical inversions of previous historical incarnations.

In the appearance of a recurring incarnation of the Godhead, tropes echoing from the earliest Vedic scriptures reveal this rebirth process with God making itself apparent to the world. In the Bhagavad-Gita, Krishna explains that as the messenger of God the being of God returns again and again: "Whenever sacred duty decays, and chaos prevails, then, *I create myself* . . . to protect humanity of its virtue, and destroy those who do evil, to set a standard of sacred duty, I appear in age after age."[22]

Is this a return that is an analogous repetition? or, as inventive communist hermeneutical thinkers interpret this as something else? Perhaps in an anomalous way? An analogous repetition relies on bios, its framework; a similar function with differing structures. For example, wings on birds and airplanes both allow the forms to fly, even though the wings on a bird may have different presentational qualities to that of an airplane. Birds typically have wings covered with feathers; whereas airplane wings are made of metal. The analogous interpretation, deriving from the Greek "analogos" and the Latin "analogous" meaning according to proper ratio and proportion, would reduce difference to a difference of surfaces with the identity of content remaining the same. As if the differing structures can always be contracted into the same content, we look different but we are all the same underneath our funny Halloween masks. Or, to make the polemical antithesis to this, difference is so different that each incarnation of Brahma, the Godhead, is so otherly that its difference fetishizes its exoticism to the point where no social bond can be discursively formed.

Brahman's reappearance as Godhead is conceptual personae as "repetition-for-itself" where the phrase "I create myself" construes a self-sustaining repetition. No empirical point around which this repetition revolves can be known by empirical standards of inquiry. Since, according to these narrative tropes, all creation exists within the mind of Brahman, the corporeal manifestation of God could happen at any moment, since all time is a construct of Brahman and we are all within that construct; all life is also integral to this liberatory process of becoming-awake.

BODHISATTVA OR ARHAT: WHAT KIND OF "BUDDHA BODY" IS THE OEUVRE LEFT BY MARX?

There are two main branches of Buddhist thought: Theravada that tended to rely on "arhat" interpretations of salvation, a term that would later be denigrated as "little vehicle" by Mahayana buddhists who prefered the bodhisattva path, and would refer to all other schools as hinayana, or "little vehicle" because the arhat seems to only care about selfish awakening. Differences between Theravada and Mahayana are nuanced, even though in contemporary times some of these categories may appear homogeneously. The key figures are the Bodhisattva in Mahayana, which are juxtaposed with Arhat in Theravada. It strikes me that there are two vastly different ways to read "Marx," and broadly speaking, Marx's oeuvre. What kind of "Buddha Body" are the texts left by Marx?

Can it be read as a "Great Vehicle" in the sense of a recurring bodhisattva vow? Transcending as a return. To reincarnate in the next life, means to return to the world in the aftermath of present dharma.

If the word "religion" etymologically arises in the context of "heilige" (as Marx uses it in German), which means "to bind" to something, especially in the way Marx writes about the purpose of religion is "binding" or "yoking" oneself to the state and to the virtues produced for workers by the bourgeoisie.

EIGHTFOLD PATH AND THE BODHISATTVA "BUDDHA MARX"

Much about those aspects of Marx's writings bear affinity with the eightfold path, not as a personal journey. "If you see Buddha in your path, kill him" as the oft cliched statement from Lin Chi tells us. The path is the awakening of the awareness that consciousness is always "yoked" to material conditions. Consciousness is always yoked to conditions of class. The eightfold path occurs as an open-ended *dispositif*—a way of exercising power within the body. Right speech, right work, right action, and so forth are the positively charged libidinal economy. An eightfold path is positively reinforced; whereas, most western Marxisms appropriate from a Hegelian methodology, thus constituting something called "critical theory" as the endless negation of negation of negation. Appropriating from the Judaic "negative theology" as in the ten commandments is negative ressentiment that speaks itself as "no . . . no . . . no . . ." Your path is your path.

Does that mean the eightfold path is an example of arhat? Or, are we supposed to be diligent bodhisattva workers with our eyes down like the dull-minded laboring horse in Orwell's *Animal Farm* who keeps pulling the plow? A sturdy, Stoic, void of imagination, of no-mind echoing the mantra: "Keep doing the work, there's bound to be an end soon, keep working." No! If we understand *pratitya-samutpāda*, then right actions, work, speech, thoughts, and so forth are always already interconnected. We are not monads; our subjectivity is nomadic; it flows, moves, shifts, connects, and coproduces. Whether we have the awareness or not is another story entirely, but we are all produced by something else and we all carry on to produce and in some cases, life consists of "anti-producers." To put it in terms known by readers of Deleuze and Guattari:

> It is impossible to separate the production of any consumer commodity from the institution that supports that production. The same can be said of teaching, training, research, etc. The state machine and the machine of repression produce anti-production, that is to say signifiers that exist to block and prevent the emergence of any subjective process [. . .].[23]

In seeing the eightfold path, many people think it merely espouses virtues of humility, quietude, and various Judeo-Christian-Islamic[24] "slave-moralities" as Nietzsche called them. This mindset is perhaps where Marxists went wrong. Political praxis was framed within a metaphysics of Judeo-Christian-Islamic yoking of God to the state. The cult of personality surrounding the leader had to take a Messianic Form. Hence, in this framework the only viable result is political theology and fascist messianism. Buddhist thought is not necessarily like that, although people have interpreted the teachings of the Buddha as if it were a political theology, I am of the opinion that this is a mistaken interpretation. Buddha literally means "awake" and the philosophy of Buddhism forms a practice to help people become awake. Simple as that. It is not a religion in the sense of binding oneself to the Buddha. In fact, one of the most quoted sayings in the Buddhist philosophical tradition is "if the Buddha is in your path, kill him." Often attributed to the ninth-century Buddhist monk Lin Chi. It is meant as a reminder to those who genuinely believe that the Buddha himself provided all of the answers, are inhibiting their own path toward awakening by turning the Buddha into a messianic figure rather than experiencing their own individual path to awakening. I see a parallel in the ways contemporary readers of Marx used to consider "what is living and what is dead" in the philosophy of Marx. In the sense that the oeuvre of writings left by Marx are intended to be useful, and if they are not, then set them aside rather than turn Karl Marx into a messianic figure with all the answers.

If we move through the tenets of the eightfold path in sequence, while this is a rudimentary prolegomenon of sorts, and if we accept the view that there are three main sites of Marxist struggle—economic, ideological, and political—then reading the steps along the path through Marx might look something like this:

1. **Right Views**: Questions can arise when the self-directed mind emerges, rather than the "mish-mash" of opinions that occur in average socialism or crude communism. A right view of the self must understand itself as a social metabolism, a species-being whose nature is constructed as a social metabolism with nature and with others through its relationship with the processes of production. Production is being and being is production. In describing Nishida's early meditation practice, I describe his Kenshō moment in a later chapter. This is important because the Japanese Zen word for "ken" (seeing or to see) is "shō" (true nature, essence). Self is revealed to be an avatār constructed from the mind of social reality. Therefore, no self-exists in any essentialist notion of discovering a fixed object that clarifies selfhood as self-identical to itself.
2. **Right Intent**: Gramscian saying perhaps says it all: the pessimism of the intellect, optimism of the will. Seizing the modes of production as a form of ontological liberation. Taking control of the ends of production

of oneself and social production of beings with others. Throwing off the yoke of "ground rent" where most of the value of production goes wasted to produce a consciousness of collective self-interest.

3. **Right Speech**: *parrhesia*,[25] or risky speech, in the sense of speaking truth to power, or saying everything openly and honestly—spreading radical thought that breaks the frame of self-referential ideological mirroring, because right speech does not mean remaining so humble that one "turns the other cheek" to advance the will of oppression through humility, nor does *parrhesia* mean saying the right thing, in the right way, to the right person, at the right time so as not to offend others. Parrhesia is fearless speech that cries out the king is not king, the emperor has no clothes, and even though they may or may not know what they are doing, the truth must be told.

4. **Right Conduct**: In the later discourses, the Buddha explicates this to be a call to understanding moral behavior objectively before trying to improve it. In some senses, the student who is disciplining themselves into right conduct is carefully reflecting upon the motives that prompt virtuous actions. In a Marxist sense, this can be best understood as the shifting ground of material conditions propels human conduct and motivation. If there are precarious material conditions, then the chaos and uncertainty will produce egoist actions. If there are secure and stable conditions of material reproduction, then the social antagonisms of class-conflict wither away, and social production creates the cultivation of a higher consciousness that is motivated by the collective good. This is assured through the creation of shared resources and shared work load, perhaps with rotating professions, and thus an economy of empathy based on rotating occupational identities.

  As Marx argues in Critique of the Gotha Program, it may be necessary to create a reserve fund for the expansion of production, the replacement of machinery, the development and expansion of schools.

5. **Right Livelihood**: In no sense is the "Buddha as corporate efficiency consultant" implied in the sense of "livelihood" because in Vedic teachings there are four types of yoga (or "yokings"): raja (body health, reintegration, psycho-psychological exercises), bhakti (love), karma (actions, work), and jnana (self-knowledge, thoughtfulness). Right livelihood is the balance between all of these activities with the purpose of being in harmony throughout life. It is the rarest thing in the world to find someone who is truly alive. This is because to live, one must be assured of the material reproducibility of the basic necessities of life. Therefore, the right livelihood can only truly occur after the wage-labor system, the state, and the mechanisms of disciplinary power that produce *dispositifs* at the micro-political level have thus withered away. In the capitalist

system, this "right livelihood" can only be caught in glimpses. Nevertheless, the highest form of flourishing can occur if and only if there is transcendence beyond the basis of inequality of material conditions, when labor power is no longer estranged from the ends of its own production, and the products are shared among those who produce.

However, if every member of society, performing a certain part of necessary work "receives a certificate from society to the effect that he has done such and such a quantity of work . . . 'equality' seems to reign supreme . . . equal right presupposes inequality," because, "different people are not alike, one is strong, another is weak, one is married, the other is not, one has more children, another has less, and so on," and so "with equal labor . . . and an equal share in the social consumption fund, one man in fact receives more than the other, one is richer than the other," and as Lenin argues in State and Revolution: "the injustice consists in the means of production having been seized by private individuals, and which is not capable of destroying the further injustice consisting in the distribution of the articles of consumption 'according to work performed' and not according to need."[26]

6. **Right Effort**: A string pulled too taut will snap. A tight yoke is burdensome. Right effort is immanent, internal to the subject, and cannot be outsourced. Labor becomes the source of wealth only through its process as a social production. As an enhancement of self and community through its productive qualities that are no longer held as property of the capitalist class.

As Marx wrote with Fredrick Engels in the *Communist Manifesto*, the proletariats are those who without means of production of their own must reduce themselves to selling their labor for a wage.[27] In the workers' state every local administrator is elected by local constituencies and the process of centralization of the modes of production keeps the fruits of labor effectively distributed and proportioned according to needs. The whole of society will become one social body and mind when "all have learned to manage, and independently are actually managing by themselves social production, keeping accounts, controlling the idlers, the gentlefolk, the swindlers and similar 'guardians of capitalist traditions,' then the escape from national accounting and control will inevitably become so increasingly difficult"[28] that the observation of simple, fundamental rules of everyday social life in common will become habit, Lenin says, in describing what Foucault might refer to as a disciplinary society as the necessary proletarian state prior to the eventual withering away of the state entirely.

Much more recent work in contemporary Marxist political theory outlines this "affective labor" as the immaterial labor power of social reproduction.

As Michael Hardt and Antonio Negri explain in *Empire*, "What affective labor power produces are social networks, forms of community, biopower," and what is truly crucial to this is the "creation and manipulation of affect." With affective production, exchange, and communication generally associated with human contact, in the newer versions of global capitalism, a capitalist realism emerges where that contact can be either actual or virtual as in the case of the entertainment industry. Problematic as it is, nevertheless the biopolitical aspects of capitalism involve labor power more and more with social interactions and cooperation. "Cooperation is completely immanent to the laboring activity itself," as biopolitics constructs its disciplinary power by moving crisis and identity politics that were once marginal directly into the central dimension of these social relations. As Hardt and Negri explain,

> Today productivity, wealth, and the creation of social surpluses take the form of cooperative interactivity through linguistic, communicational, and affective networks. In the expression of its own creative energies, immaterial labor thus seems to provide the potential for a kind of spontaneous and elementary communism.[29]

7. **Right Mindfulness**: An old saying in the Buddhist tradition goes: The mind makes a terrible master, and a wonderful slave. The mind must be trained to see beyond false consciousness. Mindfulness is summarized in the opening lines of the Dhammapada: "All we are is a result of what we have thought." Marx dialectically overturns centuries of "mind-only" consciousness that came to a crescendo in Hegelian self-consciousness. As he wrote in the Postface to the Second Edition of *Capital*:

> For Hegel, the process of thinking, which he even transforms into an independent subject, under the name of "the Idea," is the creator of the real world, and the real world is only the external appearance of the idea. With me the reverse is true: the ideal is nothing but the material world reflected in the mind of man, and translated into forms of thought.[30]

Take, for example, this passage from the Lew Ayers *Altars of the East*, written in 1956, as a Westerners observation of monks in Thailand practicing this seventh virtue:

One of them spends hours each day slowly walking about the grounds of the wat in absolute concentration upon the minutest fraction of every action connected with each step. The procedure is carried into every single physical act of daily life until, theoretically, the conscious mind can follow every step that goes into the generation of a feeling, perception or thought. A fifty-year-old monk meditates in a small graveyard adjoining his wat, because he's undisturbed there. He seats himself, cross-legged and immobile but with his eyes open, for hours on end—through the driving rain at midnight or the blistering heat of noonday. His usual length of stay is two or three hours.[31]

Imagine if the focused attention of the trained monk could be the force behind a political movement. Ayers might as well be describing someone staring off into the abyss, a gaze the monks perfect for years. To slow down the mind-movies and inner-chatterings of the mind are necessary as a precursor to the sustained attention span necessary for deliberative political discourse and direct action. Unfortunately, it results in endless navel gazing and echoes the famous line from Nietzsche: If you stare into the abyss, the abyss stares into you. Activists who fail to stare into the abyss produce theoryless praxis that mirrors the face of the master. For example, the immediatism of direct action almost always has an element of anarcho-capitalism that blunts any effective potential for transformation.

In joining theories of labor ("Marx") with Buddhist "right mind" is to reach this spirit of mindful concentration especially within the context of work (or Karma Yoga). Building merit through good actions. Immersion in an activity can help someone pay attention to what is happening, drawing attention outside of oneself, and form connections with social communities beyond the atomized individual.[32] This is one way of understanding "species-being" as drawing workers into a social context beyond individual consciousness.

8. **Right Concentration**: Friction-free capitalism is a ruse. As those who have read Marx, Engels, Lenin, Mao, Gramsci, Althusser, and so forth know, the state exists to reconcile the antagonisms of class-conflict, usually through "free and open discourses" (i.e., spectacle) that produce distractions by means of "ecclecticism, by an unprincipled, sophistic, arbitrary selection to oblige the powers that be)."[33] In effect, the postmodern biopolitical capitalist culture that has been studied so often is little more than the anarchy of social production. Concentration is so difficult because the glue that holds together this morass of chaotic conditions, the dispositif that holds together the hybrid body of capitalist antagonism is the spectacle which regulates public discourse and opinion. We are in the era of capitalist realism when the imperialist phase of capitalism has ended and the colonial subjects have begun entering into the metropoles of capital. Yet, Lenin's appraisal of the imperialist phase of capitalist expansion still holds true:

> Imperialism in particular—the era of banking capital, the era of gigantic capitalist monopolies, the era of the transformation of monopoly capitalism into state monopoly-capitalism—shows an unprecedented strengthening of

the "state machinery" and an unprecedented growth of its bureaucratic and military apparatus, since by side with the increase of repressive measures against the proletariat, alike in the monarchical and the freest republican countries.[34]

In other words, the dialectic that Engels outlines in *Socialism: Utopian and Scientific*, where the natural tendency is to have wealth gravitate toward monopolies, remains exactly the same. The technologies and mechanisms have changed. Nevertheless, state monopoly capitalism correlates with the strengthening of "state machinery" and repressive state apparatuses; therefore, the proletariat and the industrial reserve army who are most repressed and are most likely to remain subjects of the state, by this I refer to the line from State and Revolution from Lenin: "What does power mainly consist of? It consists of special bodies of armed men who have at their disposal prisons, etc."[35] are also shielded from the market forces and those whose wealth grows through the process of state monopoly capital and state repression. Therefore, the tendency among those without awareness or class consciousness to conflate the association with all forms of economic planning, scientific socialism, and centralization, with state repression, gulags, and imprisonment for disobedience. Another mistake due to the fact that the hegemonic classes own the dominant discourses and the media is to associate wealth accumulation with some intrinsic virtue within the wealthy person, as if wealth accumulation consists of an intrinsic signal of virtue within particular individuals. Right concentration in a Marxist sense might mean seeing through these ideological smoke screens.

Focus on the "ends of production" while remembering that even the Buddha told his followers one day that he had his first inkling of awakening years before he left home. While still a small boy, he was sitting one day in the cool shade of an apple tree, as he was coursing in the deep thought of nature in its beauty, he found himself in what he would later describe as the first level of the absorptions, and it was the return to that deepening of experience, as much as the disillusionment with the tinsel of life and its usual rewards of fleeting pleasures that produced nothing less than a completely new philosophy of life.

In the context of the eightfold path, one might think that the teachings of the Buddha set up some kind of negative reinforcement, or somehow force a choice between "this or that." In fact, nothing could be further from the truth. Either-or choices were created out of a dualistic way of thinking that is furthest from both the philosophies of Marx and Buddha. As the Buddha said in the Vaipulya Sutra he speaks "neither existing nor extinct, neither permanent nor annihilated, neither identical nor differentiated, neither coming nor going." A point that is illuminated by Marx. When people try to force a decision between two non-choices, the best thing to do is reframe the question in terms that expose the a priori first principles that bias the way the question is presented to begin with:

> Communism is quite incomprehensible . . . because the communists do not oppose egoism to selflessness or selflessness to egoism, nor do they express this contradiction theoretically either in its sentimental or in its highflown ideological form; *they rather demonstrate its material source, with which it disappears of itself.* The communists do not preach morality at all. . . . They do not put to people the moral demand: love one another, do not be egoists, etc.; on the contrary, they are very well aware that egoism, just as much as selflessness, is in definite circumstances, a necessary form of the self-assertion of individuals.

Notice the breaking of the false-dyad that Marx presents us with here, the choice that is not a choice. By saying, "communists do not preach morality at all" one might jump in and say, "So, communists are immoral?" remember, it is not this, not that, not preaching morality means morality is not the basis with which people are made to be moral. Morality cannot be preached through discursive measures, because moral and immoral behaviors are motivated by material conditions. A desperate person who is starving to death may steal a loaf of cinnamon bread out of necessity. Stealing means surviving in otherwise destitute material conditions and there is no discursive way to understand it, which posits stealing as distinct from greed, because greed is the bourgeois who has enough and takes more than is needed. Both are egoism. Both are guided by different intentions.

One is egoism out of desperation to survive, and perhaps there are children who depend on that act of egoism. Greediness intends to take more than needed and push an imbalance of wealth even further. Someone with wealth has the power to choose and therefore can decide one way or another. Framing all ethical choices in terms of free will means that there is a bias in the frame in favor of the bourgeois ethical a priori. The way to understand the difference between one action and any other is to demonstrate the material source of the motivation. Greed is motivated from a material source of prior existing wealth and is therefore unethical. Stealing from a position of material poverty is motivated from a material position of destitution and is manifest on the basis of survival. Greed, is not to be understood as a free will choice between "egoism" and "selflessness," but rather egoism and selflessness manifest as human behavior as demonstrative of its material source. Changing the material source of an action changes the behavior that is manifest. Marx continues:

> Communists by no means want . . . to do away with the "private individual" for the sake of the "general," selfless man. That is a figment of the imagination . . . communists know that this contradiction is only a seeming one because one side of it, what is called the 'general interest' is constantly being produced by the other side, private interest.[36]

If anything that we see in the ways "morality" is framed in debate format as if these were questions of discursive abstraction and propositional logic rather than material conditions. "Good or evil," "egoism or selflessness" are non-choices. Reading the Buddha, one clearly sees that these are precisely the tactics that the Buddha uses in many of the Sutras passed on from his followers, all the way up to more contemporary usages of the Zen kōan with the desired effect in confusing the question, is kenshō.

By demonstrating the ineffectiveness of the way the questioner framed the question, often the desired effect is to reveal the biases inherent in the way the question was framed to begin with, a subtlety often lost on many who register the kōans as a kind of flippant irrationalism, a nihilistic "anything goes!" kind of nonsensical jargon. By turning "Marxism" on to Buddhism, we can ingratiate a metaphysics that was always already there—the metaphysics of conditioned coproduction, which reveals multifaceted ways that our habits are formed out of our behaviors from previous lifetimes, and the lifetimes of our ancestors.

> Men make their own history, but they do not make it as they please; they do not make it under self-selected circumstances, but under circumstances existing already, given and transmitted from the past. The tradition of all dead generations weighs like a nightmare on the brains of the living. And just as they seem to be occupied with revolutionizing themselves and things, creating something that did not exist before, precisely in such epochs of revolutionary crisis they anxiously conjure up the spirits of the past to their service, borrowing from them names, battle slogans, and costumes in order to present this new scene in world history in time-honored disguise and borrowed language.[37]

A thesis I try to forward in this book is that the texts left by Marx are a kind of Bodhisattva Vow. Which means that the good-end of communism really has to do with assisting in the development of the highest form of human consciousness. Distributive justice without a telos amounts to a hamster wheel of production for production's sake. Work is not merely work for the sake of work itself, but a vow to devote your life to the supreme moral perfection of all sentient beings through humble service toward others.

Any great philosopher can have that effect through the re-reading of their writings even after their corporeal body is gone. Jacques Derrida may have an inkling of this in *Spectres of Marx* without fully and openly acknowledging a bodhisattva, Mahayana metaphysics in his work. In the exegesis on the spirit that is gone, but not really gone, throughout that which has an epiphenomenal effect without a corporeal presence.

In linking Marx to Buddhism there can be a tendency to read this as saying somehow Marx was a reincarnated old soul, perhaps a brahmin in an earlier life, and so forth. Nothing would be further from the truth, and nothing would register as true more commonly among ordinary New Age spiritualists, the kind of thing that one might imagine turns the vast oeuvre of Buddhist philosophy into little more than a spirituality that forms the thesis that in order for the subject to have access to the truth, the subject must transform, shift, or in some way change itself.

The truth being something other than what the subject is, and the guru presenting himself (almost always the guru is a male, unless it is Quan Yin, who is the most notable Bodhisattva in the Mahayana tradition) as someone who has an unvarnished access to the truth. The subject is supposed to ask the master,

> In what aspects and how must I transform my being as subject? What conditions must I impose on my being as subject so as to have access to the truth, and to what extent will this access to the truth give me what I seek, that is, the highest good, the sovereign good?[38]

Questions that Michel Foucault said were central to the two predominant hermeneutics of the subject in the twentieth century: Marxism and psychoanalysis, which he shows were passed forth from Greek antiquity through Christian "confessions of the flesh" through entangled, diverse, concealed, and inscribed epistemes into current discourses of power/knowledge. My hope is that by showing excerpts from the oeuvre left by Marx alongside the myriad of Buddhist philosophical texts, it will be possible to untangle Marx from psychoanalysis (the twentieth century gave us no shortage of psychoanalysis/Marxism syntheses) and that the risk of turning Buddhism into yet another form of psychoanalysis-producing-docile-bodies as a capitalist consulting firm. All psychoanalysts except say Jacques Lacan and the lesser-known attachment theories of John Bowlby fall into this category of analysis as capitalist consulting firms. Buddhism has been lumped into a Hegelian-psychoanalytical capitalist consulting firm. This book tries to expropriate Marx and Buddhism from the notion that capitalism is the "absolute universal" into which all consciousness should synthesize.

NOT-BEING: HEART, DIAMOND, AND LOTUS SUTRAS[39]

The three sutras that most aptly introduce Buddhist thought have to be the Heart, Diamond, and Lotus Sutras, which form the basis of "Mahayana Buddhism". Included in this is Chan Buddhism, as a sub-sect with its special emphasis on nothingness. These sutras are also read and studied but other non-Chan Mahayana schools. For example, the Lotus Sutra is very important for Tiantai school in China, Tendai school in Japan, and Nichiren Buddhist schools in Japan. These sects/schools are not Chan or Zen. Nishida philosophy was influenced by these teachings. Which, in turn, had an enormous impact on framing the "me-ontology"[40] of Japanese thought, as influenced through Nishida. I will simply refer to this as "ontology" throughout the book, and it should be carefully noted that Nishida does not need to be categorized as purely Buddhist, or Eastern, in the sense that his work has much to contribute to philosophy outside the matrices of religious thought. However, the references to these sutras should not go unnoticed.

Nishida's quotations of various Zen and other Buddhist scriptures, especially in the last writings, are referred to several times in each of his last works. Things like "mind that is mind because it is not mind" and "the discrimination of non-discrimination" were apparently derived directly from D.T. Suzuki's soku-hi logic, which refers to the logic of what "is and at the same time is not" from the Diamond Sutra.[41]

MARXIST THREADS WOVEN THROUGH KYOTO PHILOSOPHY

The two main "Marxists" in the Kyoto School were Tosaka Jun and Miki Kiyoshi (both of whom died in prison shortly after World War II. Most of their work has some fusion of Marxist and Hegelian concepts and Miki in particular utilizes a "proletariat awakening" as his methodology for many years, although it is unclear if Miki should be considered a marxist in the strict sense of ideological adherence to a sort of marxist-infallibility. His work, much like mine here is akin to a schizzed, or deconstructive reading of the texts of Marx. To awaken the workers through the infusion of Marxist concepts into Buddhist categories of analysis, particularly "Shinren and Honen" who were the first Pure Land Buddhists in Japan, although Pure Land Buddhism had existed for centuries before them in China and even in Japan within the Tendai sect as a practice, if not an independent sect/school.

As far as Nishida, much of his work is covertly "Marxist," and even though his students Tosaka Jun and Miki Kiyoshi criticized him for not having a theory of reification, a careful reading of Nishida's *Intelligibility and the Philosophy of Nothingness*, and "Unity of Opposites" essays reveals that these writings are laden with dialectical concepts that most Nishida scholars interpret as "Hegelian"; and yet, one of the theses I am trying to forward in this book is that these are easily appropriable into Marxist categories. To reiterate the point made previously in this chapter, Marx characterizes his dialectical method:

> the ideal is nothing but the material world reflecting in the mind of man, and translated into forms of thought.[42]

A marxist dialectical method can help us to understand what Nishida means when describing "enveloping" that seems to be interpreted in exactly the a-political way that Nishida seems to criticize when he opens his essay entitled *The Unity of Opposites* (or "absolute contradictory self-identity") by writing:

> The world of reality is a world where things are acting on things. The form and figure of reality are to be thought as a mutual relationship of things, as a result of acting and counteracting. But this mutual acting of things means that things deny themselves, and that the thing-character is lost.[43]

He then gives a definition of "poiesis" as he sees it as the world of reality as "absolute contradictory self-identity," and that this is a result of the world moving from the "formed, the product" to the "the forming, creative self-production."[44]

Whether he intends it or not is another question, but Nishida does give his readers the tools to understand how ideology reproduces material conditions in what he refers to as "enveloping"; but in almost completely Hegelian terms, the sort of conceptualization that Marx himself would have perhaps utilized in describing bourgeois-class consciousness as being a general intellect that subsumes all other consciousness in its autotelic valorization made possible through the bourgeoisie's position as the hegemonic class. Nishida does not say all this, but if you read between the lines in sections of his essay "The Intelligible World," the influences are clearly there when he writes trying to show an insubstantial self that cannot be reified because it exists beyond the realm of physical entities and can only be accessed as "spirit":

"Self-consciousness is beyond the realm of predicates," which one might take to mean that the self is not a discursive subject, a merely linguistic construction produced entirely out of language, but Nishida continues, "What is called Self or Ego is beyond the determinations of space and time" clearly, a knock on Kantian intuition as springing forth out of our phenomenological experience of ourselves as entities in space and time, and then by extension this has to be considered a criticism of Heidegger. With a Nietzschean twist Nishida continues: "it is the individual, in the abyss of the individual in space and time." Hence, the double repetition of the term individual in this sentence marks the return of the "absolute contradictory self-identity" as the inner-dialectic that Nishida later goes on to say makes us human rather than the reflexive mirroring of animality: "the world of animal instinct, the animal is desiring insofar as it mirrors the world"[45] and echoing Marx's theory of labor power as species-being, where the metabolism of our social life is accompanied by our relations in the marketplace and our social metabolism of nature (inner-human nature and external nature, which we take into ourselves through consumption); Nishida makes a similar point:

> At the transition from animal to man, we become social beings. In society there are already individuals. Society originates in poeises as center. Our conceptual knowledge must have originally developed from social production. The concept of "thing" must have originally been developed through social production. The origin of conceptual knowledge lies (I think) in the style of production, of self-forming things which have been conceived through social production.[46]

To turn back to Nishida's *Intelligible World* essay, it becomes clear that the "Universal which envelops the universal of judgment" in other words, a realm beyond mere mind-only consciousness of judgment as Hegelian concept of mind ideationally projecting onto concrete objects, it is the other way around for Nishida, because he continues by saying, "if that which determines itself through judgments is called the 'concrete' Universal, then this concrete Universal must have several planes of determination in itself, and in these planes it determines its own content."[47] Most people have interpreted this "determining" process of the concrete as either an homage to Nietzschean perspectivism where Nishida is describing a self-deciphering many planes of consciousness internal to itself as if the "concrete determines its own content" as an existential individual. Whereas a Marxist reading of this makes it clear that Nishida may have also intended to describe "concrete material conditions" that produce consciousness, not as a homogeneous "one"-size-fits-all, but as a heterogeneous differentially constructed general intellect.

A point that Nishida clarifies when writing, perhaps tipping his hand in favor of Marx:

> It is an abstract Universal, because it gives only one aspect of a single being which has its place in the concrete Universal. Which regard to the Universal in general, the abstract Universal signifies the planes of determination, where the concrete Universal determines itself.[48]

Then, echoing his sentiments later on that without saying it the animal is implied in all "mirroring" in Nishida's philosophy, the mirroring of the Universal of self-consciousness. He might as well have called it "hegemonic consciousness of the bourgeoisie appearing as if normal"; Nishida writes: "from the standpoint of the Universal of self-consciousness; it is the plane where the Universal of self-consciousness mirrors its own content."

Then, in describing anti-reification resistance as will in a non-substantialist description, Nishida writes:

"Not intentions, but will is the essence of consciousness"[49] and rather than poiesis as labor power moving material in a physicalist sense, taking lumber from a forest and making it into paper or a wooden stool, Nishida is carefully describing "will" as "knowing efficacy and effective knowledge . . ."[50] when someone says "I" am this, or "I" am that, they reify themselves insofar as their identity is "placed" on a topographical matrix of location, whereas "doing means a change, means to become different."[51] Yet, "acting as 'being' becomes full of contradiction," in the sense that the self that tries to grasp itself as a stable identity, eventually congeals into grasping onto itself as an object, and this is what causes contradictions. A mistaken interpretation of "Marxist"-philosophy turns contradictions in capitalism as if these are propositional contradictions.

Nishida gives us a clearer understanding of material conditions and the heterogeneous planes of consciousness that these conditions produce. Consciousness arises through adapting forms and formations to new arising material conditions that may provoke class-conflict and the end of all classes, or not, but the point is that the phenomenology offered by Nishida can be read as produced by material conditions. Hence, this mistake is repeated over and over in Western political theory, because "will is the last 'being' which has its place in the Universal of self-consciousness. Will is, as many pessimists say, the point of contradiction: we desire in order to end the desire; we live in order to die."[52] It may seem strangely "dialectical" for Nishida to say this, but it is crystal clear that he is evoking a critique of "dukkha" through unclenching from "being" as a substantialist physical entity in any material sense.

A lesser-known later essay from Nishitani Keiji titled "The Awakening of Self in Buddhism,"[53] as a Buddhist-existentialist, we find him arguing that even if a total class revolution were to occur where proletariat conquers the bourgeoisie and creates a classless society (as Marx hoped), to truly be free, the proletariat would still have to work on an "inner" revolution.

The essay is interesting because it takes the approach that Marxists focus primarily on "external material conditions" as the only form of revolution. Whereas Buddhists have only focused on an "inner revolution" at the level of consciousness, whereas the "external revolution" falls short of any transformative effect internal to the subject. If the revolutionaries inspired by Marx are only capable of focusing on external material conditions then the post-revolutionary society that a communist friendly organization tries to establish will ultimately reproduce the latent ideologies that carry over from the capitalism prior to the revolution, because the consciousness internal to the subject has yet to be fully transformed.

The problem of hermeneutics is the problem of "the perfect map" as the example of the impossibility of creating a perfect self-representational system.

NOTES

1. Gianni Vattimo and Santiago Zabala's work *Hermeneutical Communism* is one point of inspiration.
2. William Butler Yeats. *The Second Coming*.
3. Marx letter to Antoinette Philips. March 18, 1866.
4. Inoue Enryō, Buddhist Philosophy, *Selected Works of Inoue Enryō*, volume 7. Pg. 107–181.
5. Louis Althusser says this about Marx in so many words: Marx was not born a "Marxist"—Marx even says it about himself later on in life over the ways he believed his son-in-law Paul LaFargue was misappropriating "Marxism" from his work and he said about Lafargue: "If that is Marxism then I am not a Marxist," which would indicate a level of disdain toward those who generalize the category of "Marxist" this or that.
6. Suttanipāta, 3.6.31.
7. Political Spirituality, as opposite from political theology in the sense of Carl Schmitt's use of theology to bind religion with a messianic view of sovereignty, which is the fascist political legacy that basically every "cult of personality" in the twentieth century has utilized. A charismatic leader rises up, from the discursive position of marginality, rallies the people, and everyone winds up less free with the world

in rubble. Rather than erecting a fascist state, the goal is to offer a Marx that is a "line of flight" out of the state.

8. Bhagavad-Gita, 4.1.
9. Ibid., 4.8.
10. Sukhamala Sutta: Refinement.
11. Ibid.
12. Frederick Engels. *Socialism: Utopian and Scientific.* Translated by Edward Aveling, 1908.
13. Donald K. Swearer. "Consecrating the Buddha." In *Buddhism in Practice.* Edited by Donald S. Lopez, Princeton University Press: New York, 1995. Pg. 55.
14. Gayatri Chakravorty Spivak. "Moving Devi." *Cultural Critique* 47 (2001): 120–163.
15. A clearly fictional number that indicates a vaguely long length of time and is meant to tell us it is a story about "becoming-awake." This finds analogous temporal paralleling in Matthew 4:1 of the Gospels which depicts Jesus entering the Judean Desert for forty days to withstand temptations from and testing by the devil after being Baptized into the Holy Spirit by John the Baptist. Jesus then returns to Jerusalem and is tempted again and again, with two key temptations occurring right before the Sermon on the Mount and also while Jesus is in the midst of the Crucifixion he finds himself tested and cries out "Father, father why have you forsaken me?" what is widely considered among Christians to be his most important teachings, the point is that spiritual exercises that test the soul are crucial for "becoming-awake."
16. Kafka loosely based this story on himself as legend has it he wrote it as semi-autobiographical, even working on final drafts of the story as he died of tuberculosis in 1924.
17. Harold Talbott. The Round of Existence. *Studies in Comparative Religion.* Vol. 5, 1. Winter, 1971.
18. Karl Marx. *Capital: Critique of Political Economy.* Translated by Ben Fowkes. Penguin: London, 1990, volume 1. Pg. 90.
19. "Consecrating the Buddha." Pg. 55.
20. There are many missed opportunities for this kind of reading of the famous Socratic dialogue. The Phaedo, where Socrates is said to have uttered the lines "the soul is imprisoned by the body," as he contemplates whether or not to choose to drink the hemlock and die.
21. Louis Althusser. *Reading Capital.* Verso: London. Pg. 116.
22. *Bhagavad-Gita*, book 4: Jnana Yoga—"Knowledge," section 7–8. (emphasis is my own).
23. Gilles Deleuze and Felix Guattari. *Anti-Oedipus: Capitalism and Schizophrenia*, volume 1, 1984. Pg. 34.
24. I will continue to include Islam in the midst of Judeo-Christian-Islam.
25. Michel Foucault. *Government of the Self and Others parts 1 and 2: Lectures at the College de France, 1982–1984.* Picador Press.
26. Vladimir Lenin. *State and Revolution.* Pg. 76–77.

27. Karl Marx and Frederick Engels. *The Communist Manifesto*. Pg. 1, first footnote where Marx and Engels clearly define the difference between bourgeoisie and proletariat as the difference in property relations.

28. Lenin. *State and Revolution*. Pg. 84–85.

29. Michael Hardt and Antonio Negri. *Empire*, 2000. Pg. 292–294.

30. Karl Marx. *Capital volume 1. Postface to the Second Edition*, written January 24, 1873.

31. Lee Ayers. *Altars of the East*. Doubleday: Garden City, NY, 1956. Pg. 90–91.

32. Mihaly Csikszentmihalyi. *Flow: The Psychology of Optimal Experience*. Harper Perennial, 1990.

33. Lenin. *State and Revolution.* Pg. 19.

34. Ibid. Pg. 29.

35. Ibid. Pg. 10.

36. Karl Marx. *German Ideology*. Section 3: Saint Max. Pg. 264.

37. Karl Marx. *18th Brumaire of Louis Bonaparte*.

38. Michel Foucault. *Hermeneutics of the Subject: Lectures at the College de France 1981–82*.

39. Red Pine has done amazing translations and analyses of these from an historical perspective. See his translations of Heart, Diamond, and Lotus Sutras for further analysis; this is merely a summary en route to my work on Marx and Nishida.

40. Nishida's philosophy is referred to as me-ontology, which derives from the term "not-being" from Greek, but to avoid confusion with a misreading as if Nishida forwarded a solipsistic variation of pro-egotistical Randianism, I will avoid that phraseology wherever possible.

41. Michiko Yusa. Pg. 330.

42. Karl Marx. "Postface to the Second Edition." *Capital: Volume 1*, Vintage, 1977. Pg. 102.

43. Nishida Kitarō. "The Unity of Opposites." In Intelligibility and the Philosophy of Nothingness. Translated by Robert Shinzinger. Pg. 83.

44. Ibid.

45. "Unity of Opposites." Intelligibility and the Philosophy of Nothingness by Nishida Kitarō. Pg. 111.

46. Ibid. Pg. 107.

47. Intelligible World by Nishida Kitarō. Pg. 39.

48. Ibid.

49. Ibid. Pg. 41.

50. Ibid.

51. Ibid. Pg. 42.

52. Ibid. Pg. 44.

53. Nishitani Keiji. "The Awakening of Self in Buddhism." In *The Buddha Eye: An Anthology of the Kyoto School*. Edited by Frederick Frank, 1981.

Chapter 2

Samsara, Pervasion, and Conditioned Coproduction

"However, there is always samsara, endless transmigration, from the standpoint of the self as an objective existence. Here there is eternal delusion. Now when the self realizes its own bottomlessly contradictory identity, it discovers the possibility of object logic as one of its abstract moments. *Delusion only arises if one becomes attached to objective determination, to taking what is conceived of by object logic as concrete reality.*"

Nishida Kitarō, *Bashoteki ronri to shukyoteki sekaikan*[1]

"They are doing it without knowing they are doing it. Value, therefore, does not have its description branded on its forehead; it rather transforms every product of labor into a social hieroglyphic."

Karl Marx, *Capital* vol. 1[2]

In this chapter, I want to summarize some of the ancient and classical forms of metaphysical causality that one may encounter in the subtext of reading the Kyoto School philosophers. Some of this may seem familiar and some of it may be confusing to Western audiences, but I hope to clarify some of the ways that pervasion and conditioned coproduction (sometimes referred to as interdependent origination) serve as a pervasive methodology among these philosophers.

TWO CATEGORIES OF CAUSATION: NATURAL AND MECHANICAL

Western philosophy, until recently with speculative realism, seems to be limited to two categories of causation in metaphysical thinking. It is that Western metaphysics is founded on a standpoint of Being (as opposed to a standpoint of *Basho*) that sets the stage for a dualistic view of the world. Dialectics in the west, as appropriated into the work of Marx and subsequent Marxists, tends to view dialectics as a priori conflictual with a resulting, ensuing, as of yet to arrive resolution into peace. Therefore, the only way that Marx and those who have interpreted him can understand metaphysics is through the two methodologies—natural and mechanical causation.

Natural causation possess intrinsic qualities in nature that make things do what they do, without the need for God as a prime mover. Nature is what it is without any outside force acting upon it. Nature simply snapped into existence on its own. In "naturalism" the belief is that nature does not need God and God is not necessary for nature to exist. God chooses to create nature, but either way, there is a cosmic separation between the cause and the effect, and yet, the intrinsic qualities of a thing will activate its essence regardless of whether or not a more powerful entity exerts force and influence over its actions and behaviors.

Mechanical causation says that things happen because of an external cause. However, this philosophy of mechanical causation seems not to allow for "free will." Things happen as a sort of domino effect, and if you push the first domino in the row, the dominoes will fall in exactly the same way. It is just as if you were to turn the key to start an automobile, the car should start the same way. God as a central point is a sort of the key-starter for the universe and the universe, nature, human life, and all actions and behaviors are a result of intrinsic behavioral causes and effects. And to borrow a term from Nishida's philosophy, actions occur without any sort of "active intuition" behind them, "the case where a certain phenomenon necessarily accompanies another phenomenon, with absolutely no end or telos whatsoever, mechanical activity."[3] Mechanistic causality, it is presumed, "is on the basis of the condition given at the beginning that what subsequently appears is determined,"[4] every after effect is an identical repetitious unfolding of its "*arche*" or first principle.

Humans and nature are cast as automatons like the engine of the car starting and moving in exactly the same way. The argument of mechanical causation claims that God is at the helm, and all beings respond as pre-programmed machines. A machine does not have the intelligence to move and choose for itself and it acts based on the automatic mechanical causation.

The third methodology is the Buddhist philosophy of *Conditioned Coproduction* which means everything that is brought into being relies upon something else for its existence. There is no "being" that creates itself from out of nothing, and we are all interconnected with every other being, and vice versa. If we ruin nature, for example by cutting down all the trees in the Amazon Rainforest, we have to understand that forest land has a function that the entire world relies upon. We all rely on those trees to breathe in the carbon, so our air is clean, and so on. We are not in isolation, that is without connections with other things, such as food, air, and so on. We all need these things to work correctly for life to survive. You can have conditioned coproduction and still have the freedom of "active intuition."

VEDIC THOUGHT: THE METAPHYSICS OF PERVASION[5]

Pervasion tends to be the term for inclusive dialectics that is used in Indian versions of Buddhist and Hindu inflected philosophy. An age-old metaphysical logic from Buddhist philosophy, most likely first discovered by the logician Dignāga (480–540 AD), is that pervasion is non-conflictual dialectical metaphysics. One example of "pervasion" is smoke and fire. In the west, a logic course might discuss causality through the metaphysics of cause and effect. Is smoke "A" caused by fire "B"? If "A" then "B"; therefore, "A" must be contingent upon "B" to exist, and so forth. We can conclude that smoke is the antecedent of fire, and that everything must have a prime mover, that is, "God" in the Genesis story.

Nishida often evokes a metaphysics of kenosis, the process of God emptying itself into being. Nishida explains that nature is a semblance of universal law, which keeps stability to things that make meaning possible. The laws of nature must

> stand above unrepeatable determinate time . . . the world of nature that is above a time without content becomes a world that has been thought and, thus, being the content of thought, enters into relations of mutual activity with other contents of thought.[6]

Because things are empty, they rely on something else for their existence, form, and content. This is a position in Buddhist thought that spans all the way back to Nagarjuna who is widely considered the founder of the *Prajnaparamita sutra* schools of Buddhist thought. The idea is that emptiness (śūnyatā) means a lack of self-nature or own-being (svabhāva) and since everything is empty because lacking independence things depend on various factors and other things for their meaning. Anything assuming an absolute truth for itself falls into self-contradiction because it fails to see that its meaning derives from other sources and its interconnections within a greater context.[7] Nishida continues this into the metaphysics of what might be called "pervasion" by saying:

> Necessarily, all the contents of thinking are acting in something like what is called God's thinking. Just as it is thought that all physical force is acting simultaneously in the entire universe, all thinking is necessarily present in God. The activity of our thinking must be the manifestation of God's thinking.[8]

Pervasion conceptualizes metaphysics as a thing that always already contains the constraints of its transformational being; it is precisely the kind of thing that Nishida is challenging with his critique of "mechanical and teleological" thinking, which are classical methods of metaphysical thinking. In classical pervasion, the idea is that smoke is not caused by fire. Smoke and fire both always already pervade existence; phenomenal presences are always already there but it is a question of what materializes as an appearance. Smoke pervades, fire brings it forth, a spark, friction, the use of force brings forth the fire that burns and brings forth the smoke. It is a pathway of causation based on interdependent causality. If this happens, it calls forth that which is already there, insofar as potential becomes kinetic energy, potential becomes active power. Pervasion was the Vedic metaphysical philosophy from which Siddhartha (the Buddha) appropriated. As a Hindu, he had a readymade set of metaphysical beliefs going back to centuries that he could draw from to create Buddhist thought. Conditioned coproduction is considered a web of interconnected relations, sometimes thought to bridge innumerable lifespans. This is precisely the sort of historical fatalism and inertia that Nishida was trying to critique.

By asserting individual autonomy, one is forced into self-negation because one denies the interconnected web of karmic-historical residue.

"PRATĪTYASAMUTPĀDA"— CONDITIONED COPRODUCTION

In Pratītyasamutpāda, there is an interconnectedness unbound by finitude, and each layer of finite and infinite parts fits into greater wholeness, like pieces in a working system. Sometimes the system falls out of balance, but sometimes the system also works optimally.

Nagarjuna had his blessed insights that opened up a new awareness that samsara is effected by karma, not in a fatalistic way, but as the deeds and actions we take toward one another, and the effects are connected by that which is willed through what the Buddha called *Pratītyasamutpāda* or *conditioned coproduction*.

A metaphysical principle is "*if this exists, that exists*"; and there is an interconnected metaphysics to all life. This can be easily applied to the "general law of accumulation" in chapters 23–25 of the first volume of *Capital*. The existence of capital-wealth accumulation is only possible if there is a general appropriation of wealth away from some other class. "If capital exists, the working class exists" is the basic formula of class-conflict in capitalism. Once capital no longer exists, no other classes will exist either.

Nishida emphasizes conditioned coproduction throughout every period in his writings. It may seem odd to a Western reader who would like dialectical friction of competing arguments, even in an agonistic sense; however, Nishida writes serpentine sentences that might sound nonsensical to those with no understanding of samsara and conditioned coproduction. For example, the following passage from his essay *Unity of Opposites* reads:

> In the historical-social world, however, past and future are thoroughly confronting each other, and formed and forming are confronting each other; the formed forms even the forming, and the creature forms the creator. The single one does not only pass away into the past; it also produces a producing, and this is true productivity.[9]

NISHITANI KEIJI: THE GREAT DOUBT AND THE GREAT DEATH

Not only read as a temporal passing that haunts the living like a nightmare but Nishida also presages his student Nishitani Keiji's work on the Great Death, which Nishitani expands upon in his magnum opus *Religion and Nothingness*.[10] Stretching beyond a merely dialectical negation of a seemingly opposing argument, the Great Death constitutes the great horizon of our collective existence. "The essence of finitude is not finite. . . . It is much the same with our ordinary way of considering death: on that day in the years ahead when I die, death will, along with me, cease to be."[11]

Nihility can only be known existentially. If we stray but a step from the path of Existenz, nihility can only seem an utterly meaningless notion, devoid of reality. In fact, a great many philosophers, from a great many points of view, have come to that very conclusion. It is like a radio that has not been tuned properly and picks up only senseless static that totally blocks out the real sound of the broadcast. For only in the existential confrontation with nihility do we see the earnest life-or-death struggle for the transcendence of birth and death, escape from the unending causality of karma, and attainment of the "yonder shore" beyond the fathomless sea of suffering. It is, in other words, the struggle for *nirvana*.[12]

The Great Death serves as a cold-burning absolute zero, a black hole at the end of all existence, and the angst with which an individual might confront the certainty of the Great Death has been rationalized or completely denied as an actual fear through the mechanization of modern thinking. Nishitani explains in 1982 when there was still a massive portion of the world living under something that could vaguely be called "communism":

> In communist countries, the political institution exhibits a tendency toward totalitarianism that implies an orientation to the mechanization of institutions as well as of man. In liberal countries, the freedom of individuals under democracy is apt to be oriented to the mere freedom of the subject in the pursuit of his desires. These two differing orientations, however, derive from the same source and are bound up with one another. Here again, viewed as a whole, the problem of a mechanized civilization and political institutions can be traced back finally to one and the same source: the point from which contemporary nihilism is being generated, whether in overt or cryptic fashion.[13]

Political ideologies have attempted to "give meaning" to desires; whereas, the reality is that with the death of God, and the appearance of the finality of our existence in the Great Death, no deeper narrative meanings can be found with which human beings can attach meaning to their/our existence. The political ideology that won out, not coincidentally, was neoliberal capitalism that merely attaches meaning to life based on chasing one's innermost desires and rendering those palpable through the enjoyment of consumerism and the enjoyment of creative labor power. One still must resign oneself to the fact that the deeper metaphysical issue of the meaning of our existence still remains to be a riddle wrapped in a mystery, and henceforth, the deepest and most terrifyingly obvious fact: at the core of our existence is the Great Death.

Nishida provided a rather rosy glow to his theory of the subject and the individual when he says:

> If the individual, as individual of a world of unity of the opposites of the one and the many, is mirroring the world, then the self-determination of the individual is necessarily "desire." The individual acts neither mechanically nor teleologically, but by mirroring the world in its own Self. That I call "conscious." Even the instinct of animals, seen in its essence, must have this quality.[14]

Mirroring does not always send back an identical image, and that is not necessarily what matters in the effect of mirroring. What matters is whether the subject recognizes itself in the image that appears within the frame of the mirror, even and especially if the image is distorted. If the subject recognizes itself in the distorted image, there is always something revealing about that process of recognition. When something new enters into the frame, it is often completely impossible for the subject who "recognizes" what is already known through repetition of the same to break the frame and allow new knowledge to shift the parameters of the epistemological frame with which the subject claims to know itself, and onto which this knowledge allegedly pours out into knowledge of the world. In fact, breaking the codified frame of reference through which one truly believes they possess knowledge of and about the world is equivalent to a "satori" moment because it appears as a completely unexpected contingency. If the subject knew that the moment of awakening would occur, then it would not be a moment of awakening, it would be a mechanical or teleological extension of what was already allegedly known from the start.

In his essay titled *Unity of Opposites*, Nishida paints this picture of desire as anti-mechanical: "Desiring does not mean that we are merely mechanical or merely teleological; it means that we are mirroring the world in ourselves, it means that we make the world the medium for the formation of the self" he continues, "the environment encloses the subject and forms it. . . . the subject that subsists in the environment by submersion of the Self into the environment, is the historical subject."[15] Melting away and pouring out of the self into the environment of history are the process with which the subject is unlocked. The self-negating individuating from the absolute of the subject in the historical process is dialectically opposite to the melting away, the pouring out of the individual into the environment, conditions, and the mirroring of nature. Again, relying on kenosis, Nishida evokes a sense of self as self-sacrifice.

In Nishida's essay titled *Expressive Activity* (1925), this process of mirroring is a sort of groundless ground akin to a kenshō awakening wherein the subject discovers that the self is no self, a self-awareness of pure apperception, an unchangeable consciousness that is the ultimate foundation of the unity of experience. This is a much more prominent theme in the early Nishida. When mirroring occurs, it may be a hermeneutical stretch to apply this to political mirroring, in the sense of reimagining historical events through the mirror of nostalgia, but Nishida's thesis in his early work still relies on a bit of objectivist normativity. For example, when he writes: "When the consciousness involved in judgment makes of mental phenomena a cognitive epistemological object, the consciousness itself involved in judgment looks back upon the self itself."[16] A sort of nationalistic ipseity resounding through self-negating humility might not have been the best tactic to resist the rise of nationalism on the horizon at that time.

This is why perhaps, his student Miki Kiyoshi accused Nishida of forwarding a bourgeois philosophy because at times Nishida tended to fetishize the individual "self" as if selfhood, even as it mirrors, does so in non-ideological ways where there is always already the presumption of an autonomous individual self that self-negates as it differentiates from its interconnectedness. If the individual melts into the environment of history, forced to do so as a process of pervasion and conditioned coproduction, the question becomes: What if the environment of history is completely violent? Why would anyone want to transform history by melting into its historical environmental social context?

By the time Nishitani writes *Religion and Nothingness*, human existence is seen as subsumed almost entirely within the mechanization of daily life. The problem is not that the philosopher must quell the Great Doubt and bring certainty to an uncertain era of precariousness, but that in the midst of life in a mechanical era, the daily ordinary existence of humans in the modern era restricts our concern to our isolated self-consciousness (read: alienated and atomized consciousness), which embraces the self as if it were extended to all things. It would be mistaken to regard the Great Doubt, as its exposure to the Great Death, as a kind of psychological illness, as medical capitalism has rendered almost every sort of allegedly "marginal" form of consciousness when it makes uncertainty apparent. Nishitani's definition of *samadhi* is when the self becomes single-minded and focuses itself on the one doubt that blocks out all other experiences, and hence, the focusing of the mind into a samadhi state is not to censor out uncertainty and gain the confidence to take on life, but to understand the Great Doubt and the Great Death as:

> The Great Doubt when we press our doubts (What am I? Why do I exist?) to their limits as conscious acts of the doubting self. The Great Doubt represents not only the apex of the doubting self but also the point of its "passing away" and ceasing to be the "self." It is like the bean whose seed and shell break apart as it ripens: the shell is the tiny ego, and the seed the infinity of the Great Doubt that encompasses the whole world. It is the moment that is the "locus" of nothingness where conversion beyond the Great Doubt takes place.[17]

The Great Doubt always emerges as the opening up of the locus of nothingness as the field of conversion from the Great Doubt itself. There are those such as Mori Tetsuro and John Maraldo who describe Nishitani's worldview as extending beyond narrow Japanese nationalism. Mori argues that Nishitani focused on a view that every nation needed self-sacrifice while emphasizing a global perspective of the Buddhist "no-self";[18] whereas, John Maraldo views Nishitani from a relativistic perspective:

> I suggest that in the 1940s Nishitani did not set himself up as an advocate for state or ethnic nationalism, but of a globalism that seriously mistook his nations' capacity to negate itself and overcome its self-centeredness. If this was the case of mistaken judgment on his part, he never admitted as much not even when the Occupation forces had him suspended from his university post in a purge of intellectuals thought to have collaborated in the war.[19]

These questions have been debated ad nauseum and I do not wish to replicate those discussions here; however, the bigger existential and metaphysical questions are to the nature of our being as beings in the world. Nishitani asks these crucial questions as to the mechanization of life in the era of automated production when a vague notion commonly referred to as "science" has taken a hegemonic position among the truth discourses. Think of what he says in terms of how political discourses today tend to valorize work, the creation of "jobs" as the telos of our existence, and the formation of wealth as the basis of judging the success or failure of a life, and in the bizarre turn that the ideological superstructures take in creating consumers of culture and reifying mechanized consciousness:

> Anyone will lose interest in living if he is regarded as nothing more than a cog in a machine. For the sake of convenience, let us disregard intellectuals who have their opinions on this matter, they are willing to look at all things scientifically, *except* themselves. The more people think that only scientific truth is absolute, the more they lose interest in living. For example, if a scientist were to give faint praise to an individual saying, "You are a perfect machine." I am sure that individual would take offence, not finding such kind of perfection desirable. It really does not make life worth living . . . in fact, the individual might even commit suicide, since such a life would be too tedious. An individual cannot accept himself as merely a cog in a machine. The basic humanity of the individual threatens to disintegrate . . . the further people are mechanized, the more negative they become toward their own existence. People tend to lose interest in their lives and come to doubt there is any meaning in existence.[20]

Hence, the liberation from work through automation might be the basis of a new "Marxist" practice, as some among the accelerationist philosophy[21] have forwarded; whereas, the labor movements that tend to reinforce the valorization of factory labor are doomed to reproduce the mechanical consciousness that Nishitani forewarns will only intensify the Great Death of spirit and mismanage the fact of creeping nihilism, rather than face the Great Death squarely.

NISHIDA'S THREE ELEMENTS OF *EXPRESSIVE ACTIVITY*

Nishida's alternatives to the explanations of causality (ideology, various materialisms, pervasion, etc.) are enhancements of these philosophies. His three elements of expressive activity are forwarded in his 1925 essay *Expressive Activity* (Hyōgen Sayō) and these are as follows:

1. Content that is expressed (implying that there is also a form)
2. Expressive activity
3. The expression itself (expression qua expression)

Activity ("sayō") indicates activity that is not merely a means to an end. In this sense, to appropriate from Nishida, a "communist" activity would be the activity itself, rather than striving toward a telos that will become "communist" one day in the future.

Nishida claims that there are realms of expression, such as art and painting, which convey meaning that cannot be expressed in spoken language. Since these forms of expression exist, it indicates that there is a basic human need to complete the production of these gaps through the creation of new methods of expression. In describing this, there is a will, perhaps a self-negating will to find an inner expression of One-ness with all. Communism is suchness in the inner expression of One-ness with all, in material conditions in the actual form of lived experience. Nishida, in explaining this process of expression seeking One-ness with all, uses a material example of labor power, which he claims is always an incomplete or imperfect expression, probably as the ideal form passes into corporeal existence through the exertion of bodily labor power. He writes:

> The case of building a house can likely be thought to be one kind of actualization of the will. The built house is within us, a house that is neither wood nor stone. But in this case the content of the will is the desire to live. The desire to live is the desire that would sustain our existence in this spatiotemporal world; it arises from the fact that the will follows upon nature; it is not the content of a will that envelops the actual world, but the content of a will enveloped within the actual world.[22]

In such a clear description you see that Nishida is articulating a materialist point that human will, while not completely negated into passivity, is always enveloped by conditions, not of our choosing. Nishida also wants to make a correlation point that thinking and being are connected, rather than dualistically separate, in side-stepping the problem of state-Shintoism as the "self-awareness of God" manifest on earth in the form of fascism giving the proletariat their roots back. He does not want to forward a purely reified interpretation of materiality as pure-being. He writes, in a brief point, "what does not act is not merely passive."[23]

Verbal expression shapes thinking from subjectivity into objective, much like the strange way that the French terms "langue and parole" exemplify this point when placed in the context of the English language. A speech act is the articulation of a thought set free from the inner world of the mind, only to find itself under the surveillance of an Other as if the thought were let out on "parole," under panoptic scrutiny that reifies the expression. Our thinking possesses its possibility based on verbal expression, but pure thought, "is not subsumed within the activity of our thinking; it resides, rather, in the world of language; language is something like the body of thought."[24] It would be easy to simply take a Wittgensteinian view of this articulation of a "body of thought"; and yet, Nishida doubles down on correlationism as he wants to present a pure experience, not over-determined or mediated by discourses, but "there is an *activity (sayō)* that unites the sense that is expressed and the thing that expresses."[25] I added the italics for emphasis because the point becomes clear that Nishida is forwarding a shifting correlationist theory of mind and language. Hidden in plain sight is the influence of Marx. What "activity" unites the sense expressed and the thing expressed? It is the labor power. As labor metabolizes nature, nature (i.e., the object) changes its form; as nature is metabolized by labor power, labor power also changes its form. If anything mediates the subject and object, it is the illusion of a real being that is sensing at all. Sense is the mediation from which the delusion of being arises.

TOSAKA JUN—SHIZEN TETSUGAKU TEKI (SELF-NATURE-PHILOSOPHICAL-PROCESS)

Tosaka Jun was a key member of the Kyoto School, and along with Miki Kiyoshi was one of the earliest contributors to the Kyoto School to set himself on the path of a firmly Marxist trajectory. Tosaka's writings are a treasure trove of unique concepts, most of which only make sense in the original Kanji.

Some key examples are his use of the term *"Ronri"* meaning "theory" and *"Riron"* which means "logic." In his lectures "The Role of Natural Science to Society," he vacillates to exemplify a dialectical materialist process of logic in the natural sciences of the self (*shizen kagaku*). Self ("*ji*") as studied by the social sciences must be understood as having a dialectical process, rather than an objective basis. Science must understand human behavior as a dialectical becoming within history, and if revolutions are the locomotives of history, then class-conflict is the basis of dialectical materialism within capitalist class relations. If social science fails to see the dialectics of class-conflict that forms the basis of social relations, then science becomes a reified system of false consciousness.

For example, Tosaka writes that "In order to understand a wave, one must also have a theory (*ronri*) of the wave (*nami*)" The term wave, or "*nami*" means undulation or movement. Whereby Tosaka is rendering this as a political mobilization, a wave of activity, is not "*hitoshi ka*" equal and identical with what went before, as if there are "*mujoken*" or unconditional and objective renderings of human behavior outside of historical conditions. "*Riron*" (theory) must take into account the "*wa mu ron*" or the certainty of the contingency of the nothing, whereby "*ronri-dogu*" (tool logic) is put forth and called to mind within the context of numerous logical systems of philosophy. This rendering of logic as a dialectical process between "*ronri*"/theory and "*riron*"/logic, Tosaka produces a term that does not exist in English, "*ronri ku teki*," or the equivalent of indicating a method as "scientific" except in terms of logic, so it would be "*Logictific*" which calls to mind the famous text from Georg Wilhelm Hegel, the title rendered as *The Science of Logic*. Utilized within a philosophical context, the natural sciences inadequate to fully understand the depths of human nature, one might utilize Tosaka Jun's term, a term that has no equivalent in English: "*shizen tetsugaku teki*" or the self-nature-philosophical-process.

Existentialism may seem appropriate as a close affinity with this concept; however, the "*nami*" (the wave, as in "tsunami" without the tsu/"sage" qualities of natural science, or the kami as natural spirits from the mythos of land in shintoism), it means a class movement without a metaphysical message from the cosmos attached to a natural disaster, as if a tsunami were a hermeneutical message from the Gods. Tosaka Jun's thesis is that science must not study natural phenomena, including human behavior, as if there is some concealed metaphysical first principle to be discovered and understood once and for all, rather than the lived "nami" of history as undulating, billowing, flowing, at times surging, cresting, and falling temporal flow: a cascading at times, a stasis at other times, and movement that indicates being within a place in historical time.

Tosaka Jun's main question in his 1930 essay, *The Principle of Everydayness and Historical Time*, is the issue of historical time and its distinction with everydayness, the latter being an essentialized version of ordinary time and sunken-every-dayness from Heideggerian theories of time. Tosaka's thesis avoids a phenomenology of time where what is studied is not the direct experience of ordinary time, rather, what survives in its independence after as before and outside of the mind is the process of reality, that which cannot be wished away is the constitutive basis of reality, even in its ebb and flow of changing historical conditions via class-conflict, changing forces and conditions of production, and so forth.

Humans obtain this status of historical beings when humans can produce their own history and future. Humans obtain the ability to control their history, present, and future when humans become producing beings, rather than foraging, hunter-gatherers who find resources by chance. When humans become tool-making beings who can create fire, use hunting tools, and perform basic tasks of agricultural mastery such as planting seeds and cultivating land brought humans into historical time because these processes created mastery over the ends of production in ways that were unlike our animal ancestors. Aristotle's point that humans are the speaking animals emphasizes "logos," speech, language, and logic as the basis with which human beings differ from other animals. At the transition from animal to the human being, we become social animals. As we became tool-making and tool-using creatures, we developed the ability to conceptualize and narrativize the meaning of our existence. The conceptual basis of our existence emerged as we needed language because our lives depended on social production. Without language, there is no thinking, and language accompanied a common social activity, and common production. Conceptual knowledge is true insofar as it is productive according to the style of its productivity.[26]

Surprisingly, in 1932–1933 Tosaka Jun writes a brilliant set of essays on the politics of humor and tragedy. Brief, albeit dense, these essays were written during the rise of fascism in Japan. At that time, tensions were brewing with China as the so-called January 28th incident where acts of war were enacted between China and Japan and Shanghai was demilitarized, and the fascists of Japan were already arresting leftist academics and public figures in the early 1930s. Some 30,000 arrests had occurred from 1930 to 1933 by the fascist-run Ministry of Home Affairs; therefore, his essays were a sort of profile in courage. He writes that a "relatively, intellectual primitive emotion becomes visible as laughter. One hears that most animals can show anger, but only primates can laugh."[27] As language extends beyond merely speaking to other forms of expression as well, all these styles of expression become possible when people can reproduce the conditions of existence. When humans become tool-making beings, labor power emerges, and humans can produce for basic needs.

Comedy = humor = irony = paradox = critique, as Tosaka points out, there is a backside and a frontside to every signifier. When a backside is brought forward into contact with the frontside, the exposure of what is concealed is what forces the subject to laugh. As society creates these wells of emotions by choking off various forms of expression, the rotary motion of pent-up potential energy is released in the form of the joke, which seizes upon the concealed backside of what appears as the frontside of the thing. The pressure of the backside of the thing conceals negativity/wickedness that is only exposed through the joke, and hence, the rise of fascism is understood in one way, as the explosion of pent-up wicked "backside" desires in tragic and violent forms rather than farcical comedic forms that are agonistic. It is the transference of class-conflict onto a tragic, wicked backside that takes form through violence misdirected. "The logic of laughter gradually makes plain the viciousness, negativity, and criticalness that is inherent in its logicality."[28]

We all have fixed expectations that are presupposed. For example, in the use of a cliché like prior usage in this essay of "ideological superstructure" if I were to change the terms to "ideological stupid structure" it may appear as a misuse of the words. The reader may presume the lack of knowledge, and it may seem offensive or belittling toward someone else; however, the use of the inverted expectations, "when consciousness is surprised by the successful betrayal of expectations" is something that almost never translates well in a dry academic piece of writing, but it also tends to elicit laughter in a live lecture because there is a common expectation that is "regulated in a suitably precise way" and are the necessary conditions for laughter.[29] Whereas tragedy needs to be grounded in a historical necessity and a particular earnestness or gravity must find its expression in tragedy for tragedy to be acknowledged as such. When society is completely awash in spectacle and absurdity as humor, then the tragic has been completely effaced from public-popular culture. The effect of this is the denial of the Great Death. The society of the spectacle has tipped the scales in favor of a kind of slapstick comedy where the tragic undertones of this "backside" that is exposed in comedy may not factor into the fixing of received expectations, which are undermined by turning/exposing the backside in the frontward facing side of the joke.

Obviously, in a fascist regime where censorship creates a highly repressive set of cultural conditions and people are being locked up for the slightest anti-government jabs, for Tosaka Jun to write an essay about the politics of comedy at that time took massive courage.

Phenomenology, as the predominant lens through which popular variations of "Zen" trickled into the west with its focus on the principle of presence, focused on phenomenology of everydayness and ordinary-being-as-presence at the moment. Whereas the exposure of limitations toward the principle of factuality (*jijisusei*) is the representation of time as clearly evident (明白—*meihaku*), the presence of the present extends into the past and future as if the principle of presence carries with it the residue of normativity from now into the past and the future. As there are limitations on an individual life, with death looming over each of us individually, a lifespan only lasts a temporary amount of time, the continuation of historical progress from one lifespan into the next reaches an aporia at the point of generational transference of progress accomplished. Each successive lifespan starts with birth and ends with death following the paths of the stages of life (student, householder, retirement, sannyasin).

Historical time extends beyond the span of lifetime, and thus, historical time cannot be reduced to ordinary everydayness. Historical time is the progress of the ends of production that accrues beyond one lifetime. For example, as historical progress is always a promethean compromise, its outcome is only measured in technological advancements such as the automobile rather than the locomotive, the locomotive rather than the horse and carriage, or today, the irreparable damage that will occur as a result of all aspects of life being bonded with digital technologies. Once labor power reaches a technological advancement, there is no turning back; if efficiency is gained, there is no turning back, there is no return to the time prior to that invention.

Tosaka's thesis that "it is the parsing (*kizami*—i.e., notching, parsing, incision, cutting, etc.) itself that makes time possible."[30] And later, Tosaka draws a distinction that makes his point clearer, the notching/parsing/cutting of time is only possible if we do not analyze time through the lens of phenomenology, which emphasizes temporality (*toki*) rather than time (*jikan*)—with *jikan* you have to understand as "*jikaku*" and selfhood as the parsing of one lifetime truncated by the bookends of birth and death. Temporality (*toki*) tends to bleed into conflation with eternity, even though "eternal things are the exact opposite of temporal things."[31]

MU! AND NON-CONSEQUENTIALISM

The Gateless Barrier is typically acknowledged by scholars to be the first collection of kōans in Zen philosophy, collected by Wu-men (*Mumon*), who was a thirteenth-century master of the Lin Chi (Rinzai) school. This collection consists of forty-eight kōans and they initiate a different sense of nothingness, a different sense of awakening, enlightenment, and perhaps a much more antagonistic notion of these concepts than Mahayana Buddhism, which emphasizes compassion, mindfulness, and nothingness as a provocation to contemplate in stillness. Zen, at least in these early kōans, gives readers and practitioners an "active" understanding of practice, much closer to how Nishida Kitarō writes about active intuition. As shifting conditions, rather than the stereotype of a docile body in sitting yoga (i.e., meditation), Mu! is a sudden evocation of an unforeseen contingency that brings the subject into an awakening.

The spitting of the cat in two by the Zen master in the fourteenth koan "Nan chuan Kills the Cat" or the statement that Buddha mind is a "dried shitstick" in koan 21 "Yuan Men's dried shitstick" reveals the non-consequentialist philosophy of the "Mu!"-satori moment in Zen awakening. Non-consequentialism is the normative ethical theory that denies the rightness or wrongness of our conduct, which is determined solely by the goodness or badness of the consequences of our acts or the rules to which those acts conform. Mu! awakens us not to the comfort of knowing that things will be alright but that we have cosmic paternal overseers singing us lullabies to sleep. Awakening opens up *in-finitio* (infinite and unfinished) possibilities with no comfortable guarantee of a soft-landing in "good" consequences.

KENSHŌ: THE KŌAN OF CHAO-CHOU'S DOG

What was Nishida's enlightenment experience? Apparently, a bit anticlimactic. Nishida first wrote of "pure experience" in 1908, after studying meditation for ten years. He allegedly had a kenshō experience in the summer of 1903. Kenshō is the Japanese Zen word for "ken" (seeing or to see) "shō" (true nature, essence), which occurred after meditating extensively on the "Mu!" koan, otherwise known as Chao-Chou's Dog. It reads:

A monk asks Chao-Chou, "Has a dog Buddha-nature?"
to which Chao-Chou replies: "Mu!"

It is one of the first koans given to novices to meditate on the nature of reality as beyond good and evil. By meditating on this koan, you learn about nondualism. If Buddha nature is everywhere, then of course a dog has Buddha nature. But, the dog has a different consciousness to that of a human being. We must be aware to not anthropomorphize the dog's nature. In other words, if the dog does possess Buddha nature, it would be of a kind so patently different from human consciousness that its Buddha nature might not make sense in any meaningful way to us as humans.[32]

This is to speak the unspeakable that there is no inside or outside to the Buddha nature when that nature is understood as radical nothingness. Mu is a sense of nothingness that opens up what Wu-men called the *The Gateless Barrier*, you see that there are no obstacles and the gate opens because to begin with there was no gate. If there was a gate, it was a mental barrier constructed from within the mind. Once the mind is cleansed of unnecessary barriers the gate opens without effort. The barrier is Mu and this is tricky in how simple it is to understand since Mu means nothing. The mental barrier is constituted by that which is not-being.

Tathāgata is another term for Buddha nature, which is the essential nature of all things, and indeed the universe itself, which is completely empty, yet full of boundless vitality and innumerable myriad beings with dynamic possibilities. When asking if the dog has Buddha nature, the monk is asking if the dog has Tathāgata, which is not a simple yes or no question. The dog is and is not, and yet, this nature of its both being and being not, which sounds contradictory, yet koans are not to be understood through the lens of propositional logic. In Western logic, a contradiction is invalid because in Western logic there cannot be a statement where p∧~p which is held to be true at the same time.

Kōans are beautiful and confounding to Western philosophers who are trained to think along the lines of their training, which tells them to posit the validity of a statement by running it through the rigors of logical truth tables. Zen does not look at truth from that perspective. What if we did not look at the philosophy of Marx from the perspectives that confine it by these restrictive categories of logic. Not that all logic is "bad" per se, but what if there are new methods available in the open-endedness of the communist ontology?

Mu! means nothingness, and it could be considered a vital concept in all of Nishida's philosophy. In a later letter to his colleague Watsuji Tetsurō in 1930, he would write

> What I mean by "nothingness" (*mu*) is closer to the warm heart that Shinran[33] possessed, which acknowledges everyone's freedom and embraces every sinner (although I don't know whether Shinran actually put it into words this way). While I appreciate Eastern culture as profound and precious, I cannot deny my longing for Western culture, which is a great development of rich and free humanity.[34]

Reportedly, Nishida passed the famous "Mu!" koan test and then wrote in his diary:

> 7 AM, listened to the talk. Evening, a private audience with the master. I was cleared of the koan "Mu." But I am not that happy. Subimori is going to study abroad. I have to rely on myself. It's no use counting on the others. The new koan: "Stop the Peal of the Bell."[35]

The sixteenth kōans in *The Gateless Barrier* reads: "Yun-men said, See how vast and wide the world is! Why do you put on your seventeen-piece robe at the sound of the bell?"

Zen practice gives the awareness of the bell, as silence surrounding the sound. Mindfulness is strengthening presence as awareness is pulled away from centering your practice on the bell, the sounds around, and the silent stillness within you (samādhi). If anything, if the sound of the bell puts you off your way, then use it as a way to snap back into mindful practice (put your seventeen-piece robe back on, so to speak, get back into the dressage of mindful practice). In these kōans, you can see that perhaps the "antagonism" in some forms can snap a person back into practice. You hear the sound of the bell and return to the sound, perhaps the sound helps to present the mind with a focal point with which to snap out of the dreadful dream-state and return the practice to mindfulness. Being with the Mu presents itself as a contingency outside of the individual and the narrow realm over which the individual may exert control. In other words, the bell and the sound are a contingency external to the subject. To put it into terms Marx may have used, when the bell provokes the practitioner to put back on the seventeen-piece robe, the practitioner's consciousness is awakened back into awareness as a product of material conditions.

Peal of the Bell koan must refer to case 16 of the Wu-men koans which asks:

"Does the sound come to the ear, or does the ear go to the sound?"[36] In other words, there is no "I" to hear, but rather is the sound itself an entity that finds the ear, which then experiences "it"? In other words, the formulation of Nishida's "pure experience" is given a more thorough detailing in his first book-length work *An Inquiry into the Good* (*Zen No Kenkyu*), where Nishida writes one of his most famous passages, something that must seem perplexing to Western philosophers:

> It is not that experience exists because there is an individual, but that an individual exists because there is experience. I thus arrived at the idea that experience is more fundamental than individual differences, and in this way I was able to avoid solipsism.[37]

What if there were a way to understand the camera obscura in connection with the Zen koan? Instant, sudden, abrupt, and completely unexpected awakening from the slumbers of the ideological camera obscura. Koans do not produce a narcosis effect, a state of stupor, or drowsiness. A koan awakens!

The intended effect is called kenshō. The subject is stunned into awakening as self-knowledge. Kenshō opens up self-knowledge to the anti-essentialism of the self. The self discovers it has no prior objective essence. What the self thought it was, was revealed.

It is as if a curtain is raised and there is nothing behind it.

Another example of this is Dōgen's remarks throughout the Shōbōgenzō. For example, the "Immo" which reads that the sound of the bell is not a matter of the clapper striking the bell, nor the bell resounding from the clapper, but the "ringing of the ringing," or the saying that "when the donkey sees the well, the well sees the donkey," and that "the donkey sees the donkey, and the well sees the well," with the implication of solipsism apparent, Dōgen then remarks that it is the act of seeing, implying that it is in fact subject-free.[38]

Dōgen's paradoxical approach to awakening is given when he says things like, "without silent abiding, there is no delusion." Without first sitting silently, the subject may persist in endless pre-reflective consciousness without any awareness of the delusionary status of their consciousness. Hence, statements such as these from Dōgen serve as distant early forms of ideology critique. What it means is that without quiet meditative reflection, a subject may simply whirl around embodying a consciousness completely enveloped by pre-reflective (read "ideological") habits. Acts of reflection pre-suppose a more basic pre-reflective consciousness; inward-looking self-reflection can become a delusional endless trap as well. Therefore, to awaken from the slumber of delusion means that one detaches from the belief that an objective-self-essence is there to be discovered. However, the early use of dialectics in Chan Buddhism gives us the sense that there is a busy-ness of being where the initial consciousness of human beings cannot see itself as living in the midst of a delusion. The early stages of meditation practice reveal the delusion to us through practice. By slowing down, the delusion is revealed, thus, allowing the arising of the self-observant/observant-self. Alienated from the ebb and flow of the world, this self-observant self is an effect of experience that can only be experienced and possesses no objective thingness there awaiting discovery.

To understand the importance of a philosopher you must understand the context out of which the philosophy arises. Nishida says this throughout his published writings that consciousness emerges from narrative and narrative begins from history and the world. While these are not ready-made, there is always a subjective side to the ways human beings can interpret. It is important to remember what Nishitani Keiji says at the beginning of his pinnacle biography on the life of Nishida Kitarō. In explaining what drew him to study under Nishida Kitarō at Kyoto University, Nishitani Keiji explains: "the place Nishida held in the soul of a simple student like me seems to mirror on a broader scale the position he has held in the post-Meiji Japanese mind."[39]

Capital has an implacable aspect to it that resonates at the realm of intuition beyond what is physically manifest. There is a "fetish" aspect to the commodity because capital itself has substantial and non-substantial aspects to it. To put it into Nishida's verbiage there are aspects of capital that resonate within the intelligible and unintelligible worlds. By enveloping consciousness capital is here and beyond, immanent, and transcendent, and this is what makes it so difficult to resist.

Nishida Kitarō is an immensely important anti-fascist critical theorist who could be of great importance to a thoughtful prolegomenon to a philosophy of praxis (*Jissen tetsugaku jōron*).

Interpellation interpellates subjects as individuals. Selfhood is called forth out of nothing. The idea of empty selfhood spans back to early Japanese Buddhist texts. Marx had some engagement with Buddhist writings in the early 1860s until the publication of *Capital*, but the influence of Buddhist philosophy is a subterranean one at most. If the self is the reification of social relations, then the self does not exist in any a priori sense except as a subject beckoned forth to be recognized. The Kyoto Philosophers most likely to engage with this notion of selfhood ("ji" 自己), perhaps as interpellated rather than "ipseity," are Tosaka Jun and Miki Kiyoshi, more so than Nishida Kitarō whose selfhood is closer to an "ipseity" of Nietzschean origins.[40] Nishida uses "Jiko" early on in *Zen No Kenkyu* up to and throughout his religious worldview essay.[41] He also utilizes (自己が自己を写す)—"*Jiko ga jiko o utsusu*" self-reproducing-self which he claimed was influenced by Royce but can readily be appropriated into Althusserian-Marxist categories of the self as ideologically reproduced. Whereas, Tosaka Jun utilizes "Ji" in terms of (自然科学) "*shizen kagaku*" or natural science indicating the reification of the self in the human sciences which creates a false consciousness of naturalness to something referred to as "human nature." Tosaka Jun's thesis is quite convincing. His work echoes other twentieth-century philosophers whose work has obtained a wider readership within the continental tradition; for example, Michel Foucault's critique of the social sciences.

Selfhood is a "synthetic" concept and not synthetic in the Kantian sense as if the self is synthesized as a logical synthesis of propositional statements brought together. Self is synthesized from an amalgamation of other constructed concepts one of which is derived from a social context. A dialectics of social synthesis rather than a Kantian synthesis derived out of abstractions. Social conditions are not analytical concepts. In other words, capitalism is not a priori given and should never be understood as an intrinsic outgrowth of human nature. It is not that you define "human being" analytically by defining it in terms of the "synthetic" concepts that are particular to capitalism.

ZEN NO KENKYU (AN INQUIRY INTO THE GOOD/ THE GOOD MEDITATION, THINKING)

It is impossible to summarize a work like *Zen No Kenkyu* in the matter of a few brief pages, even if it is an early phase of Nishida's writing where he is like the young Marx, a nominalist. "Good" is not a particular behavior within specific contexts circumscribed by particular conditions; "the Good" takes the form of a universal abstraction knowable through the category of pure experience. Another book explaining a book might illuminate some of the opaqueness to someone whose sole background might lie completely within the boundaries of the Western philosophical tradition. Perhaps a good place to start is with a Japanese writer who is not Nishida who explains a crucial difference between the emphasis on *"kokoro"* (soulfulness) and *"iki"* (Japanese aesthetic of space) which may be unfamiliar to Western phenomenology, one might add that this description of the Japanese toilet is idiomatically left out of Slavoj Zižek's eurocentric triad of French, German, and British toilets as indicative of ideologically representing deconstruction, idealism, and pragmatism.

Jun'ichirō Tanizaki's *In Praise of Shadows* (1933)

> Every time I am shown to an old, dimly lit, and, I would add, impeccably clean toilet in a Nara or Kyoto temple, I am impressed with the singular virtues of Japanese architecture. The parlor may have its charms, but the Japanese toilet truly is a place of spiritual repose. It always stands apart from the main building, at the end of a corridor, in a grove fragrant with leaves and moss. No words can describe that sensation as one sits in the dim light, basking in the faint glow reflected from the shoji, lost in meditation or gazing out at the garden.

The novelist Natsume Sōseki counted his morning trips to the toilet as a great pleasure, "a physiological delight" he called it. "And surely there could be no better place to savor this pleasure than a Japanese toilet where, surrounded by tranquil walls and finely grained wood, one looks out upon blue skies and green leaves."[42]

> "As far as I know the West has never been disposed to delight in shadows . . . they paint their ceilings in pale colors to drive out as many shadows as they can. We fill our gardens with dense plantings, they spread out a flat expanse of grass."[43]

Since the basis of early modern Western philosophy typically relies on a Cartesian Cogito, a thinking "I" is taken for granted. Therefore, Nishida's statements may sound absurd when he makes statements like: "It is not the case that there is first an individual who has experiences; rather, there is experience first and then the individual."[44]

In a lot of ways, Nishida is also including himself in these discussions, and rightfully so, but Nishida's work does not necessarily carry the same baggage as a westerner whose spatial awareness had been conditioned to prioritize a sense of knowledge as a process of bringing a thing out from the darkness into the light. For example, Plato's *Divided Line and the Allegory of the Cave*[45] produced a Western approach to epistemology favoring enlightenment and the optics of light over the shadowy figures in the cave, and objects obscured by shadows. Imago, simulacrum, and things that are obscured by darkness, obstructed by other objects, or exist beyond the horizon of what is visible are less likely to be called forth into our awareness as an object of care. Thusly rendering many existing things unintelligible.

Nishida's approach is considered meontology, a study of nothing, and this includes that which the Platonic theory of knowledge considered unintelligible. Nishida's epistemology if the self takes a much different approach than the Platonic-Cartesian method of pulling oneself out of darkness to find a factual kernel of truth about oneself. As it is based on kenshō, Nishida's methods are not starting based on describing a discoverable essence of the subject, as stated earlier in this chapter, the discovery is that there is no self in any substantial sense, even if Nishida gets into trouble with his colleagues for perhaps essentializing humility and the melting away of selfhood into the mirroring of environment, even in the midst of violent circumstances such as the rise of fascism in Japan.

Ishihara Yūko has proposed that the unitary mode of self-awareness is foundational for Nishida, but self-awareness in the full sense is a dialectical process moving back and forth between the modes of unity and difference. Ishihara shows that Nishida recognized both reflective and pre-reflective self-awareness, but that awareness shifts between differentiated and undifferentiated awareness.[46] Nishida consistently implies a related phenomenological sense of consciousness as that which appears. As Nishida states, "experience reflects itself within itself," in his *Basho* essay of 1926, he still affirms the manifesting power of self-awareness as it extends into and reflects its place in the world. The self is understood to be placed into a context that is greater than the substantial form of the individual self.

Masao Abe's diagram in his introduction to *Zen No Kenkyu* is shown below.

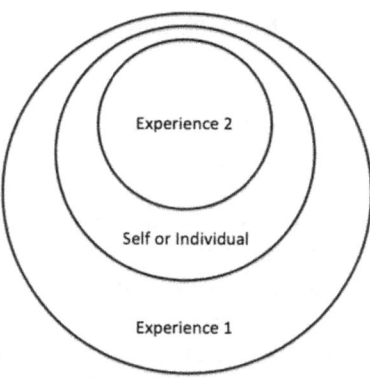

"An individual exists because there is experience."

The "self" might merely be an effect of active, yet involuntary behaviors. The "self" is tacking on experiences, as a shadowy non-substantive, non-entity effect of the base of social experience,[47] which later on in the text Nishida refers to as "God,"[48] but for the sake of consistency, we might as well call this the spirit of material conditions; spirit is self, as much as corporeality is spirit, and vice versa. "The universe is not a creation of God, but a manifestation of God."[49] The metaphysics is the metaphysics of samsara. God is not separate looking in on creation, but immanent within it, corporeal as much as spirit; if there is a God, God is not remote, even though for Nishida, when he speaks of God in his early texts, it is in terms of a transcendent force above and beyond nature which pours itself out into corporeal being, there is often a kenotic vision of God.

Nishida begins this book by stating that his understanding of "pure experience" is as though "without the least addition of deliberative discrimination"[50] in the sense that pure experience involves the subject in an immediate relation between subject and object. Immediate in the sense of no perceived gap in either space or time. The example Nishida uses is of a musician harmonizing so fluently with the flow of the music that at the same time the musician can play in anticipation of what will happen next. The music and musician form a seamless connection with the performance because the musician acts on intuition and the performance seems to happen automatically.

Past experiences synthesize so smoothly with the subject's involvement with the present that there is a sequential experience of time occurring reflexively—a "pure experience" that feels seamless. This is because there is no felt gap between perception and thinking, a distinction that needs clarification. A little later in the book, Nishida will explain that he sees the difference between perception and thinking as a commonly misunderstood problem of internal and external origination of thought. Perceptions are typically understood to be input from external objects stimulating a sensory perception. Thoughts are typically considered the processing of internal abstractions. From this the problem is simple: Where does thought arise?

Perceptions stimulate inputs that produce internal mental images that to think must imply that there is something thought about, going back to the Greeks up to and including Husserl; thought is understood as "noema," a thought that is thinking about a thing. These internal abstractions are understood to be about something, and yet, there are limitations to this method of epistemology. If perceptions are inputs from something, and thinking is about something, then the internal abstractions that constitute the thought process itself must rely on mental images produced by consciousness. The mental images are the material with which the abstractions of thought can work.

However, as Nishida says, "a mental image, regardless of its type, never stands alone, for it inevitably appears in some relation to the whole of consciousness."[51] To make this point clear, there are two ways that this statement from Nishida can be understood. As a view from the atman/brahman conceptualization of inner and otherly soul as constitutive of the world in the mind of the Gods and, of course, these are Gods that are in this world, the "whole of consciousness" is "God" as the sum of all sentient consciousness on earth; or, the whole of consciousness means "general intellect" in the sense Marx uses it here:

> Nature builds no machines, no locomotives, railways, electric telegraphs, self-acting mules etc. These are products of human industry; natural material transformed into organs of the human will over nature, or of human participation in nature. They are organs of the human brain, created by the human hand; the power of knowledge, objectified. The development of fixed capital indicates to what degree general social knowledge has become a direct force of production, and to what degree, hence, the conditions of the process of social life itself have come under the control of the **general intellect** and been transformed in accordance with it. To what degree the powers of social production have been produced, not only in the form of knowledge, but also as immediate organs of social practice, of the real life process.[52]

This becomes clearer when we understand how Nishida effaces the distinction between inner and outer worlds of consciousness, by giving a lucid description of base and superstructure without explicitly saying so: "consciousness derives meaning from its relations to other consciousnesses—meaning is determined by the system to which consciousness belongs."[53] The system is understood here to be the ideological "superstructure," which will be explained a little later in this chapter. What else could Nishida be describing other than the immaterial cogitations of ideology at the level of thought (the cogitations of mental imagery within one's own mind as a product of belonging to a system of consciousness) then when he says:

"Even when circumstances in the external world are such that action does not occur, the will is still functioning."[54] What is still functioning as a "will" if corporeal bodies are not moving around traversing space? It must be the movement of thought as immanent within the mind. Earlier, Nishida already established that you do not need to wait for the totalized knowledge of general representation to occur prior to analysis occurring, because if an abstracting process is occurring, then analysis occurs as well.

"All consciousness is systematic, and no representation arises alone—it necessarily belongs to some system."[55]

Nishida explains that this "synthesis of pure experience . . . is not present in thought, because if one thinks about the present, it is no longer present."[56] Thinking about thinking snaps our awareness into the process of thinking, whereas the sort of pure experience that initiates Nishida's inquiry into the good has to begin from the immediacy of the pure experience itself because the concept of "pure experience" derives from a rather beginner's mind passage from William James who says the pure experience is, "the instant field of the present, only virtually or potentially object or subject as yet . . . it is plain, unqualified actuality, or existence, a simple *that*; and the doubling of it in retrospection into a state of mind and a reality intended thereby, is just one of the acts."[57] Something may arise to our attention, and as yet, the qualities of the thing in the sense of what makes it this thing rather than something else, those qualities are not yet understood. In pure experience, the object has no differential qualities, and in this sense, there is an openness of possibility, because the mind has not yet attached a categorical understanding to the immediate experience.

Some events on the other side of the world may influence our perceptions. A peace agreement between warring countries on the other side of the world may not fall into the frame of our immediate attention, but that event may have an enormous impact on our lives in ways we may never be fully aware of. What is beyond the sphere of our attention is not necessarily beyond the realm of what actually exists, and sheds influence onto perception. As Nishida explains, this is a complicated process because "pure experience coincides with the sphere of attention," in that pure experience can only experience what arises before our senses and what enters the parameters of our windows onto the world. Our attention gathers our focus into a frame with which consciousness can perceive the world, but "pure experience is not necessarily limited to a single focus of attention."[58] There is an indication that he means something beyond can enter into the frame of our attention, even breaking or rearranging the frame itself, from beyond what is visible, while our consciousness remains only aware of that which is presented through system/structures. Most of the actions of the will, the thinking through of the perceptible, happens below the surface of our awareness. This pure experience happens without thoughtful deliberation, choice, or voluntary decision-making.

Nishida refers to "trans-experiential" things as an intuition of ideal things most commonly occurring in the field of art and religion. Talented people in these fields tend to tap into a shared sense of what is "beyond," that is, the "pure land" or a "*u-topos*"—some enhanced ideal beyond what is a hope, a shared sense of that hope. Therefore, it is hope immanent within a community.

When the synthesis of pure experience occurs, it does not even appear as such, because there is a seamlessness to it, a unity that "occurs by itself, and coalesces on its own,"[59] and it is an automatic, perhaps impulsivity to immediate experience that is dangerous. Because as Nishida himself points out, "All consciousness develops systematically,"[60] and the synthesis of difference into an apperceptive unity, can be quite problematic when "that which advances thinking is not voluntary activity."[61] When there is no voluntary will behind intentional acting, then a grammatical subject that differs may merely trigger a series of associations where its otherness is considered merely a difference in appearance, rather than a difference in kind, and vice versa.

Language represents a thought; it stands in and gives form to communicable thought; yet, within capitalism a meaning emerges from the singularity of the relation of the expression to the assimilable signifiers with which a subject makes sense of it. Structures of value, in capitalism, are meaningless. Meaning is always deferred, events are deferred, enjoyment is deferred, and we are awash in chronic, identical repetitive presentations of meaning, with no end. This is the "machinic" association of value rather than the "tool" use of the capitalist political system. Capital is always undoing and decomposing itself, even as "capital" is a subjectless social edifice, it is structured around not-being as an object. Capital is a flow, a movement, an action.

In addressing this problem indirectly, Nishida draws on a Buddhist philosophy of mind saying, "Thought has its own laws. It functions of its own accord and does not follow our will."[62] One must then ask Nishida, who is thinking if it is not following "our" will? Who are "we" in this case if "we" are not our thoughts? There is some other aspect of ourselves that is not directly inextricable with "thought" neither with what we "think about"? Then, who are we? and what is thought? It calls to mind an old saying from Buddhist philosophy, "the mind is a terrible master, and a wonderful servant." We must "yoke" the mind, or else it will be as the "Rutting elephants roaming wild do not cause as much devastation in this world as the roaming elephant, the mind, let free, creates in Avīci and other hells."[63] This is one example of many from the eighth-century Buddhist, Santideva where spiritual defilement occurs when the mind roams free to think by way of its own laws. Many of these ancient Buddhist philosophies of mind portray the mind as if it were an untamed wild animal set loose in civilization. When the animal destroys civilization and wildly places the human mind on the path to Avīci, which is considered the lowest rung in the deepest pit of hell, Avīci is reserved for those who have done the worst things, like killing a bodhisattva or arhat.

Marx, in some places, substitutes another "master pillar of the production of wealth," for the "social individual" in the sense that the telos of communism is the socialization, or the artistic, scientific, and development of every individual thanks to the reduction of working time to a minimum and to the extension of leisure time. Labor's appropriation of his own universal productive labor force creates a new social subject, conscious, knowing, and able.

Ideology is the unwitting desire set free in the pursuit of enjoyment in the form of commodity fetishism. Ideology is thought that does not follow our will, but the will of desire as reflexive motivation to pursue immediate enjoyment in a mechanical circularity without end.

In general, people are conditioned to believe that "my" experience is what is real. That there is a real entity called the "self" in which it is presumed "my thoughts" and "my feelings" are uniquely my own. Material of thought is derived from the perceptive inputs from the world, out of which "arise" thought processes.

NISHIDA'S HUMAN BEING, 1938 ("NINGENTEKI SONZAI" OR HUMAN "ENEMY, POINT, TELOS," OF EXISTENCE)

One might also render this title *The Pointedness of Human Existence* because "teki" may be translated as "point, enemy," or perhaps even "enemy, or target" it becomes tricky. Is Nishida referring to the being of beings in its human form as focused on a particular point? Or, the targeted focus of attention placed on an enemy as a symptom of estrangement with "self and other" and dehumanizing others by seeing separation when there is none?

In the later era of Nishida's work, starting in the 1930s until the early 1940s, some have categorized his thought as moving into meditations on a dialectical world-matrix involving acting beings.[64] At that time, Nishida's student Miki Kiyoshi had already published his 1936 work, *The Study of the Human*, where Miki offers an interpretation of philosophical anthropology from a Marxist perspective.

Miki emphasized that self-awareness is the basis of philosophical anthropology, but this does not mean that self-awareness is simply immediate knowledge; it has always to be mediated.[65] "Our standpoint of philosophical anthropology is one of acting self-awareness. It does not disembody human beings but grasps them in their subjective and social existence."[66] Nishida may have been responding directly to Miki on this subject.

John Maraldo has argued, quite convincingly, that Miki and Tosaka were so influential on Nishida's work in the 1930s along with Tanabe's critiques must have encouraged Nishida to take history more seriously than he had previously, and began to turn his attention to bodily action, active intuition, and then later the religious worldview.[67]

Perhaps, there is no place in Nishida's work where we see a more obvious example of working through the problem of *entfremdung* "estrangement" and *entäußerung* "externalizing" than in the opening of this essay where Nishida writes,

> The world of historical actuality is the world of production, the world of creation. Although to speak of "production" is to say we make things and that the thing is something made by us, it is nevertheless the case that the thing, as an utterly independent thing, conversely affects us and, indeed, that the acting itself by which we make things is born of the world of things. While things and self are utterly opposed and utterly contradict each other, *the thing affects the self and self affects thing; as contradictory self-identity*, the world itself forms itself, moving in active intuition from the made to the making.[68]

Nishida continues, "In the actually existing historical world, what is seen in active intuition is necessarily what has been formed in expressive activity." Production forms the horizon line; it structures the visible, the ideological horizon of what appears to the subject. What can be seen is what is rendered apparent by being produced, and since consciousness and labor's self-identity is returned to it through what it produces, what is rendered apparent is what is being produced, and therefore the being of beings is rendered apparent through production, being is produced as well.

Production as generality frames perspectives on first principles of truth. Since first principles are the aspects of the ideological super structures that are invisible, the Genesis of the inapparent first principles occurs at the level of production Nishida's aporic-koan should make sense: "We both must and cannot think that in the world there is a beginning."[69] If consumption constitutes the singularity of consuming that particular use value, singularity happens once and only once, after which there is no return, the subject is shaped by what it consumes. For Marx, what is consumed is shaped by what is available from the general horizon of production as "determined by social-accident" of which "products fall to individuals" on the basis of class.[70]

With a single subject (an individual or a nation, a community) consumption is returned as a product, back to the subject. What the subject produces is returned in consumption, and the subject is shaped by what it metabolizes in consumption. The demand for art is created by the production of art and the consumption of art is what cultivates the subject for a more refined aesthetic taste. A piece of technology that is not used is the only technology in potential and therefore has no use value.

In a society, consumption is mediated by exchange after "selling" or otherwise expropriating the product of labor through sale after setting a price. A shifting subject, rather than as a stable substance. If anything, this is one of Nishida's most important concerns, especially when writing one of his later essays *Human Being* (1938) where he says "Our knowledge arises from the fact that we, as singularities in the historical world, see the thing in expressive activity." It is the objectification of the epistemological object under inquiry (for example, what is "human nature") that tends to objectify and absolutize what in actual reality is produced by the myriad beings of shifting temporary social relations. The object is fetishized and concretized when it should be viewed as an abstraction, an avatar out of a groundless ground, a dynamism animated by historical subjectivity. Labor power moves historically toward ever higher forms of abstraction and intensification of potential power, the ontological antagonisms of which can burst forth into actual kinetic energy. The mediation of value through the schematic of money places strict limitations on this production force; however, we can only know what the more developed form will be after it exists in the forms of actually existing communist ontologies.

NISHIDA'S CONTRADICTORY SELF-IDENTITY (MUJUNTEKI JIKODŌITSU)

Following are some of the keywords in the phenomenological analysis offered by Nishida: Mu means nothing, and this concept bears heavily in the context of the Zen koan tradition, as it is an instructive "nothing" often associated with awakening. Jun means a secondary order, a turn, a shift. *Teki* is often translated as "dialectic" but more closely it may indicate a point, an enemy in the sense of a focused self, or selfhood gathering focus into a single point also estranges and separates from itself in other places, and as a term that indicates a process. When Tosaka Jun uses *"teki"* in the context of *ronri-teki* it may mean "logical dialectic" but another rendering may not make sense in English, "Logicific" as in an active process of utilizing logic akin to changing the word "science" to "scientific" which gives us a strange sounding neologism in the English language, and another representation of the Hegelian title: "Science of Logic" or the dialectical process of utilizing logic in a scientific sense: "Logicifical" knowledge. Jiko is self as akin perhaps to "ipseity" or self-referential identity. Jikaku means awareness, self-aware, awake; derives from "ji" meaning self and *"kaku"* meaning aware. *Dōitsu* means equal, common, as in common people under the same flag, and it might mean something akin, but not identical to the German word *"geist"* or the spirit of a community that draws a group together under a common spirit of togetherness.

In the context of a contradictory self-identity, it means that there would have to be an "observant self" that you can turn back to and reflect on what to do, an observant perspective within the self, some folks call it "God" when in fact, it might be just a deeper plane of existence, a higher self within themselves, but also a resistance to the spirit of a community as formed external to the self.

This metaphysics of the observant self is one hermeneutics of Nishida's *ningenteki sonzai*, but one has to ask whether or not the self-contradictory self is aware of itself as such? In my reading of Nishida through Marx, one might align the self as a commodified form of labor power, alienated from itself, as embodying an antagonistic-dialectic immanent within itself as indicated in passages like these in the *Grundrisse:*

> The simple fact that the commodity exists doubly, in one aspect as a specific product whose natural form of existence ideally contains (latently contains) its exchange value, and in the other aspect as manifest exchange value (money), in which all connection with the natural form of the product is stripped away again—this double, *differentiated* existence must develop into a *difference*, and the difference into *antithesis* and *contradiction*.[71]

The phenomenological existence of labor as a commodity within capitalism means that labor must present itself as both productive forces and as an exchange value. It must manifest exchange value, which is then expropriated from it, and brings it further into alienated/estranged ways of being, without realizing it is happening. Labor is reduced to a commodity, without knowing it. Remember Nishitani's point that the one thing that a person cannot see clearly as a machine is itself, neither the labor power nor the capitalist can see beyond the limitations of this ideological horizon line. This is what "structural" analysis is, the structures are perhaps visible, yet, do not contain any modicum of consciousness of itself. If, as Hegel says, "Spirit is a bone," then we must also follow up with his lesser-known lines later on in the *Phenomenology of Spirit* that the bone does not possess self-awareness, yet it is the basis of human life, without it, human life would not exist. Force is enacted by notions concealed behind the physical interactions between entity and entity.

Describing the elements of *Expressive Activity*, Nishida turns to Fichte's concept of *Tathandlung* as a form of self-awareness that allows for the self to see itself, something that he has to mask in a German Idealist cloak when this idea of the self-observant self-stretches back far into the history of Buddhist thought.

In his essay *Expressive Activity*, Nishida has this to say:

> To clarify that the idea sees the idea itself, we must turn to Fichte's concept of *Tathandlung*. According to Fichte's conception, we can never arrive at the profound internal unity of acting and knowing. In self-awareness we can say that truly to act is to know, and to know is to act. For such self-aware activity to come into being, however, there must be a standpoint that transcends self-awareness. From the standpoint that unifies the personal and the suprapersonal, the self and the not-self, we can make a cognitive epistemological object of the content of the person. We should even say that it is precisely such a standpoint

that is the standpoint of true intuition. When we say that the knower and the known are one, the "one" is no more than a cognitive epistemological objectified "one." Even though we speak of an infinitely productive activity that is without ground, this is an activity that has been rendered a cognitive epistemological object."

If there is a "God" it is not a central point, "God developing in world history is nothing more than something like a merely conceptual empty time at the heart of nature."[72]

NOTES

1. Nishida's last publication titled *Nothingness and the Religious Worldview* has also been translated as "the Place of the Nothing" or "the Logic of Place" and the *Religious Worldview* shows his work coming full circle as the *Basho* essay was one of his earliest publications. Italics are my own emphasis. As with any erudite philosopher Nishida draws upon many influences. In this section, I would like to try and unpack influences on his work from "samsara" that tends to be understood more about Tibetan Buddhists and Vedic traditions that draw from Hinduism.

2. Karl Marx. *Capital Volume 1*. Pg. 166–167. This is the famous line often cited by Slavoj Zizek that describes "ideology" in a Marxist sense. The thoughtlessness of going through the motions without understanding why, and the second portion of this text makes it clear that the "social hieroglyphic" that labor is transformed into is money.

3. Nishida Kitarō. *Expressive Activity*. Pg. 39.

4. Ibid. Pg. 41.

5. Th. Stcherbatsky. *Buddhist Logic*, volumes 1&2. Dover Press, 1955.

6. Nishida Kitarō. *Expressive Activity*. Pg. 46.

7. John Krummel. *Nishida Kitaro's Chiasmatic Chorology*. Pg. 36–44.

8. Nishida Kitarō. *Expressive Activity*. Pg. 47.

9. Nishida Kitarō. "Unity of Opposites." In *Intelligibility and the Philosophy of Nothingness: Three Essays*. Translated by Robert Schinzinger, Pantianos Classics, 1958. Pg. 91.

10. Nishitani Keiji. *Religion and Nothingness*. University of California Press, 1982.

11. Ibid. Pg. 170.

12. Ibid. Pg. 174.

13. Ibid. Pg. 87.

14. Nishida. *Unity of Opposites*. Pg. 87.

15. Ibid. Pg. 98–99.

16. *Expressive Activity*. Pg. 45.

17. Nishitani Keiji. *Religion and Nothingness*. Pg. 21.

18. Tetsuro Mori. "Nishitani Keiji and the Question of Nationalism." In *Rude Awakenings: Zen, the Kyoto School and the Question of Nationalism*. Edited by James

W. Heisig and John C. Maraldo. Honolulu: University of Hawaii Press, 1994. Pg. 325–326.

19. John Maraldo. "Questioning Nationalism Now and Then: A Critical Approach to Zen and the Kyoto School." In *Rude Awakenings: Zen, the Kyoto School and the Question of Nationalism*. Honolulu: University of Hawaii Press, 1994. Pg. 355–356.

20. Nishitani Keiji. "Mechanization." In *The Philosophy of Nishitani Keiji: 1900–1990 Lectures on Religion and Modernity*. Translated by Jonathan Morris Augustine and Yamamoto Seisaku. Edwin Mellen Press: Lewiston, New York, 2012. Pg. 63–66.

21. Nick Srnicek and Helen Hester. *After Work: The Politics of Free Time*. 2020.

22. Nishida. *Expressive Activity*. Pg. 59.

23. ibid. Pg. 51.

24. Ibid. Pg. 53.

25. ibid. Pg. 55, italics are my own.

26. Nishida Kitarō. *Unity of Opposites*. Pg. 107.

27. Tosaka Jun. *Laughter, Comedy, and Humor*. 1932–1933.

28. Ibid.

29. Ibid.

30. Ibid.

31. Ibid.

32. Thomas Nagel's thesis is just this in his famous essay "What Does it Mean to be a Bat?"

33. Shinran (1173–1263)—a Pure Land Japanese Buddhist Monk, student of Hōnen.

34. Letter no. 595, 4 January 1930, NKZ 18:396–398.

35. Diary, 3 August, 1903. NKZ 17:119.

36. *The Gateless Barrier*. Koan 16. "The Peal of the Bell."

37. Nishida Kitarō. *An Inquiry into the Good*. Preface. Pg. xxx.

38. Masao Abe. *A Study of Dōgen: His Philosophy and Religion*. State University of New York Press: Albany, 1994. Pg. 92.

39. Nishitani Keiji. *Nishida Kitaro*. Pg. 3.

40. Friedrich Nietzsche. *Beyond Good and Evil* § 207 is the first known use of the term "ipseity." Nietzsche coins the term in a slightly different version where he says "However gratefully one may go to welcome an objective spirit—and who has not been sick to death of everything subjective and its accursed *ipsissimosity* [Ipsissimosität: coinage from ipsissima, 'very own']!—in the end one has to learn to be cautious with one's gratitude too and put a stop to the exaggerated way in which the depersonalization of the spirit is today celebrated as redemption and transfiguration, as if it were the end in itself: as is usually the case within the pessimist school, which also has good reason to accord the highest honors to 'disinterested knowledge.' The objective man who no longer scolds or curses as the pessimist does, the ideal scholar in whom the scientific instinct, after thousandfold total and partial failure, for once comes to full bloom, is certainly one of the most precious instruments there are: but he belongs in the hand of one who is mightier. He is only an instrument, let us say a mirror—he is not an 'end in himself.'"

41. Uehara Mayuko. *The Conceptualization and Translation of Jikaku and Jiko in Nishida Kitarō*.
42. Jun'ichiro Tanizaki. *In Praise of Shadows*. Pg. 4.
43. ibid. Pg. 30–31. obviously, this is a matter for another book, but the allusion is to "clearing" in a Heideggerian sense, but also in literature, the presence of clarity, of being brought forth into the light, summarized in the lines that the thicket is no sacred grove, the opening epigraph to James Fenimore Cooper's Leatherstocking Novels.
44. NKZ 1:4.
45. Plato's Republic lines 509–521.
46. Ishihara Yūko. "Later Nishida on Self-Awareness on Self-Awareness: Have I Lost Myself Yet?" *Asian Philosophy*, 21 (2011): 2. Pg. 193–211.
47. ZNK. Pg. 138.
48. ZNK. Pg. 158.
49. ZNK. Pg. 158.
50. ZNK. Pg. 3.
51. ZNK. Pg. 13.
52. *Grundrisse*. Notebook VII, Chapter on Capital.
53. ZNK. Pg. 15.
54. ZNK. Pg. 20.
55. ZNK. Pg. 21.
56. ZNK. Pg. 5.
57. William James. "Does 'Consciousness' Exist?" In *The Writings of William James*. University of Chicago Press: Chicago. Pg. 177–178.
58. ZNK. Pg. 6.
59. ZNK. Pg. 7.
60. ZNK. Pg. 9.
61. Ibid.
62. ZNK. Pg. 13.
63. Santideva. Guarding of Awareness. in the *Bodhicaryavatara*. Pg. 34.
64. John Krummel. *Nishida Kitaro's Chiasmatic Chorology: Place of Dialectic, Dialectic of Place*. Indiana University Press, 2015.
65. Miki Kiyoshi. *The Study of the Human*. 1936.
66. ibid.
67. John C. Maraldo. "Nishida's Ontology of History." In *Japanese Philosophy in the Making I: Crossing Paths with Nishida*. Chikosudō Press. Pg. 239.
68. Nishida Kitarō. "Human Being." In *Ontology of Production: Three Essays*. Translated by William Haver. Pg. 144. My own italics to emphasize the use of alienation and estrangement from the oneself inherent in Nishida's use of "contradictory self-identity."
69. Ibid. Pg. 144.
70. Ibid. Pg. 89.
71. *Grundrisse*. Pg. 147.
72. *Expressive Activity*. Pg. 51.

Chapter 2a

Dialectics

Ideology, Reproduction, and the Falling Rate of Profit

There has been scant engagement with Kyoto School Marxism and Japanese Marxism published in western academic journals. Besides Kojin Karatani's 2008 article *Beyond Capital-Nation-State*,[1] among the essays published in *Rethinking Marxism*, most of the work of "rethinking" Marx tends to focus entirely on French and German philosophy within the continental tradition. Karatani's work argued in favor of abandoning "the architectural metaphor of base/superstructure that has come to inform historical materialism since Marx and reconstruct a Marxian theory of social formation around the notion of 'exchange' (Verkher)."[2] This is because there has been a much more thoroughgoing engagement with the second and third volumes of *Capital* among Japanese Marxists than there has been among the so-called Western Marxists, the latter staying almost entirely within the parameters of "critical theory," and super-structural critiques of culture and ideology studies. My contention is that through careful readings of the second and third volumes, offered by Japanese Marxists listed in this paper, a deepening of our understanding of the economic base, reproduction, and the falling rate of profit can offer a much more cogent analysis of capitalism.

For example, a myriad of papers is written on Althusserian Ideological State Apparatuses and reproduction. Yet, Althusserian analysis can be enhanced rather than rebuked through the ways that Japanese Marxists such as Tosaka Jun rebuked a fatalistic reading of "conditioned coproduction" that makes more sense by returning to the second and third volumes of *Capital* where Marx brought a thorough detailing of his analysis of social reproduction, and as an addendum to this, the engagement is fully fleshed out in the notebooks that would later be published under the title *The German Ideology*. In his *La philosophie de Marx*, Étienne Balibar drew attention to the enigma of the complete disappearance of the notion of ideology from Marx's texts after 1850. In *The German Ideology*, the omnipresent notion of ideology is conceived as the chimera that supplements social production and reproduction; yet, the moment Marx engages in the "critique of political economy," what he encounters in the guise of "Commodity Fetishism" is no longer an illusion that "reflects" reality but an uncanny chimera at work in the very heart of the process of social reproduction.[3]

The problem is that there must be a vehement criticism of the perspective that brings Japanese Marxists into conversations as saying something particular about "Japan" or reading Kyoto Scholars as ethnically particular to something like a "Japanese context" without stripping away the particular historical context. There are ways to engage with this work without fetishizing Zen in their work as a manifestation of "heilige" (or salvational messianism so common among the western religions critiqued by Marx), rather than engaging with non-western Marxists through a silly binary of positive or negative attitudes toward something vaguely referred to as "ego." One can better understand Marx when he says, in *The German Ideology*, that the ego and its negation are manifestations of material conditions. Ego or non-ego are never matters of choosing moral asceticism or not, being humble or selfish, but are a product of lived conditions of social reproduction that produce the tactics of ego-self-representation. Whether or not a moral code of conduct allows egoism or not, when desperate material conditions put workers in life and death situations, egoism will emerge as the conatus or will to survive. This is echoed in Nietzsche's addendum to Darwin in a brief, all too brief section of *Twilight of the Idols*,[4] where Nietzsche correctly asserts that the flaw in Darwin's theory of evolution is that Darwin failed to fully understand "intelligence" as a skill that manifests among the physically weak who must adapt in order to survive. Brute strength in corporeal form is not the only tactic that the physically weak can use to pull at the levers of power to empower themselves. Intelligence might be read as "ego" and it might be read as the adaptation of culture into ideologies that become sympathetic to the plight of the weak, something that Nietzsche was skeptical about, but cultural critics who engage with Nietzsche and Marx seem to conflate the two in favor of a Marxist, allegedly sympathetic reading of ideology as adaptable insofar as it cultivates compassion toward a society based on needs rather than abilities.

These titles include works by some Japanese intellectuals known to western scholars such as Kojin Karatani's *Marx Towards the Centre of Possibility*,[5] a series of publications Karatani published in 1973, translated by Gavin Walker; along with Walker's own text *The Sublime Perversion of Capital: Marxist Theory and the Politics of History in Modern Japan*,[6] which offers a new generation of scholars a historical materialist analysis offered by political philosophers in early modern Japan (Uno Kuzo, Noro Eitaro, and Yamada Moritaro); along with the translations of Tosaka Jun's writings offered by several top scholars in *Tosaka Jun: A Critical Reader*.[7] William

Haver's *Ontology of Production: 3 Essays by Nishida Kitaro*[8] was one of the first to offer a fully "communist" interpretation of Nishida's philosophy; yet, there seems to be a disconnect between the scholars working in history departments, needless to say, the contributions of Harry Harotoonian's *Marx After Marx*[9] and his brilliant and erudite gathering of sources into a fusion of historical materialist analysis with political philosophy. With the discussions with scholars who work on the Kyoto School and have limited, if no engagement with the works of Marx. Many book length studies engage from a Hegelian,[10] Nietzschean,[11] or phenomenological perspective.[12] As admirable as those works are, there seem to be two "contrapuntal" discourses going on in the western reception of Kyoto School philosophy. Those who juxtapose with Marx and those who do not, and what I hope to do is to bring these pieces of literature into conversation with one another in a rethinking of Marx among the Kyoto Scholars.

The problems outlined in this chapter are clearly not behind us in that very little progress has occurred. None of the recent works in this area, including the monolithic contributions of Slavoj Žižek to the field of ideology studies, has approached this subject from the perspective of placing Karl Marx's writings on ideology, most notably *The German Ideology*, in conversation with Antoine de Stutt de Tracy, the originator of the word "ideology".

IDEOLOGY AND ANTOINE DE STUTT DE TRACY (1754–1836)

The invention of the word ideology has been attributed to Antoine de Stutt de Tracy (1754–1836) during the French Revolution's Reign of Terror. This was an especially violent era in the French Revolution; some disagreement occurred between historians about the exact timeframe, but it took place somewhere between the Autumn of 1793 and the Summer of 1794. Most would say that it definitively ended with the execution of Maximillien Robespierre who promoted the use of violence, fomenting an already violent situation. During this time there were many public executions. de Tracy was imprisoned and awaiting trial when he was the first person on record to use the term "ideology." He did so with the intention that this would be a positive mechanism that governments could use to prevent the kind of mob rule that occurred during the Reign of Terror.

de Tracy viewed this new form of political science as a subcategory of zoology in the sense that its purpose would control the biological impulses of the masses as if one were controlling an animal in a zoo to make it docile. By controlling the four faculties that comprise conscious life, perception, memory, judgment, and volition, one can control the basis of "sensuous" life.[13] In fact, after the French Revolution, de Tracy worked as a counselor of Public Instruction and drafted circulars for the professors of the central schools. In these circulars, he stressed the crucial role of ideology in each subject studied by the young elites in the French education system. History was to be taught from Enlightenment texts, but only after a firm introduction to the principles of ideology and legislation, which would ensure students would not regress into past moral and metaphysical superstitions. It was based on objective assertions that would undermine religious vaguery, and it was more than a "science of ideas" in that there were no ideas toward which one would uphold as if from a sanctified standpoint.

de Tracy's work emerged in the same era as the three critiques written by Immanuel Kant at the end of the eighteenth century. It should come as no surprise that Tracy's work has been almost completely forgotten whereas Kant's critiques are taught as a virtually omnipresent force in most college philosophy courses. This is because de Tracy's work attempted something that seems absurd, not just in the hindsight of Immanuel Kant, but more crucially because Karl Marx offers a scathing critique of objectivist ideology from which a general objectivist epistemology, the likes of which was forwarded by de Tracy, has not recovered. According to de Tracy's view of ideology, it was a kind of knowledge containing the validity in the grammar and logic of all possible science. Yet, his ideas were truncated because the only way to make objective knowledge of everything possible is if it does not question itself, and does not question the legitimacy of its own foundations, limits, or turn the gaze toward the roots of its own representation.[14]

It is also clear that among the students of Condillac, of which de Tracy was one, an emphasis is laid upon sensuous life as the basis of knowledge. Tracy's magnum opus, a five-volume work titled *Éléments d'idéologie* (1817–1818), presented his ideas as "Ideology Strictly Defined" in his first volume. The fourth volume of the *Eléments d'idéologie* he believed would be the introduction to a *second* section of the planned nine-part work which he titled *Traité de la volonté* (*Treatise on the Will and Its Effects*). Thomas Jefferson translated the book into English and retitled the volume *A Treatise on Political Economy* that undoubtedly served as a guide for many of the early American political leaders who would want to avoid a similar Reign of Terror occurring in America.

Therefore, the continued use of the terms "sensuous" life by Marx throughout *The German Ideology* can be viewed as a rebuking of state ideologies. One cannot say strongly enough that Marx, if carefully read, always uses ideology in a pejorative, rather than a propagandist sense of the word.

For example, one of the most famous excerpts from *The German Ideology* makes this clear:

> The production of ideas, of conceptions, of consciousness, is at first directly interwoven with the material activity and the material intercourse of men, the language of real life. Conceiving, thinking, the mental intercourse of men, appear at this stage as the direct efflux of their material behaviour. The same applies to mental production as expressed in the language of politics, laws, morality, religion, metaphysics, etc., of a people. Men are the producers of their conceptions, ideas, etc.—real, active men, as they are conditioned by a definite development of their productive forces and of the intercourse corresponding to these, up to its furthest forms. Consciousness can never be anything else than conscious existence, and the existence of men is their actual life-process. If in all ideology men and their circumstances appear upside-down as in a *camera obscura*, this phenomenon arises just as much from their historical life-process as the inversion of objects on the retina does from their physical life-process.[15]

These comments from the young Marx clearly indicate that he was distancing himself from the philosophy of Hegel. And it was not until later on in the first volume of *Capital* where he devotes sixteen pages to the topic of ideology in the section titled: "The Fetishism of the Commodity and its Secret." This is the section of *Capital* that contains one of the most infamous phrases that Marx pens to describe ideology: "they are doing it, but they do not know that they are doing it."[16] When taken out of context it appears to be a rather condescending statement against the working class. However, a closer reading is required to carefully understand what Marx meant by the "it" that is enacted without awareness.

What Marx does to open this section is begin from an Aristotlean concept of labor by describing the four causes[17] of a product in the subtext of the opening salvo of the chapter.

> A commodity appears at first sight an extremely obvious, trivial thing . . . whether we consider it from the point of view that by its properties it satisfies human needs, or that it takes on these properties as the product of human labor. It is absolutely clear that, by his activity, man changes the forms of the materials of nature in such a way as to make them useful to him. The form of wood, for instance, is altered if a table is made out of it. Nevertheless the table continues to be wood, an ordinary, sensuous thing. But as soon as it emerges as a commodity, it changes into a thing which *transcends sensuousness*.[18]

The four causes are all outlined here. The material cause is the raw materials, the cherry, maple, or oak wood that is taken from the nature and metabolized through the labor process. The formal design is laid out, as Marx says later, that the worst human architect is superior to the best bee because "the architect builds for the cell wall in his mind before he constructs it in the wax."[19] In the change of forms from a tree trunk into a carefully crafted table, the efficient cause for this transformation is the laborer who carefully handcrafts the lumber into a table using skilled woodworking processes. The final cause is the table that is used to serve food, entertain guests, bring a family together for meals, any number of pragmatic uses. It is what Marx says at the end of this passage that differentiates him from prior Aristotlean philosophy. When a commodity becomes a commodity it "transcends sensuousness." Many people have studied this as a philosophical debt to Hegel, and undoubtedly there is no hidden influence there that one can obviously see Marx drawing on Hegel's philosophy of absolute mind, and absolute spirit, to which Marx was attempting to concretize the ideational in the form of the commodity. Creating a breadcrumb trail leads back to the material conditions and the modes of production, overdetermined by social relations. Critiques of ideology are not merely discursive re-arrangements of the language games that trap us in a falsely framed perspective on reality.

One might say, as Marx did in *The German Ideology*, "They forget, however, that to these phrases they themselves are only opposing other phrases, and that they are in no way combating the real existing world,"[20] and the inversion of ideology that Marx saw subsuming both old and young Hegelians at that point consisted in starting from consciousness instead of material reality. As it says in the Dhammapada, one must shed the yoke of both good and evil to obtain nirvana. Good and evil are illusory as categories and serve as snares that the wealthy use to trap the meek.

For example, in lengthy discussions, much ink spilled to discover that Aufhebung is understood to be the renunciation of pleasure that is eventually the sublation that occurs when transposing the raw contingent real into the order of symbolic necessity, and there is always some aspect of this raw real that resists integration into the order of the symbolic, and yet, this is precisely what both Marx and Nishida say is the effect of religion as understood to be ideological tools once they become the opiates of the masses, where the exploited go to mollify their suffering and return to the systems of exploitation as if it were God's will. It is clear that both Nishida and Marx have major problems with religion serving that function.

IDEOLOGICAL SUPERSTRUCTURE

It is not through the use of overt propaganda that desire becomes entangled with capital. The structural aspects of capitalism fundamentally misrepresent or occlude its own structures of power—the sensuous forces and relations that condition its own cognitive activity. For Marx, the sensuous is the domain of both social production and reproduction, and this is exactly what remains inapparent to the subject. If the subject has a consciousness that is produced by material conditions, the ideological superstructure is that which cannot render itself visible within the frame of its material conditions as such. If ideology rendered itself apparent, it would no longer be ideological.

Consciousness systematically occludes the sensuous forces that condition its own cognitive activity. Ordinary social consciousness is ideologically enveloped and necessarily misrepresents social reality, and this is why the political economy is ideological through because it can only mischaracterize its relations through this camera obscura (the ideological lens) which is why it inverts, distorts, and presents what is false as if it were real, without being aware that it is doing so. In *The German Ideology* and the early economic manuscripts, he is already laying out the terrain of ideology to distinguish between what is sensuously real from that which ideology recognizes as truthful. As Marx set out his cogent critique of political economy, he does so with the assertion that classical political economics up until that point has only approached economic and political questions from an ideological perspective, with de Stutt de Tracy, among others, blinded by their own categories, they think they are analyzing the world in an objective sense. Marx introduces categories of analysis that they were not seriously considering, such as class, labor, exploitation, surplus value, and these changeable categories that make up the contingent and historical nature of social relations.

Rather than a-historical or "objective" categories that can be discovered as if these were facts, Marx inquires into the categories of social relations as created out of productive activities that can change on the basis of class, property, money, and all the categories on which classical political economy usually begins rather than asking where these categories originate. This is a new "genesis" in the sense that Marx offers a new starting point: the reality of labor and the concealed exploitation of labor as a working class.

CULTURE INDUSTRY

Typically, the "culture industry" is understood to produce ideologies in the form of a spontaneous false-consciousness subject to systematic misrepresentation of sensuous forces and material relations that condition the cognitive activity of a subject blinded by ideology and ignorant of this blindness. For Marx, the sensual is a domain of social production and reproduction which is often inapparent to cognitive awareness of our social reality. Political economy had only been able to see the social relations and relations of production through an inverted lens of ideology, that is, through a "camera obscura." As Marx writes:

> The production of ideas, of conceptions, of consciousness, is at first directly interwoven with the material activity and the material intercourse of men, the language of real life. Conceiving, thinking, the mental intercourse of men, appear at this stage as the direct efflux of their material behaviour. The same applies to mental production as expressed in the language of politics, laws, morality, religion, metaphysics, etc., of a people. Men are the producers of their conceptions, ideas, etc.—real, active men, as they are conditioned by a definite development of their productive forces and of the intercourse corresponding to these, up to its furthest forms. Consciousness can never be anything else than conscious existence, and the existence of men is their actual life-process. If in all ideology men and their circumstances appear upside-down as in a *camera obscura*, this phenomenon arises just as much from their historical life-process as the inversion of objects on the retina does from their physical life-process.[21]

BOURGEOIS SELF-ENJOYMENT/CRUDE COMMUNISM

It is without question that capitalism has most certainly not put an end to patriarchal relations. However, there is a way in which Marx and Engels are correct to assert that capitalism can adapt a hierarchical class system to matriarchal forms of consumption. Marx has an interesting section toward the end of *The German Ideology* where he moves close to the kind of psychoanalytic work that those on the left pursue in post-Lacanian terms. He writes:

> The philosophy of enjoyment was never anything but the clever language of certain social circles who had the privilege of enjoyment. . . . It sank to the level of edifying moralizing, to a sophisticated palliation of existing society, or it was transformed into its opposite, by declaring compulsory asceticism to be enjoyment.[22]

Here, Marx is showing his firm commitment to class politics and revealing the predominant discourses of revolution offered by consumerist bourgeois ideologies are always atomistic and allegorical in nature—a morality of the individual, rather than infused with class consciousness. Capitalist liberalism frames every question of power in terms of individual choices, thus naturalizing market forces as if it were an extension of human nature, rather than an imposition that traumatizes and reshapes human nature. It is an aporia question in the sense that many people cannot see beyond this at all. To illustrate the appropriative qualities of say, "crude communist"/atomistic liberation of the drives through the use of early phase brand marketing, let us turn to the stunning work of Edward Bernays.

The two photographs that follow are examples of early marketing techniques that evolved from the work of Edward Bernays, who was the nephew of Sigmund Freud and inventor of the term "public relations" which he coined because after working with Woodrow Wilson and moving into corporate marketing campaigns he felt the word "propaganda" had a negative connotation to it. His first major project was working with the Wilson Administration to build public support for the "Great War" as World War I was called back then. Hooking people in based on hope and change, Bernays decided that the best strategy was to sell the war through the idea that Wilson was "bringing democracy to the rest of the world," a campaign that exceeded all expectations and won Wilson the popular support that he desired.

These two ads for cigarettes stem from Edward Bernays's appropriation from the women's suffrage movement as a way of selling a phallic-appearing commodity to women in order to alleviate the guilt associated with smoking at that time. Equality of representation within the capitalist private property framework only reinforces this kind of Commodity Fetishism. Freeing the repressed drives into equality of unequal positions is a reproduction and social reformation of capitalist relations.

ALIENATION AND ESTRANGEMENT

What Marx draws on in his early notebooks on Estranged Labor is clearly influenced by a response to Fuerbach and Hegel. The ways that labor power has its product expropriated away from itself by capital means that the working class loses control over the ends of production and thereby gives up the power to create self-consciousness through the process of working toward an end that would be defined by the workers themselves. Handing over the fruit of labor is a process of "entfremdung," estrangement, or externalizing "entäußerung" away from aspects of "gattungswesen" or species-essence. Marx's vocabulary has a connotation in German with exposure or bringing risk onto oneself by putting oneself into a position of risk, as in exposing oneself to risk in an economic sense of opening oneself up to economic liability.

Whereas in Hegel consciousness estranges itself, in Marx it is labor that is thrown into alienating material conditions where it must hand over the product of its work and loses the power to create consciousness for itself. What labor produces presents itself as an object alien from the producer. The realization of labor is its objectification, and labor metabolizes what it has from nature into the objectified form of its labor power, the commodity, which it then metabolizes into itself as the singularity of consumption.

1. Alienation of the product, of production—labor feels no connection to the thing it produces; the greater the product, the less he is himself; labor itself becomes an object, outside him independent and alien, self-sufficient, hostile, and separate from the worker.
2. Alienation of species being—separation from other people in a general form, how one feels a part of a unified community, a natural self that comes forth as part of a greater whole, a greater universality.
3. Alienation of worker and owner—labor is a mode of a fundamental practical activity that has been stripped away from the worker and handed over to the owner in exchange for a wage, the worker feels little or no connection to the thing that it produces and thereby rationalizes the time spent in production in terms of the money earned; by giving up half the day, one realizes the time spent in exchange for wages, there is no loyalty to the firm.
4. Alienation of workers to themselves—spending life toiling in exchange for money, workers find that they have lost their integral sense of identity with themselves, and have separated their personal identity from who they are for most of their daily lives.

The problem, the aporia, the impasse that occurs when we couple the process of alienation with the theory of consciousness forwarded by Marx is that this process of alienation and estrangement happens and appears to the worker as a completely unproblematic process because the worker grows alienated as it is subsumed within false consciousness. The process of alienation would not appear problematic at all, it would seem as if the fall into alienation is the way things have always been and should be.

THEY SHOOT HORSES, DON'T THEY?

No novel can match Horace McCoy's 1935 novel *They Shoot Horses, Don't They?* in unwittingly describing the capitalist wheel of samsara under the influence of the kleshas that arise in subsumption. It is not a beautifully written novel. It contains no flowery passages that are worth quoting for their prosaic imagery, or for any sort of salvational quality in the aesthetic wonderment. McCoy paints no rosey pictures, and it does not transport the reader to a fantasy world of the imagination to escape the grim realities of life. It is a harbinger of doom, the first of its kind brought forth by an existential master from within the American experience.

Simone de Beauvoir called it the first existentialist novel to have appeared in America, and the novel is not about the talent and inspiration of the author, and certainly contains no discernible plotline that could keep anyone's attention span. The characters are paper-thin and the ingredients that usually make for a good novel are nowhere to be found. Standard criteria of what makes for entertaining reading is really not what makes the novel compelling. The main character, Gloria, is a neurotic mess, depressed to the point of suicide and throughout the competition she annoys everyone with which she comes into contact. What makes the novel compelling is that the structure of the narrative conveys the material conditions of desperation within capitalist reproduction (i.e., the wheel of samsara).

In McCoy's story, a set of characters gather to compete in a marathon dance competition at an amusement pier somewhere near Hollywood—the Great Depression. Contestants pair off with a partner and try to win prize money by being the last couple left dancing. They must continue dancing for an hour with a ten-minute break. The dancers contrive ways to maximize their time in the most productive ways. Some of the more experienced professional dancers offer advice, like learning to eat while going to the bathroom, eating a sandwich while you shave, sleeping on your partner's shoulders while dancing, with the entire vortex of time centering around productive labor staying in the contest. It is an allegory about the physical exhaustion of staying on the wheel of samsara in a capitalist society where work extends into all areas of life. The spectacle of the dance marathon is used to sell tickets and we hear one audience member say, at one point, "Let's go to the dance marathon and watch the human suffering." To add to this allegorical story is the fact that toward the end of the dance marathon the competition devolves into a horse race. A circle is drawn on the floor and contestants are herded into galloping and strutting around this samsaric circle in competition and the last place couple is eliminated from the competition.

The circular nature of the dance competition that devolves into something akin to a horse race renders an obvious comparison between the wheel of samsara and capitalist reproduction. Coincidentally, the novel *They Shoot Horses, Don't They?* was published in 1935; precisely, the same year as Nishida Kitarō's essay, the *Standpoint of Active Intuition*. While it would probably be a stretch to think that the novel carried any influence on the work of Nishida and his students, the story was a favorite among Western readers of Marx because McCoy's novel conveys such stark imagery of workers beset with the desperation of being circumscribed by conditions not of their choosing, and yet, remaining fully beholden to the prevailing ideologies of work. For that reason, the story serves as an alarming allegory to beware of ideology, even in the most desperate of situations. It is reminiscent of the famous lines from Marx in the first volume of *Capital*: they are doing it, without knowing they are doing it.

"THEY ARE DOING IT WITHOUT KNOWING THEY ARE DOING IT"

One of the major contributions to philosophy from Karl Marx is the overcoming of a purely Aristotlean metaphysics, the residual effects of which can be felt all the way up to and including the alleged "idealism" of the German idealists, among them include Hegel. Marx once and for all shows that there are no "independent" substances. A substance is the ontological property of a thing that makes it what it is, without qualification from another property. In the philosophy of Marx, we see that thesis most clearly criticized in section 4 of the chapter on Commodity Fetishism in volume one of *Capital*: "The Fetishism of the Commodity and its Secret"' that starts with an homage to Aristotle, which Marx quickly criticizes.

Marx starts this chapter with an uncited use of Aristotle's four-causes, a theory of causality drawn from Aristotle's Physics[23]—the material, formal, efficient, and final cause of a thing creates its use-value.

If and when anything is created, it is created as a combination of elements. The material cause is the material that the object is constructed with, for example, an oak tree. The formal cause is what the object will become after labor carves up the oak tree into the form of a coffee table. The efficient cause is the being that works to make the thing, say a craftsman who is an experienced carver, or a factory that puts lumber through machines to mass-produce coffee tables from a ready-made template. Lastly, the final cause is how the object is useful. A coffee table has the use-value of holding coffee, or showing off books that nobody reads while resting their legs on it, zoning out in front of the television.

All of this metaphysics is fine and good if the end of production is simply "use-value" to create products to sell them to be useful to consumers. This classical political economy implies a kind of principle of sufficient reason, whereby Leibniz takes the low-hanging fruit of Aristotlean four causes and argues that if there is an efficient cause, there must be a principle of sufficient reason. If something brings something into existence through the use of its own labor, that labor must be guided by some kind of intelligence (the efficient cause of life is God, who creates us for his use, etc.). If human beings exist there must be an efficient cause, like a carpenter who creates a table, or a potter who uses clay to make a vase. As Lacan shows us in his lectures on Psychosis, the fastest way to go psychotic is to take the search for meaning in every miniscule occurrence seriously.[24]

Conflating all-causality with some metaphysics of meaningfulness is exactly the problem I hope to overcome by turning to Zen-inspired philosophy from the Kyoto School. It seems that the problem is when the telos of exchange value extends beyond merely the usefulness of the commodity in its consumption. "The mystical character of the commodity does not therefore arise from its use-value."[25] It exists in its potential as exchange value, to be sold, traded, exchanged, purchased, and transferred for money.

"The mysterious character of the commodity-form consists therefore simply in the fact that the commodity reflects the social characteristics of men's own labor as objective characteristics of the products of labor themselves, as the socio-natural properties of these things."[26] It is the hidden obverse that sustains the apparent "objective characteristics" of social relations. Following is the full quote that often gets truncated to mean something unintended by Marx:

> Men do not therefore bring the products of their labor into relation with each other as values because they see these objects merely as the material integuments of homogeneous human labor. The reverse is true: by equating their different products to each other in exchange as values, they equate their different kinds of labor as human labor. *They do this without being aware of it.* Value, therefore, does not have its description branded on its forehead; it rather transforms every product of labor into a social hieroglyphic.[27]

Searching for a meaning behind the social hieroglyphic of value might reveal that value is grounded in money, but this is wrong; the social hieroglyphic is labor itself, the crystallization of labor power in the form of the commodity, a power that is gradually estranged/externalized from the laborer.

HISTORICAL MATERIALISM

Karl Marx never pens the words "historical materialism." This concept was first invented by Frederick Engels in his 1880 book *Socialism: Utopian and Scientific*. Marx wrote an introduction to the book, but there should be clarification between Marx and Engels on this topic as the concept itself may have conflated with the philosophy of Marx.

When Marx pens the line, "history weighs like a nightmare on the brains of the living," he unintentionally veers into the samsaric territory. He was talking about the material of karmic rebirth and past lives in the sense of the historical materialism of class struggle.

Marx did not invent the phrase "historical materialism." It was a term coined by Frederick Engels in summation of how Marx may have interpreted the dialectic of history in terms of material conditions. If material conditions produce consciousness, and consciousness is formed from social relations and the processes by which humans produce and reproduce themselves in the form of material needs, then history is not over and done with, humans inherit the present from the sum total of social relations that have occurred prior to "now."

Karma and historical materialism can forward the exact same hypothesis if and only if people understand that Karma is "action" and "work." Whereas, for Marx, History "weighs like a nightmare on the brains of the living" and forms the present as conjured from the past as the sum total of history as hitherto the result of class-conflict. In section C of *The German Ideology* on "Saint-Max" titled "My Self-Enjoyment," you see the work of a historical materialist emerging in ways that have an impact on how the West might misinterpret Zen as a form of self-help to enhance personal enjoyment. "Self-enjoyment" emerged after the decline of feudalism and the transformation of landed nobility into an extravagant pleasure-loving aristocracy of monarchical societies. Self-enjoyment was the emerging ideology of the ruling class of property owners and it was given a generalized character and addressed to every individual as if without distinction.

The ideologies of the hegemonic class, as if reflexively, do it without knowing they are doing it; the presuppositions of the hegemonic class become the general norms. Even in the dialectical negation of the predominant ideologies, there is a resentment of those acting as self-negative assertions on the level of edifying moralization, "by declaring compulsory asceticism to be enjoyment."[28] How deeply run the roots of the pleasure principle when finally Zen washes ashore in the West and falls into the hands of those whose sole teloei are narcissistic enjoyment and maximal productivity.

There are ways that history "yokes" the proletariat to the present mode of production at the level of ideology. In outlining his theory of interpellation, the Italian Communist Louis Althusser was best known for his work on understanding how the ideological superstructures form the basis of "yoking," in the sense of reinforcing the dominant modes of production. The example that Athusser uses is described in the following passage taken from *Ideology and Ideological State Apparatuses* titled "On the Reproduction of the Conditions of Production":

> As Marx said, every child knows that a social formation which did not reproduce the conditions of production at the same time as it produced would not last a year.[29] The ultimate condition of production is therefore the reproduction of the conditions of production. This may be "simple" (reproducing exactly the previous conditions of production) or "on an extended scale" (expanding them). Let us ignore this last distinction for the moment.

DIALECTICAL MATERIALISM/DIALECTIC OF PLACE

Dialectical materialism has long been understood to be the philosophy of Marxism, which is distinguished from the science of Marxist thought as historical materialism. The term was most likely first used by Georghi Plekhanov in 1891. It later took on a sort of life of its own as every major communist revolutionary made use of this concept in some way, shape, or form. Lenin's *Materialism and Empirio-Criticism* (1908), Stalin's *Dialectical and historical materialism* (1938), and Mao Tse Tung's *On Contradiction* (1937) all rely heavily on the concepts of dialectical and historical materialism in some way. My argument is that this is precisely the kind of misreading of Marx that led to the problems of the twentieth-century communist appropriations of wrongheaded praxis. Even the most basic readings of Marx reveals that some of the presumptions of dialectical and historical materialism are severely flawed.

The combination of materialism and dialectical transformations in effect transforms both. Properly understood, the materialism of dialectical materialism is not reductive, and does not reduce ideas to matter asserting the ultimate identity of truth in any reified form. Rather, the idea is that matter can exist without mind and never vice versa. Mind is historically emergent from matter and remains dependent upon it; however, "science" and its applications to economics often sees objective facts as such, when in reality these are a product of class-conflict, which blinds even the most astute observers of a science of economy. All this is detailed in a matter of a few short paragraphs in a burst of brilliance by Marx in the introduction to the *Grundrisse*.

By beginning with the sense-certainty of something called "population" these "Abstract determinations lead to the reproduction of the concrete by way of thought," and the Hegelian misstep is to

> conceive the real as a product of thought concentrating itself, probing its own depths, and unfolding itself out of itself, by itself, whereas the method of rising from the abstract to the concrete is only the way in which thought appropriates the concrete, reproduces it as the concrete in the mind.[30]

The point is to remake the concrete through poiesis, the metabolism of nature through labor power, with an awareness that "human being" is one category of life within an interconnected dialectic of causality, a basho no benshōhō (dialectic of place).

SIMPLE REPRODUCTION

Thus starts chapter 23 of the first volume of *Capital*, wiping away the mystical illusions of samsaric rebirth to give way to a materialist perspective on cycles of material reproduction.

> Whatever the social form of the production process, it has to be continuous, it must periodically repeat the same phases. A society can no more cease to produce than it can cease to consume. When viewed, therefore, as a connected whole, and in the constant flux of its incessant renewal, every social process of production is at the same time a process of reproduction.[31]

What, then, is the reproduction of the conditions of production?

Perhaps to understand the subtlety in the question one has to understand the rest of what Frederick Engels writes in these letters after the death of Marx:

> The question has been approached very "materialistically" in opposition to certain idealistic phraseology about justice. But strangely enough it has not struck anyone that, after all, the method of distribution essentially depends on how much there is to distribute, and that this must surely change with the progress of production and social organization, so that the method of distribution may

also change. But to everyone who took part in the discussion, "socialist society" appeared not as something undergoing continuous change and progress but as a stable affair fixed once for all, which must, therefore, have a method of distribution fixed once for all.

All one can reasonably do, however, is 1) to try and discover the method of distribution to be used at the beginning, and 2) to try and find the general tendency of the further development. But about this I do not find a single word in the whole debate.[32]

SOCIAL REPRODUCTION[33]

"The productive time is longer than the working-day."[34]

Capital as a social relation is a dynamic phenomenon that takes on different forms at different points in the circuit. If we start with capital in the form of money, it is transformed into commodities through the production process (labor power and machine power). This form of money at the beginning of the production process is called "capital advanced" whereby the money put forth by capital at this stage is done so with the expectation that the investment will return, with a surplus value at the end of the circuit of production, distribution, and consumption. Relations of production are constituted by the ownership of productive forces, and under capitalism the most common form of ownership of productive forces is in the hands of the bourgeoisie who own factories and corporations; whereas, the proletariat constitute the working class who only own their labor power which they must sell into relation with capital, to earn a wage. By saying that the productive time is longer than the working day, Marx in the second and third volumes turns to a more expansive view of the ways capitalism gets a grip on day-to-day life.

Marx carefully works through what he calls the reproductive schema, and it takes up a vast portion of the second and third volumes of *Capital* as well as portions of the first volume. It breaks down into two ways that "surplus value" can be invested at the end of the circuit of capital—simple and extended reproduction.

1. Extended production is money put back into the means of production (*extends the next round of production, it becomes the "capital advanced" into the next circuit of money capital*). This investment may speed up the turnover rate in the next go around by improving, repairing, replacing, or sustaining the technologies used in production (i.e., an investment in fixed capital) or labor power (i.e., variable capital, hiring more workers, which poses problems we will get to in a second).

2. Simple reproduction is money put into means of consumption, "enjoyment" (*singularity*, consumption only happens once and deteriorates the product, capital burned up in wages where the workers spend paycheck on shoes, food, going to the movies, etc; the deterioration inherent in consumption means that large investments in "means of consumption" makes capital lose profits, go bankrupt, etc. This kind of social production, "humanism" we can call it, burns through the capital, if capital invests too much in this second "humanist" social reproduction he will not remain a capitalist for very long).

Simple reproduction is surplus value used in consumption. It is burned up as a singularity. Extended reproduction is surplus value used to increase production, it means accumulation and a return on investment used in the next round of production. Wage laborers are variable capital. Human workers are not as efficient. Humans get sick, have emotions, demand more money, and tend to burn up earnings in the singularity of consumption. The only other option is to invest in machines. Machines can continue to produce through the night, they do not need breaks, weekends, and never call in sick. Machines are the ideal workers that capital desires, because production can continue while the workers are asleep, away, etc. However, the basic condition of capital is that someone needs to consume the products in order to bring money back into the next round of production. This means human consumers must purchase products, and products as they are consumed are always singularities.

Once consumed, the use-value is used as one thing at one moment in time. By this, it is clear that Marx means the "ends" of production, the consumption of basic needs, food, clothing, and shelter, all of which deteriorate over time. This means that the basic condition of simple reproduction necessitates resources to move back into production, in order to keep the singularity of consumption continuing. Consumption must equal variable capital (labor and wages) and surplus value, or else the capitalist goes bankrupt, and in order to prevent that from happening there are all sorts of tactics that the capitalist uses to turn the screws on the workers (lower wages, cut benefits, "downsizing," and "outsourcing" to lower-paid areas of the world, etc.).

$ = capital advanced into (V), with (V) = wages for the working day, means less efficiency because living labor, actual human workers, create more uncontrolled variables, such as more cooperation which enhances efficiency, also creates opportunities for workers to communicate about wages, to form unions, to strike, and fight for better working conditions, benefits, because they are on the shop floor together, becoming friends, forming social relations outside of work, and so forth. Plus, with a human worker, the production stops. A human worker needs rest, sleep, lunch breaks, weekends to recharge, vacations, benefits and the workers get sick and call into work from time to time. And, the obvious health hazard is known as death: "The owner of labor power is mortal."[35] Human labor power is unreliable and costly. It leads to the falling rate of profit in the decision to invest between machines and labor power; capital loses its share of consumers if its investment is spent on machines, but it gains production efficiency if it invests in machines, although at the loss of consumers who are not earning wages. Hence, this is the contradiction posed by the automatic factory.

FALLING RATE OF PROFIT: CONSTANT OR VARIABLE CAPITAL

The problem of capital's reproductive schema is simple; this is the contradiction known as the falling rate of profit. The falling rate of capital is summarized in volumes two and three of *Capital*.

The theory itself is quite simple and Marx repeats it over and over in the second and third volumes of *Capital*, in some of his best work, albeit in an incomplete form that was not fully revised before his death. The tendency for profits to fall boils down to a simple contradiction in the mode of production itself. Capitalists want to maximize profits. One way to do this is to increase and develop more efficient technologies. As technologies are created and production becomes more and more efficient, human labor power becomes less and less important. Now, the big lie that workers are sold is that the worst thing in the world is to be replaced by a machine, even though most workers loathe their jobs, the valorization of work ethic has this stunning tendency to keep people stuck in jobs they hate. However, as technology emerges, the real problem that capital faces is the problem of overproduction. Efficiency increases, the output of products increases, more supply of products means less value can be placed on each commodity in terms of the sale price. We see this all the time as new technology hits the market. Its price starts extremely high and then it gradually drops to the point where something that was excruciatingly expensive before is not too expensive in a matter of time. As production processes become more and more efficient, the price of a thing becomes less and less. Hence, the capitalist is hit with a very strange situation. In capitalism, the more common the product becomes, the less valuable it becomes as the market becomes saturated with that product. Hence, the capitalist has every motivation to keep products scarce so as to maintain just enough market saturation where the product is at a price that makes sense to maintain profit. In addition, the demands of workers for higher wages and better working conditions always tend to interfere with the increase in profitability of the corporate firm.

The falling rate of profit is about the ways that technology always makes production more efficient, and yet, if the capitalists as a collective class figure out a way to make their production maximally efficient and lay off all human workers throughout the entire society, and hire only machine labor, or artificial intelligence as labor power, then the other quagmire that the bourgeoisie would be faced with is who will buy the commodities that are produced? There has to be someone with a wage in order to spur on consumption, and so capital is also forced to keep some semblance of human labor power on the payroll of collective capital, and so a strange set of contradictions emerge.

While book-length studies have been written to try and disprove the theory of the falling rate of profit, most notably, the thesis forwarded by Japanese economist Nobuo Okishio, famously known among economists as the Okishio Theorem which basically takes an apologetic tone for the stagnation of wages in exchange for higher profits in late capitalism. The Okishio theorem states that the way around the falling rate of profit is to keep wages stagnant, and therefore, as new technologies are developed that increase output, the stagnation of wages means that the sale of more and more products will result in an increase in profit for the corporate firm, even if the price of the product plummets due to an increase in supply, the best way the firm can navigate around this is to increase market share.

Of course, the two things that bourgeois economists typically fail to think about are the finitudes of the global market. The market share has a fixed world within which to grow its market share, what happens when there are no new markets to gain? The big crisis happens.

The other thing that bourgeois economists fail to take into consideration is that with the stagnation of wages, there are less and less consumers with purchasing power with which to purchase the commodities that the corporate firms are selling. Hence, bourgeois economics almost never sees the economy the way Marx wrote about it in the volumes of *Capital* and the *Grundrisse*— as a syllogism consisting of "production, distribution, and consumption." Consumption is driven by wages. Hence, the credit crisis in the last forty years since the stagnation in wages, in order to spur consumption, the banking industry has to extend untenable lines of credit to the working class in order to prop up consumption and give the delusion that the "falling rate of profit" is a myth, that capitalism is infallible, and that it will continue forever. The best way to keep extending these credit markets is to have the state bail out the banks when the credit markets are over-extended. When debt runs too deep, the banks can have this debt canceled and paid off by the taxpayers, the state is capital and capital is the state.

Capital advanced is the capital put into the production process, the investment put into a "turnover" (a round of production), the amount of capital advanced must return a sum of profit that is greater than was the capital advanced to begin with, then there must be enough left over in profits to forward another round of investments into the next "turnover" with still more profits left over next time around. Labor is the basis of value and the value of what the worker makes decreases as the worker makes more. We are all confronted with the decreasing world of the value of things in capitalism, and because ideology elides the social nature of this contradiction, it appears to be the most natural and inevitable process in the world.

An increase in capital advanced can only fall into one of two categories: *Constant or Variable Capital.*

More investment in constant capital (machines, constantly producing, do not break, you are assured more or less what you will get out of the constant capital) means greater output, faster turnover time, lower costs per unit, greater profit due to lower costs per unit, less consumption for workers through wages because the capital advanced does not wind up in workers' hands (i.e., not in potential consumers hands).

An increase in variable capital means lower output due to limitations on human kinetic power (machines surpass human labor power), increased wages, increased cost per unit because humans make less at a less efficient pace and demand wages, less profit for capital at the end of the "turnover," and the society enjoys an increased consumption for workers since work is done by human labor power they earn wages and therefore have money to buy commodities, the downfall of which is that consumption deteriorates the product. Advances in technology make for lasting technological changes whereas human labor power stagnates production, increases consumption, and once consumption happens (food eaten, clothing worn, cars driven and gasoline burned, houses heated in the winter, etc.) that product is gone forever.

Categories of simple and extended reproduction make this a little more complex: If a capital (capital could be worker-run factories or community co-ops with capital left at the end of production, or a capitalist who owns and contributes no labor power) spends its surpluses on simple reproduction (its own consumption, it takes the "surplus value" and buys a nice vacation, or a beautiful car, or something that takes value out of production) then capital expended in enjoyment means that surplus value has been taken out of "extended reproduction" or the surplus value that can be reinvested into production to extend, and perhaps even enhance the next cycle of production, the next round of turnovers. Simple reproduction is enjoyment, but it takes surplus value out of extending the production process.

Remember, consumption is "singular" and enjoyable, it happens only once, and it is the fetish of consumer society wrapped up in the commodity form as the basis of enjoyment. Extended reproduction is not enjoyable, but it might have to do with creating new factories, investing in better equipment, and other resources that put wealth back into the means of production to extend the life of the capital. These things extend the productive capacity of the next round of "capital advanced" and restart the circuit of capital. Eventually, Marx presumed that the technology developed by capital would foster the creation of a factory run by automatons, dubbed the "automatic factory."

AUTOMATIC FACTORIES AND ZERO-WORK UTOPIAS

Marx has two places, maybe more, where he carefully describes the development of the automatic factory. In the first volume of *Capital* in the chapter on Machinery and Large-Scale Industry and in the infamous section in the *Grundrisse* notebooks, referred to as the "Fragment on Machines."[36] What Marx envisions is a world made possible by the rapid development of technology in capitalism where an automatic factory can extend production to the point where there is no end to the working-day for the machine. Because one of the "good" things that capitalism does is to create advanced technology, even if it forms conflicts between "constant and variable capital" in the process, the basic instruments for automatic production eventually emerge. Marx writes that the automatic factory is the combined cooperation of many orders of working people, and as a vast automaton composed of various mechanical and intellectual organs, acting in uninterrupted concert for the production of a common object, "the automaton itself is the subject, and the workers are merely conscious organs, coordinated with the unconscious organs of the automaton, and together with the latter subordinated to the moving force."[37]

There are all sorts of grants now are to try and create automatic factories to rid the world of work entirely, that is, to get rid of "Karma"-yoga (the virtue accrued through works and deeds). The result is not "zero-work utopias" but a division between engineers and displaced unskilled laborers.

> The essential division is that between workers who are actually employed on the machines (among who are included a few who look after the engine) and those who merely attend to them (almost exclusively children). More or less all the "feeders" who supply the machines with material which is to be worked up are counted as attendants. In addition to these two principle classes, there is a numerically unimportant group whose occupation it is to look after the whole of the machinery and repair it from time to time, composed of engineers, mechanics, joiners etc. This is a superior class of workers, in part scientifically

educated, in part trained in a handicraft; they stand outside the realm of the factory workers, and are added to them only to make up an aggregate. This division of labor is purely technical.[38]

A new division of labor develops between the educated technicians (i.e., the engineers, the STEM students, Science, Technology, Engineering, and Math), and the "disposable life"[39] of the displaced unskilled laborers. A displacement rendered fully internal to the ideological matrices of real-subsumption because "All work at a machine requires the worker to be taught from childhood upwards, in order that he may learn to adapt his own movements to the uniform and unceasing motion of an automaton."[40]

Hence, the priority of labor as caretaking toward machines takes precedence over the development of human consciousness for the sake of personal creativity, or "caritas" as the Greeks called it, "trading skills" in exchange for the benefit of developing the talents, skills, and creative capacities of what was once referred to as a "soul" of a human being.[41]

Hence, it is no wonder that with the emergence of automated factory production and the development of a new hegemonic class of "engineers"' who possess hegemony over technological maintenance of the machines that production relies upon, there is also a turn to "posthumanism" in the humanities and the most egregious kinds of self-effacing, abhorrent animal-studies in philosophy. It is one thing to study animals, while still acknowledging the superiority of human "logos" (the ability to think, act, produce, use language, logic, and Math), but it is an entirely different thing altogether to posit a bizarrely common ethos that all animals are equal in intelligence to human beings. As Aristotle said, "Humans are the animals (zoe) who can speak (logos)" that is a major difference between us and animals, and in the next section there is a brief, all too brief, explanation of why this Aristotlean understanding is important to the project of Marx. Yet, it is an inadequate thesis to explain "general intellect" and I will continue by exploring theories of metaphysics derived from what, for the sake of brevity, we might call "Vedic Thought" (pervasion, interdependent origination, and inclusive dialectics).

NOTES

1. Kojin Karatani. "Beyond Capital-Nation-State." *Rethinking Marxism*. September 3, 2008.
2. Ibid.
3. Étienne Balibar. *La philosophie de Marx*. La Découverte: Paris, 1993.

4. Nietzsche. *Twilight of the Idols, Raids of an Untimely Man #14*.

5. Kojin Karatani. *Marx: Toward the Centre of Possibility*. Translated by Gavin Walker. Verso: London, 2020.

6. Gavin Walker. *The Sublime Perversion of Capital: Marxist Theory and the Politics of History in Modern Japan*. Duke University Press: Durham, 2013.

7. Ed. Ken C. Kawashima, Fabian Schafer, and Robert Stolz. *Tosaka Jun: A Critical Reader*. Cornell University Press: Ithaca, 2013.

8. William Haver. *Ontology of Production: 3 Essays by Nishida Kitaro*. Duke University Press: Durham, 2012.

9. Harry Harotoonian. *Marx after Marx: History and Time in the Expansion of Capitalism*. Columbia University Press: New York, 2017.

10. John Krummel. *Nishida Kitaro's Chiasmatic Chorology: Place of Dialectic/ Dialectic of Place*. Indiana University Press: Indianapolis, 2015.

11. Ed. Bret W. Davis, Brian Schroeder, Jason M. Wirth. *Japanese and Continental Philosophy: Conversations with the Kyoto School*. Indiana University Press: Indianapolis, 2011.

12. John Maraldo. *Japanese Philosophy in the Making Volumes 1 & 2*. Chukosodo Press: Nagoya, 2017.

13. Emmet Kennedy. ""Ideology" from de Stutt de Tracy to Marx." *Journal of the History of Ideas* 40, no. 3 (June–September 1979). Pg. 353–368.

14. Michel Foucault. *The Order of Things: An Archaeology of the Human Sciences*. Pg. 240–243. A wonderful section on "Ideology" and the way that Kant was in discourse with Destutt de Tracy. Michel Foucault may have tried to pose Destutt as a philosopher of French Idealism, a powerful counterpoint to Kant, Schelling, Fichte, Novalis, Holderlin, and Hegel and the German "Ideologists" as Marx would call them.

15. *German Ideology*. "The Essence of the Materialist Conception of History."

16. *Capital Volume 1*. Pg. 166–167.

17. *Aristotle Physics*, Book II chapter 3: "The Four Types of Cause."

18. *Capital Volume 1*. Pg. 163.

19. Ibid. Pg. 284.

20. *German Ideology*. Pg. 36.

21. Karl Marx. The *German Ideology*. "The Essence of the Materialist Conception of History, Social Being and Social Consciousness."

22. *German Ideology*. Pg. 441.

23. *Aristotle Physics*. Section 2 chapter 3. "The Four Types of Cause."

24. Jacques Lacan. Seminar III: The Psychoses, 1955–1956. Pg. 9. "One of our psychotics tells us how foreign the world is which he entered some time ago. Everything has become a sign for him. Not only is he spied upon, observed, watched over, not only do people speak to, point, look, and wink at him, but all this—you will see the ambiguity straightaway—invades the field of the real, inanimate, nonhuman objects. Let us look at this a bit more closely. If he encounters a red car in the street—a car is not a natural object—it's not for nothing, he will say that it went past at that very moment. Let us inquire into this delusional intuition. The car has a meaning, but the subject is very often incapable of saying what it is. Is it favorable?

Is it threatening? Surely there is some reason for the car being there." Conflating all-causality with some metaphysics of meaningfulness is exactly the problem I hope to overcome by turning to Zen inspired philosophy from the Kyoto School.

25. *Capital Volume 1*. Pg. 164.

26. Ibid. Pg. 164–165. Is there a more Zizekian line in all of Capital? No, I am afraid not.

27. *Capital Volume 1*. Pg. 167.

28. Karl Marx. *The German Ideology*. "My Self-Enjoyment." section III: Saint-Max. Pg. 441–442.

29. Letter from Marx to Kugelmann on July 11, 1868 which reads: Every child knows a nation which ceased to work, I will not say for a year, but even for a few weeks, would perish. Every child knows, too, that the masses of products corresponding to the different needs required different and quantitatively determined masses of the total labor of society. That this necessity of the distribution of social labor in definite proportions cannot possibly be done away with by a particular form of social production but can only change the mode of its appearance, is self-evident. No natural laws can be done away with. What can change in historically different circumstances is only the form in which these laws assert themselves. And the form in which this proportional distribution of labor asserts itself, in the state of society where the interconnection of social labor is manifested in the private exchange of the individual products of labor, is precisely the exchange value of these products.

Science consists precisely in demonstrating how the law of value asserts itself. So that if one wanted at the very beginning to "explain" all the phenomena which seemingly contradict that law, one would have to present science before science. It is precisely Ricardo's mistake that in his first chapter on value [On the Principles of Political Economy, and Taxation, Pg. 479] he takes as given all possible and still to be developed categories in order to prove their conformity with the law of value.

On the other hand, as you correctly assumed, the history of the theory certainly shows that the concept of the value relation has always been the same—more or less clear, hedged more or less with illusions or scientifically more or less definite. Since the thought process itself grows out of conditions, is itself a natural process, thinking that really comprehends must always be the same, and can vary only gradually, according to maturity of development, including the development of the organ by which the thinking is done. Everything else is drivel.

The vulgar economist has not the faintest idea that the actual everyday exchange relations can not be directly identical with the magnitudes of value. The essence of bourgeois society consists precisely in this, that a priori there is no conscious social regulation of production. The rational and naturally necessary asserts itself only as a blindly working average. And then the vulgar economist thinks he has made a great discovery when, as against the revelation of the inner interconnection, he proudly claims that in appearance things look different. In fact, he boasts that he holds fast to appearance, and takes it for the ultimate. Why, then, have any science at all?

But the matter also has another background. Once the interconnection is grasped, all theoretical belief in the permanent necessity of existing conditions collapses before their collapse in practice. Here, therefore, it is absolutely in the interest of the ruling classes to perpetuate a senseless confusion. And for what other purpose are the sycophantic babblers paid, who have no other scientific trump to play save that in political economy one should not think at all?

But satis superque [enough and to spare]. In any case it shows what these priests of the bourgeoisie have come down to, when workers and even manufacturers and merchants understand my book [Capital] and find their way about in it, while these "learned scribes" (!) complain that I make excessive demands on their understanding.

30. *Grundrisse*. Pg. 101.
31. *Capital Volume 1*, Chapter 23: Simple Reproduction. Pg. 711.
32. Frederick Engels letter to C. Schmidt. London, August 5, 1890.
33. *Capital Volume 2*, Chapters 18–21.
34. Ibid, Chapter 13: Production Time. Pg. 317.
35. *Capital Volume 1*. Pg. 275.
36. *Grundrisse*. Pg. 690–712.
37. *Capital Volume 1*. Pg. 544–545.
38. Ibid. Pg. 545–546.
39. See Giorgio Agamben's *Homo Sacer* for the fullest description of this; and for the earlier incarnation of this "bio-politics" see also Michel Foucault's last portion of the *History of Sexuality volume 1*.
40. *Capital Volume 1*. Pg. 546.
41. See the Euthyphro Dialogue; section 10a-16 on 'trading skills' with the Gods.

Chapter 3

What Is Communism?
Mu!

WHAT IS COMMUNISM? MIKI KIYOSHI'S "KYŌDŌSHUGHI" OR COOPERATIVISM

If someone were to ask "What is communism?" it seems like the person is asking a fairly straightforward question when in fact it is an immensely absurd question. Begging the question sneers of naive quiddity as if the term itself possessed any objective sense and as if philosophers merely adorn objects with words. If we take this analytical approach, then the result would be a fairly straightforward answer. Communism means community. The etymology of the word is linked to the messianic use of the term "communion," the history of which over codes much of the presumptive messianism associated with its revolutionary potential. The communist revolution was brought on by a vanguard figure to save the masses from their exploitation and alienation in toil and turbulence, not of sin, but of life in capitalism.

One common misunderstanding is that communism is a kind of forced equality of wages. This could not be further from the truth. In fact, in some of the last writings that Marx published, he resoundingly criticized that view. In his *Critique of the Gotha Program*, Marx clearly states that the equality of wages is a bourgeois sense of equality. Since the bourgeoisie are those who are motivated by profit-driven intentions and whose consciousness is produced by the material conditions of bourgeois-class consciousness and given the bourgeois status of hegemony over the production of the dominant discourses in the culture, there is no question that this would become the predominant view of communism. In other words, the view that Marx espouses an "economic determinism" would only become prevalent among capitalists whose reified consciousness makes it impossible to carefully understand the nuanced ways that Marx forward the communist hypothesis as a revolution against the wage-labor system. In other words, Marx is talking about communism as a rebuking of capitalism qua capitalism as an ontological wholeness, changing as it may, there are stable economic forms at its core, wage-labor being one of those forms. Marx writes that quality of wages results in a bourgeois equality where there is an inequality of rewards for inequality of skills, talents, and abilities. Hence, in his *Critique of the Gotha Program*, Marx was already forwarding the oft-quoted criticisms of communism, but as a way of outflanking the bourgeois on the left, thereby revealing just how expansive the communist revolution must be to overturn capitalism, even at the level of the wage-labor system.

Those interested in the question of communist ontology can approach the question from a western perspective of the "quid and the quale"—What is it? What are its qualities? Realizing that Kyoto School Marxist Miki Kiyoshi worked through this ontological question.

Miki's work often fosters a view that may appear out of step with many Western Marxist discourses. His view is that life is both pathos (emotions, feelings, expressions, creativity) and logos (speech, logic, language, reasoning) with pathos as an expression of the unbearable in common narratives that are functional insofar as they contextualize political struggles in the context of mythos. By mythos it is clear that Miki has in mind a kind of political theology, the mythmaking process of religious and political discourses. One can imagine Marx when he writes that religion is the opium of the masses, the cry of an oppressed soul[1] that the presumption among many leftists inspired by Marx is that in a free communist society the need for religious mythos would no longer be necessary.

If there is repressed pathos among the working class, then there will be a repressed pathos in political life. If you take away the repression, the corresponding mythos will also wither away. For Marx, mythos is the ideological construction of life in exploitation. Religions are mythmaking institutions that only serve as an escape from excruciating and unbearable conditions. For Marx, that is all that the political theology of religion can and ever will be. This is a thesis I push even further in the political theology of the state in the fourth chapter of this book.

However, Miki posits a disconnect between subject and object in these unbearable conditions where one must also be aware of political ideologies that seize upon unbearable conditions to mythologize the possibilities of a nostalgic revival of the past. Religions are supple ground for a political nostalgia that will only result in political impotence. Nevertheless, for Miki the purpose of political action is to mobilize progressive visions of a future connected with love, caritas, eros, and the positive pathos of hope. In Miki's interpretation of Marxism, the problem of nostalgia is a recurring problem. Although Miki does not look at history homogeneously as a nightmare weighing on the living, history can be a resource for inspiration for activists. It is a matter of revealing the repressed histories of the agency.

For Miki, communism is not a goal or a good end. Communist practice is an ongoing process. Miki refers to this process as "kyōdōshughi" or cooperativism. If we look closely at the ways Marx actually wrote about communism, we can clearly see that this is closer to what he had in mind, rather than the typical definition of communism as the government forcing equality of wages, or even the bizarre western obsession with associating Marx's oeuvre with "dialectical materialism," which is a term first used by Georgy Plekhanov. Marx never used the term "dialectical materialism" or historical materialism in any of his works. Therefore, Miki Kiyoshi's writings on cooperativism may bear a closer understanding of what communism means as contained within the writings of Marx.

UTOPIA RENDERED ACTUAL: COMMUNISM AS POSITIVE SELF-CONSCIOUSNESS

The early notebooks from the young Marx were written at a point when Marx moved to Paris in October of 1843 until late 1844. After soaking in much of the intellectual life of Paris, he had his theories dissipated in firsthand experiences of the rapidly changing sensuous life of material conditions in the cosmopolitan city of Europe at the time. His direct contact with the working and living conditions of the Parisian proletariat shaped his intellectual perspectives. The discovery of the working class and with that the commitment to communism emerging from the real movement of actual conditions, a point he would later develop in the *German Ideology*, were already present in kernel-form. In 1844, Marx's definitions of communism still take a semi-developed, highly naive humanist perspective that reflects this youthful optimism.[2] Jean-Francois Lyotard's line regarding the work of the young Marx is, "In the 1844 manuscripts, the proletariat is Christ."[3]

At this point, the approach to communism is categorical with Marx starting clearly defining the categories of communism and then, in the attention deficit disorder of youth, he was only twenty-six when he wrote these notebooks, toward the end of the section "Private Property and Communism" he sort of drifts off and loses his place.

His categories are as follows:

1. Crude communism
2. Political communism
3. Communism as positive transcendence of private property

4. Communism of the "whole man"
5. Communism as "negation of negation"

By the last few categories, Marx stops giving titles to the sections and the meaning of communism is left to the inference of the reader. Plus, Marx drifts into vague Hegelianisms where the reader has to create an imaginary subtext to infer what "negation of negation" means—what is negated? These questions become clearer as Marx develops as a writer and researcher in the three volumes of *Capital* and the *Grundrisse* notebooks. Marx is still a young man here and this is obvious in how he seems to be rambling a little. These are notebooks and not the work of a polished thinker; however, the 1844 notebooks do contain the core of his philosophy.

Communism works in levels and most of the revolutions that occurred in the twentieth century under the banner of "communism" basically never went beyond "crude communism" and, obviously, Marx was not a Nostradamus-type prophet who could predict the future, but there is a way that this description of the lowest form of what is referred to as communism cannot develop beyond this crude form when it is surrounded by, and never transcends the base of private property relations. Crude communism mirrors capitalism on a collective level. By opening up free labor without getting rid of wages and private property, crude communism reproduces exploitation.

Crude communism is a shabby kind of open-liberalness that one might see when the word is misused as if to reduce the term communism to open-discursive communication and you often see it unreflectively promulgated among conservatives and moderate liberals who do not understand how property relations factor into inequality between men and women. Today, this crude communism might resemble the open consumption of products without any ethical standards. What Marx describes as "crude communism" is the lowest form of that signifier akin to a kind of anarcho-capitalism.

Crude communism is best understood through the work of Slavoj Žižek as the failure of the father function, the crisis of the superego in late capitalism. Postmodern late capitalism's permissive hedonism is precisely what Marx identified as "crude communism," because when there are no rules, consumers are stuck in an infantile stasis and can only be expected to act like misbehaving children. The parents (i.e., the state), following the trajectory of the path of least resistance, will never transcend the libidinal trappings of the pleasure principle. Since there is no struggle for the objects of desire, at least in the sense of an obscurantist postmodern hedonism that offers phantasies of direct contact with the thing beyond the phenomenal realm, there is no need to struggle for the "real thing" and consumers are left in a consumerist-utopian cocoon. The trauma that occurs is when that cocoon is torn away, and one must enter actual material conditions that do not offer a perpetual imperative to enjoy. Reality is founded on cosmic meaninglessness and it is far more enjoyable to escape into the inauthenticity of these cocoons of pleasurable consumption (i.e., crude communism as a not yet fully formed communist-larval subject); and one can also become infantilized by the promise of the simulacrum of imaginary lures that promise what can never be—a reality that is better than the real thing, the surplus value of enjoyment that always escapes our grasp.

The state that signifies a "big other," is a paternal force that the narcissistic ego sees as something to throw off of itself, and the crude communist vision of freedom winds up echoing the call of the previous capitalist epoch. In this crude communism, you can imagine someone enacting the role of a child rebelling against the parental guidance of the state to put its hands in the cookie jar. Crude communism resembles what Herbert Marcuse would later call "repressive desublimation."[4] In this early, anti-repression phase of crude communism, the instincts are unleashed. As the effective subjugation of instincts is created by human social institutions and not nature, the return of the repressed primal drives produces an open sort of violence. While Marx could never put these concepts into Freudian terms as Herbert Marcuse did, he did imagine this early phase of communism along the lines of the kind of free cosmopolitanism. Marx absorbed this interpretation by living in Paris while writing these notebooks. These are the sort of thing that gives consumers a dopamine-rush without changing the "base" structures of private property and the ownership of the means of production.

In these early notebooks, Marx begins to seriously forward the thesis that there is a uniquely human consciousness that emerges around labor power. The way we as humans can form the object of our consciousness by orchestrating labor power toward an end that we can envision ahead of time. If there is production, then there is always an end toward which production aims. Production is organized labor power and with some planning many problems can be solved. While other animals do this in a rudimentary fashion, the particular skill that humans have is that we can utilize language in highly skilled and complex ways to communicate so as to orchestrate our labor power efforts in a collective effort that can unlock the hidden magnitude value of our collective productive capabilities.

Early, crude communism is still a community "territorialized" by nation-states and private property. And since life would still exist within a wage-labor/slave system, the cognitive associations with capitalism persist. Also, the problem at this phase, and most people working in Marxist theory no longer use the developmental phase theory of history, is what Georges Bataille referred to as the transition from "restricted to general economy."[5] Jacques Derrida also seized upon this particular portion of Bataille's three-volume work the *Accursed Share* where the problem is described:[6] "the sleep of reason, produces monsters" the subject can either be a "free subject" unsubordinated to the "real" order of things and occupy itself only with the present,

> for the subject is consumption insofar as it is not tied down to work. If I am no longer concerned about what will be, but what is, what reason do I have to keep anything in reserve? I can at once, in disorder, make an instantaneous consumption of all that I possess. This useless consumption is what suits me, once my concern for the morrow is removed.[7]

This is exactly what "yolo" culture of postmodernist late capitalist ideology imposes upon its subjects to compel consumption, what Mark Fisher calls the gradual cancellation of the future under the crushing inertia of now, now, now,[8] and Slavoj Žižek's various critiques of the failure of the father function and the injunction to enjoy as the predominant method of ideological control.[9]

Later, in the *Communist Manifesto*, Marx and Engels write that there can be capitalism that removes misogyny and racism. In 1844, the young Marx was not so naive as people are led to believe by correctly claiming that there can be something that refers to itself as "communism" and reproduces sexism, racism, forms of social hierarchy that are symptomatic of capitalist ideologies.

The next communist form is political communism where society retains representational democracy as a function of state power. People still live under the rule of force. This is the problem with the twentieth-century manifestations of what is referred to as "communism"—it was always political communism, which Marx was correct to point out can be either "democratic or despotic" which, unfortunately in the case of most so-called communist governments in the last century, the label of despotism was most appropriate. This is because communism, up to this point at least, has been a social experiment only attempted within the tactical framework of seizing state power. Political communism has been the aporia of radical politics.

Thirdly, the stage after the withering away of the state is something that has yet to happen. Marx considers this "communism as a positive transcendence of private property," when the people open up communal property relations, you have a complete return of man to himself as a social human being.

Without the government enforcement of borderlands, because the state no longer exists as a political entity, it becomes clear that Marx had in mind a kind of free-nomadism, open mobility of labor power, free-circulation of goods and services because the "syllogism of production, distribution, and consumption" (and, one might add circulation) will no longer exist under the tyrannical hegemonic control of bourgeois interests. The technologies of production and the means of production in factories, digital technologies, and so forth will still exist; however, the world would most likely see an explosion of productivity because wealth will no longer be wasted in the hands of the few. This will result in a material abundance the likes of which the world has never seen. In this sense, "communism is the riddle of history solved, and it knows itself to be the solution,"[10] which is exactly the view of communism that Miki tries to open up as a process rather than a telos in his interpretation of collectivism.

The last stage is when human consciousness is no longer experienced through its annulment, its negation, but as a "positive self-consciousness" that is no longer barricaded by the state and class-conflict. "Communism is the negation of negation and the actual phase necessary for the next stage of historical development in the process of human emancipation and rehabilitation."[11]

Negation of negation here implies a society that has completely transcended the antagonisms of class. It is now the imaginary promise of a fully realized community, rendered completely actual.[12] Once the promise of the automatic factory, as written about by Marx in the first volume of *Capital* has been invented and the production of all basic needs (food, clothing, and shelter) can be produced automatically, there will be a reservoir of resources that can be distributed based on needs, rather than abilities.[13] However, this illuminating vision of the future is dimly lit, as the automatic factory also pulls workers further into a "division of labor" that is "purely technical,"[14] those who find solidarity with the guilds that preserve themselves as caretakers of the machines and those who are unskilled on the margins of the locus of factory production and social engineering.

UTOPIA RENDERED ACTUAL: WORLD-HIST ORICAL-EMPIRICALLY-UNIVERSAL-BEING

There is no indication that Marx closely read any ancient Vedic scriptures, except through his friend Karl Friedrich Köppen. Another Young Hegelian, Köppen published a two-volume study *The Religion of Buddhism* in 1857–1859. When they visited each other in Berlin, Köppen gave Marx these volumes as gifts in 1861. It is not my intention to study the effect of these volumes on Marx. However, this interaction between Köppen and Marx may reveal a subtle undercurrent of Buddhist thought in the writings of Marx at and around the time of the publication of the first volume of *Capital*.

If we assume an implicit connection where Marx was reading some early western research into the practices of Buddhism, this may change our understanding of how Marx understood the "general intellect" as "*pratiitya-samutpāda*"—conditioned co-production. The age we live in now carries with it the unbelievable possibility of connecting the world into a global market, something about which readers of Marx remain cautious. Because while markets necessitate a global set of distribution and supply chains, the logistics of which require advanced communication and transportation technologies, which means the world can become connected in new and wonderful ways as long as these connections do not reproduce class inequalities of property and power. It also means that a "general intellect" can connect the working class in ways unimaginable in Marx's time. These possibilities offer new opportunities for solidarity as well as misinformation and alienation. False consciousness can spread just as easily as the idea that workers of the world must unite to throw off the chains of oppression and take control of production.

These tendencies of capital to link up the world into a global market were already foreseen by Marx in a germinal form. The way the world has become hypnotized by technologies like cell phones, internet, and media have only served to bring workers further into the disciplinary power of "docile bodies" and the orbit of "opinion propagators" of the dominant class. A tendency we can gather from reading Marx that he foresaw, when writing about the ways that every technology that enhances productivity ties up the worker's time to a greater and greater extent, and in capitalism the technologies that flourish are the technologies that serve the end of production and ultimately become used as a means of organizing and regulating the behaviors of an entire class, through individual interpellation and expressive capabilities inherent in the ideology of lifestyles, expression, and identity. In other words, the only technologies that interest capital are those that foment the politics of atomization and the politics of consumption through the immediacy of crisis-driven general economies of power. As capitalism socially evolves, all that it gives us are commodities that solicit us with evermore perverse desires ad infinitum.

In conceptualizing his concept of the "world-historical-empirically-universal-being" of communist ontology in the *German Ideology*, Marx was inspired by Hegel's "absolute spirit" and world history as a concept bears an affinity with these early historical articulations of recurring liberatory "spirit-being" that emerges as needed when conditions manifest this spirit as necessary. If social institutions are merely objectification of absolute spirit, and this collectivist understanding of "absolute spirit" forwarded by others in the Young Hegelians as well as perhaps Marx, then this embodiment of the absolute spirit is the revolutionary class that makes the wheels of production (i.e., samsara) continue to turn. In fact, most world religions have some aspect of the crisis that foments the emergence of new metaphysical belief systems, and it would be absurd to think that this absolute spirit can be embodied by a single individual figure. For a metaphysical system to gain traction, there must be something ready-made within the material conditions of the time that produce the world-historical-historical-empirically-universal-being, at least at the level of the mythos.

UTOPIA RENDERED ACTUAL: SPECIES-BEING

In the early Marx, labor power is crucial to forming human consciousness because it brings individuals into sensuous contact with the social realm beyond their atomized existence. By going into the realm of work, as producing and consuming beings, every human must talk, interact, behave, and socially interact with others beyond themselves. In his early manuscripts, Marx calls this "species-being." A social species-being is formed through the sensuous contact that is necessary for production to reach its end. Every product must be brought into the market, and therefore it must be sold. To accomplish this goal, humans must bring themselves and their products into contact with others. People interact in the marketplace and the products that are sold must be consumed and therefore metabolized.

In the early Marx, there was still hope that this sensuous contact unconcealed alienated labor from its atomized distance and bring atomized individuals into the community through the sensuous contact with other beings (i.e., the recognition of oneself as part of a "species-being") and a contributor to the whole of society beyond selfish needs. Later Marx in the three volumes of *Capital* sees that as capitalism develops, the eclipsing of use value by exchange value creates another set of enormous barriers further alienating workers from themselves and the machinations of capital that may move as automatons rather than guided by any form of intelligent design.[15]

In the early manuscripts, Marx grapples with this problem of alienation through the lens of species-being as the unifying possibility that unmasks alienating relations to uncover a deeper kernel of compassion and general need. "Communism as the complete return of man to himself as a social (i.e., human) being."[16]

"Communism, inasmuch as it negates the personality of man in every sphere, is simply the logical expression of the private property which is this negation." A very sort of Zen thing to say is that the self-negation (a term Nishida often employs), if it negates the unique personality of a person, is not "communism" but symptomatic of the alienating aspects of the private property system that forces labor to shed its individualism to set out into the icy waters of the labor market, where laborers are interchangeable parts in a dehumanizing capitalist machine. Therefore, communism is the

> positive abolition of private property, of human self-alienation, and thus the real appropriation of human nature, through and for man. It is therefore the return of

man himself as a social, that is, really human, being; a complete and conscious return which assimilates all the wealth of previous developments.[17]

Thus, the early humanism of Marx hinges on naturalism in the sense that there is a natural human being that exists and capitalism strips away that underlying humanity. By circumscribing the conditions of species-being under the wage-labor system, labor power is cast into alienation where the product of its labor is taken away. Communism is imagined as the panacea in the mind of the young Marx,

> it is the genuine resolution of the conflict between man and nature and between man and man—the true resolution of the strife between existence and essence, between objectification and self-confirmation, between freedom and necessity, between the individual and the species. Communism is the riddle of history solved, and it knows itself to be this solution.[18]

The young Marx was still a humanist with a lingering influence from natural law theory. A true believer in a "good intuition" innate to all human beings. Marx still forward the thesis that evil is an epiphenomenon of material conditions. Human beings forced into the material conditions of the market can only produce based on becoming a self-interested species-being motivated solely by profit. In this case, Marx outlines private property, alienating conditions of labor. In this case, alienation is defined by Marx as conditions of production where laborers possess no power over the ends of production. What they make goes somewhere else and is sold for the benefit of business owners. Private property is protected by the force of law, which protects the rights of the bourgeoisie to exert control over the distribution of goods. In the capitalist system, the only "telos" of this process is the sale of products for profit, not the consumption of products to fulfill needs. The sale and exchange of products for profit eclipses the motivation to provide value to customers based on use.

The communist hypothesis is simple and profound. If you can revolutionize property relations, consciousness will also change. However, to make that move Marx must posit "consciousness" as epiphenomenal to property relations. Consciousness must be understood as an after-effect of property relations, and he must posit a priori goodness in human beings to make that move. In doing so, he implicates his early philosophy in the prelapsarian Edenism and the messianism of communist salvation. In the hindsight of twentieth-century vanguardism and those sorts of projects resulting in horrifying totalitarianism, this kind of thesis is now completely obsolete.

Humans are not blank slates born innocent and corrupted by social forces as if to fall out of Eden through the temptations of the marketplace. Humans are in fact animals who can talk and, for the most part, what humans have to say is irrational and violent. The only way to make sense of it is to see the factors that determine these ideologies by shifting from what Nishida calls "self-consciousness"—our own opinions as atomized subjects toward the "universal of judgment" where consciousness can transcend its ipseity (jiko) to a consciousness that possesses an awareness of the universals that "determine this intelligible world"[19]—that is, material conditions, class-conflict, and, even though Nishida intends for this to be a judgment at the realm of spirit, there are ways that the universal of judgment loses its political dimensions once the materiality of the position of these determinations of self-consciousness melt away into the ethereal realm of spirit. A powerful revolutionary consciousness is reduced to a rather clichéd version of the flaky eastern guru. Nishida, in a way, in his early writings echo a similar naiveté seen in the young Marx.

Yet, Nishida does make some interesting points that can apply to our understanding of class-conflict as constitutive of ontological difference. When he says, "when things are thought of as parts of one whole, it means that the concept of acting things is lost, that the world becomes static."[20] If we think that "all is one" then, in the midst of class-conflict and hierarchies of power that emerge out of the general laws of capitalist accumulation, our mind as a subject of ideological thinking censors out substantive differences of class. This is exactly what differentiates the Kyoto School from flaky new age guruism as "zen" has incorrectly trickled into the West as a form of corporate consulting to maximize productivity.

As early as *Zen No Kenkyu*, Nishida insists that there is an intrinsic human demand for congruence between our knowledge, feeling, and will. This is to say, equality is not necessarily about an equal distribution of things, as Nishida also points out, materialism puts people at odds with spirituality, and spirituality puts people at odds with materialism. Carving up equal shares of scarce resources strips away the spiritual ethos of compassion and the spiritual ethos distracts people from materiality of presence by turning awareness to noumenal realms extending beyond appearances. The gamble of pure land in the next life distracts from the exigencies that require our present attention. Our knowledge gives us a systematic development of epistemological methods. Falsely affirming the notion of objective truth as obtainable through identically reproducible procedures. This is the false consciousness of ontological objectivism and the tedious polemics against mystical nihility. More often, what passes as truth are blockages on creative capacities, concealments, and confinements of ontological innovations, and deflationary processes that exhaust collective ethical commitments.

Therefore, Marx at this similar impasse turns his attention to constructing "species-being" as the basis of this theory of human nature. Humans must reproduce material conditions to survive. In a society that has the division of labor, this means that the emphasis shifts from "communal by nature" to "social by necessity." We all must go to the market to get our daily bread.

FROM COMMUNAL BY NATURE TO SOCIAL BY NECESSITY

The *German Ideology* was written in 1846, only a few short years after his time in Paris. The notebooks remained unpublished until long after the death of Marx, in this case, not until 1932 by the Marx-Engels Institute in Moscow. Again, this shows crucial information about the depth of nuance with which Marx carefully formulated a communist ontology. Some have argued that Feuerbach's concept of "species-being" constituted the "epistemological foundation of Marx's concept of human nature," and most of the other major concepts in the early works derived from Feuerbach's reading of Hegel.[21] Interestingly enough, the *German Ideology* contains the only reference to Buddhism in his published manuscripts, in a passing statement about Max Stirner and his views on Hegel.[22]

In the *German Ideology*, false consciousness fails to see what is already there.

> Communism is for us not a state of affairs which is to be established, an ideal to which reality will have to adjust itself. We call communism the real movement which abolishes the present state of things. The conditions of this movement result from the now existing premise.[23]

In the early manuscripts, the indications are that Marx was working under the epistemological bias that "man" is by nature communal, in a few short years he begins to abandon that conceptual a priori. The *German Ideology* represents a path out of humanism, rather than a clear break with it, which leads to a rather subtle difference that is crucial to understanding this change in tone. The concept of species-being is replaced in the *German Ideology* and in subsequent works by a material connection between humans. No longer is there a claim that man is communal by nature, but that he is social by necessity.[24]

The *German Ideology* is the last book where Marx proposes a quasi-humanist understanding of communism as regaining a lost and alienated essence. Freedom is regained by recapturing control of the ends of production. Communism is still thought to unfold out of "real movements" rather than an idea pressed upon a reality that rejects its ideas. To make that thesis stick, a new theoretical problematic was inaugurated. As Marx works through this unintended break with humanism, he perhaps stumbles upon the rare opportunity to create a wide-open vista for thought. Marx discovers that for centuries philosophers and scientists had been relying on the faulty problematic of human nature as a fixed object. Historians studied history as if humans existed external to historical and social conditions. In the 1844 manuscripts, Marx does not yet see clearly the problems that arise in stating that communism solves the riddle of history[25] as overcoming alienation brings man back into its essence as a social being, there is a reification of man as an object that is, in its purely prelapsarian forms, "good," yet the alienation thrust upon man in unnatural conditions of capitalism forces the fall into wickedness.

In the *German Ideology*, Marx is deeply concerned about the division of labor and to create a communist society it would be necessary for individuals to

> re-establish their control over these material powers and abolish the division of labor. This is not possible without a community ... the illusory community in which, up to the present, individuals have combined, always acquired an independent existence apart from them, and since it was a union of one class against another it represented for the dominated class not only a completely illusory community but also a new shackle.

To rid the modes of production of the division of labor there is a very utopian view that there would be no specialization and therefore the free production and free labor necessary is based on the free use of land.

> For as soon as the distribution of labor comes into being, each man has a particular, exclusive sphere of activity, which is forced upon him and from which he cannot escape. He is a hunter, a fisherman, a herdsman, or a critical critic, and must remain so if he does not want to lose his means of livelihood; while in communist society, where nobody has one exclusive sphere of activity but each can become accomplished in any branch he wishes, society regulates the general production and thus makes it possible for me to do one thing today and another tomorrow, to hunt in the morning, fish in the afternoon, rear cattle in the evening, criticize after dinner, just as I have a mind, without ever becoming hunter, fisherman, herdsman or critic. This fixation of social activity, this consolidation of what we ourselves produce into an objective power above us, growing out of our control, thwarting our expectations, bringing to naught our calculations, is one of the chief factors in historical development up till now.[26]

Looking closely, all of the examples that Marx provides to illustrate his point about communism are activities external to factory or agricultural production. His critique of capitalism seems to start from resisting the conditioned co-production of the capitalist modes of production and the ways that it casts a cash nexus upon all aspects of labor power. Marx was seeking alterity to production in factories and agri-business. This is a pastoral image of the worker taking command of the ends of labor power, and it is a bit reminiscent of the Romantic Period of poetry because it paints an idyllic image of nature and the return to the noble savage, the prelapsarian Eden before the fall of capitalism. This is still "early/young Marx" we are dealing with in the *German Ideology*. Marx wagers a gamble that the removal of the division of labor will result in a new social consciousness rather than anarchical relations that reproduce capitalist individual atomization. The structuralist aporia: if a revolutionary event must originate within power structures that it rebels against, the event can only reproduce the violence that it rebels against.

> Communism differs from all previous movements in that it overturns the basis of all earlier relations of production and intercourse, and for the first time consciously treats all natural evolving premises as the creations of hitherto existing men, strips them of their natural character and subjugates them to the power of the united individuals. Its organization is, therefore, essentially economic, the material production of the conditions of this unity; it turns existing conditions into conditions of unity.

And in making a crucial point, rather than the "projective" aspect of what is mislabeled communism that squashes all singularity and individuality, "the reality which communism creates is precisely the basis for rendering it impossible that anything should exist independently of individuals, insofar as reality is nevertheless only a product of the preceding intercourse of individuals."[27]

The atomized individual is always within the community as such. No atomized individual qua atomized individual. Our commons, the land, sea, and sky are grounded in our relation to the earth itself. Unfortunately, the earth has been appropriated into a source of ground rent. Hence, Marx can say that ground rent forms the basis of the mode of production.[28] Our awareness of ourselves as social beings is enveloped by the appropriating forces of ground rent as inexorably linked to the state.

Modern life is always already within a dynamic social ontology, always connected through our reliance on the earth and modernity puts all life in an evermore precarious relation of interconnectedness with all the other moving parts of the world market system.

In his four-volume work *The Ontology of Social Being*,[29] Georg Lukács devotes the second of these volumes entirely to examining the question of ontology in the work of Karl Marx. Lukács starts his volume with a perplexing thesis, claiming that Marx never outlined his ontological view, and therefore it is up to scholars to go back to his texts and synthesize the works into something that would resemble a communist ontology. Lukács work attempts to do just this, and clearly this has had an impact on much of the work I am attempting here; however, in these volumes, there is literally no engagement with any sense of Buddhist ontology, which distinguishes my thesis from other attempts at an ontology derived from Marx's oeuvre.

There is much that can be gleaned from Lukács reading of Marx as an ontological philosopher. For instance, in addressing the significance of the 1844 Economic and Philosophical Manuscripts he remarks,

> it is not the least aspect of these texts that for the first time in the history of philosophy the categories of economics appear as those of the production and reproduction of human life, and hence make it possible to depict social existence ontologically on a materialist basis.[30]

One must wonder if something more expansive can be appropriated from a "Marxist" ontology in the sense spoken about by Martin Heidegger in his introduction to Being and Time. Clearly, Heidegger was not a "Marxist" and for anyone who has read Being and Time closely, there are numerous points of disagreement between Heidegger and the work of Karl Marx, yet his statements early on in his text bear a resonance with the thesis I forward in this book. The study of life as an academic exercise has fragmented the perspectives that each disciplinary category can utilize to study its subject. Heidegger calls these as *regional* ontologies. Psychology looks at human life through the lens of the psyche; Biology looks at beings based on a certain ontology, bios, or life. Political science, or what Marx called political economy, calls into question the ways that humans organize into communities and govern themselves. Economics might look at the way material needs are met through exchanges, markets, labor, and such. Yet, these regional ontologies have a very biased view of the "being of beings" in the sense of a *fundamental* ontology. The being of beings extends beyond the closed hermeneutic circle of political and economic interestedness. This is not to say that people are always a-political, or apathetic, and could care less about politics, but that politics is a biased, unnatural perspective cast upon people as if to be an ensnaring referential surface—an ontic surface, a transcendental aesthetic that takes itself in its facticity as its surface. Beyond this very few venture into the depths of the ontological, or the deeper underlying structures of reality as a living creative being, rather than as an object. What Marx does in his ontology is to reveal the reification of our "objective" sense of human nature. Our labor power always metabolizes nature, and vice versa; therefore, our nature is a result of history and social relations.

Chapter 3

The word "ontology" seems to have been invented by German intellectuals about 200 years ago, and breaks down into the Greek words "on" or "ont," which means "being" or "existence," and "logos" which takes several different meanings in the original Greek, from logic to reason, and Aristotle even uses the term in a statement, "Man is the animal that can speak," that claims "logos" is the particular quality of reflective speaking and the use of language that is specific to the being of being human. Ontology is the study of being, with humans as beings capable of reflective speech in the sense of the philosophical discussion.

To frame an ontological mode of inquiry, in Western Philosophy, one must begin with the question of the quid ("What is it?") and the quale ("What are its qualities?").[31] In the West, the entryway into the question of being is different than most entryways into the question of being in Buddhist thought. In asking what is it? The question is framed as if we are describing an object. Perhaps someone might think of this object in hindsight of previous political projects that attached the epigram "communism" to something that went horribly wrong.

In western logic, this is misunderstood as a problem within propositional logic. Forwarding a thesis that is then met with a counter-thesis until either one thesis loses out or there is a synthesis of the two opposites. Marx is writing philosophy in an entirely different way, from the basis of material conditions. We cannot solve this problem by route of a contradiction or a dilemma. If you say something is and also is not itself this approach poses a contradiction. A thing cannot be what it is and its negation. A contradiction is known as P * ~P. It poses a major problem and is considered problematic. A statement that claims something like: if P therefore ~P, if something is proven to be true therefore its negation is also proven to be true, this is even worse, it is called a dilemma. A dilemma can pose a strange tension to the mind that views this dilemma as problematic.

Something that is proven true in relation to its negation is common sense spanning back to the basic teachings of the Buddha in the Heart Sutra[32] summarized by the simple phrase spoken by the Buddha, "Form is Void, Void is Form," you see the core teachings of Buddhist ontology, the contradiction and the dilemma become the centerpieces of Buddhist logic:[33]

When the Bodhisattva was coursing in the practice of transcendental wisdom, in the deep course of prajnaparamita, looking and saw the five skandhas—form, sensation, perception, volition, and consciousness—were empty.

"Oh Shariputra, Form is Void, Void is Form;
Form does not differ from Void, Void does not differ from Form;
whatever is Void, that is Form, whatever is Form, that is Void![34]
The same is true of feelings, perceptions, impulses, and consciousness!

Oh Shariputra, all dharmas are marked with Emptiness:
they have no beginning and no end; dharmas are not arising, not increasing, not decreasing,
they are neither imperfect nor perfect, neither deficient nor complete.
Therefore, Oh Shariputra, in emptiness, the five essences of sentient beings do not exist: there is no form, no sensation, no perception, no volition, no consciousness.
There is no eye, no ear, no nose, no tongue, no body, and no mind.
There are no forms, sounds, smells, and tastes. There are no touchable or objects of the mind, no sight organs, no hearing organs, no smelling organs, no taste organs, and no mind consciousness element.
There is no ignorance or extinction of ignorance, no decay and death, nor extinction of decay and death.
There is no suffering, no origination, no stopping, no path, no cognition, there is no attainment whatsoever, nor anything to attain.
There is nothing to accomplish and so Bodhisattvas can rely on the Perfection of Wisdom without trouble.
Being without trouble, they are not afraid.
Having overcome everything upsetting, they attain nirvana.
All Buddhas who appear in the three periods fully awaken to the utmost, right and perfect Enlightenment because they have relied on the Perfection of Wisdom.
Therefore, one should know the Perfection of Wisdom is the great mantra. It is the unequaled mantra, the destroyer of suffering."

Because of this truth, listen to the mantra:

Gate, Gate, Paragate, Para Samgate Bodhisvaha!
{Gone, Gone, Gone beyond, gone utterly beyond. Oh, what an Awakening!}
Iti prajnaparamita-hridayam samptam.
{This completes the Heart of Perfect Wisdom!}

In this most influential sutra, you can already see common themes often linked to existential nihilism as if the Buddha is the cosmic echo of Ecclesiastes "Vanity of vanities, all is vanity," as if life must carry this expectation of fulfillment and meaning, and when someone has the realization in sannyasin that life is an empty carousel going around and around and when you get old your heart dies. Heart Sutra "form is void, void is form" rarely gets a Marxist reading. Along with pervasion that originated with early Vedic texts are the *Bhagavad-Gita*, the *Rig Veda*, and the *Upanishads* which constitute the earliest Hindu texts. Pervasion also tends to inform Theravada Buddhism in India, Southeast Asia, Vietnam, Thailand, Burma, Singapore, and informs its dialectic in the way these texts exemplify Brahman as transcendental self and atman as immanent self as one and the same. There is no separation between the Gods (and/or God) and self, there are also one and many Gods, one and many selves.

It is easy to see that the Heart Sutra reveals the Buddha to be a social constructivist, that consciousness is formed on the surfaces of social interactions, which anyone who reads Althusser on interpellation can easily understand.

Human sensuousness is rooted in human practice. The social constructivism is implicit in the a priori of the senses as "void" awaiting sensory perceptions that will fill them, only to be emptied yet again, cleansed, in a process of unlearning, renewal. One must unlearn the conditioning of capitalist ideologies, undo the material "conditions" that condition one to envy the wealthy, lust after commodities, and realize that this is the path to suffering, because "there is no attainment whatsoever, nor anything to attain." Life is the path, rather than the telos, and perhaps, as many contemporary readings of Marx have begun to think in this way in lieu of the fall of many so-called "communist" states, to think of communism this way, as a planned path with strategies to outmaneuver suffering from commodity attachments and reification, rather than a ready-made telos that the communist state must "obtain" and force upon its subjects.

In short, a metaphysical inquiry that thinks through its other as not simply a negative term, specter, or spirit, of the first principle out of which it is supposed to be made identical, but as that which corroborates its identity and endows its truth with power, as it is, rather than as a "standing reserve" to be pacified and domesticated into something akin to what Foucault referred to as "docile and useful bodies."

What must be understood is the rise of immanent, horizontal power structures; there are vertical, hierarchical systems of appropriation that are elided, and virtually all of these systems of power are a direct result of what Marx called the General Law of Accumulation. As capital gains a hierarchical position, stockpiling more and more wealth, the uneven expansion of capital must rely upon areas where slaves and exploited wage-labor produce the uneven forms of accumulation.

To make my point clear, these exploited laborers are concealed from consumers in a process that fetishizes the enjoyment of consumption and the mystical, ethereal magnitude value of the commodity form. Marx calls this concealment the "hidden abode of production," and if the commodity form takes special emphasis in capitalist consumption, then exploited labor power is the void which is concealed from representation in the capitalist system, and its matrices of production and social reproduction.

Not only referring to existing wealth inequality, uneven wages, uneven wealth distribution in actual forms of monetary wealth, and resources unevenly hoarded, this General Law of Accumulation also effects knowledge production as well. What one might call in a Foucaultian sense "power/

knowledge" is what forges the "developmental fallacy" that Enrique Dussel says informs Enlightenment philosophy and history from Adam Smith and John Locke through Hegel, some interpretations of Marx, and even up to the work of Jurgen Habermas. Tracing this Eurocentric view of modernity back to Hegel, Dussel writes:

> In the *Vorlesungen uber die Philosophie der Weltgeschichte*, Hegel portrays world history (*Weltgeschichte*) as the self-realization of God, as a theodicy of reason and of liberty (*Freiheit*), and as a process of Enlightenment (*Aufklärung*).
>
> In Hegelian ontology, the concept of development (*Entwicklung*) plays a central role. This concept determines the movement of the concept (*Begriff*) until it culminates in the idea, that is, as it moves from indeterminate being to the absolute knowledge in the *logic*. Development . . . unfolds according to a linear dialectic; although originally an ontological category, today it is primarily considered as a sociological one with implications for world history. Furthermore, this development as a direction:
>
> Universal history goes from East to West. Europe is absolutely the end of universal history. Asia its beginning.

Dussel continues with a point that I would like to have resonated throughout this book:

> But this alleged East-West movement clearly precludes Latin America and Africa from world history and characterizes Asia as essentially confined to a state of immaturity and childhood (*Kindheit*).[35]

Particularly in that last part of the quote, you see the oblivion of the Enlightenment thinkers to the fact that their position of stature is a direct result of being situated in a privileged position within systems of uneven social-economic power. The only thing that is missed is that out of the western philosophers, the figure who looms largest as being completely aware of this is Karl Marx who points out: "Force is the midwife of every old society which is pregnant with a new one. It is itself an economic power,"[36] and the invention of capitalist power was not this peaceful sort of transition where workers choose to go into factories out of some sort of democratic choice inherent in the free-market. No, "Money . . . comes into the world with a congenital blood-stain on one cheek, capital comes dripping from head to toe, from every pore, with blood and dirt."[37] Routinization into being a "docile and useful body" was accomplished through overt displays of violent force "agricultural folk were driven from their homes, turned into vagabonds, and then whipped, branded and tortured by grotesquely terroristic laws into accepting the discipline necessary for the system of wage-labor."[38]

Marx was clearly aware that the colonial powers of so-called modernity were not so peaceful in the strategies that they employed to turn the world into Enlightened hard-working morally elevated beings, with part of the point in the Marxist project as the undermining of mechanisms of production that, in privileging the site of ontology, try to oversee "the nothing," the emptiness of uncultivated abyssal nothingness, as potential "standing reserve" (to borrow from Heidegger) that the emptiness of non-being must be transformed into something productive, even if that something is a docile yet useful body. While in western metaphysics the "nothing" provokes angst, it is because non-being cannot be reified, even as capital attempts to make the magnitude value of all reality into an existing commodity with use value, in Buddhist thought (and since Siddhartha Gautama was born a Hindu and trained in Hindu thought one can include those trajectories in this analysis) there is a way that these philosophies are unworried by "nothingness," and do not feel compelled to force the transformation of nothingness into something useful.

MODES OF PRODUCTION: THREE TYPES OF PRODUCTION IN THE *GRUNDRISSE*

Labor produces commodities and produces itself in labor as a commodity. What Marx meant by "mode of production" and more specifically "production" can mean literally tangible products like commodities, but it is clear that Marx also intends a broader definition of "production" to include the production of life through social relations. What labor produces presents itself as an object alien from the producer.

Production overdetermines how humans relate to one another because a society that does not reproduce its basic conditions will soon go extinct. Thus, viewing each other like products, commodities, and use-values. In capitalism, people are treated as a means to an end (to make profits) instead of as intrinsically valuable beings. In capitalism, the value of human beings is judged as a result of being productive. For a worker, being unproductive means you are not selling the one commodity that you own, your labor power, and if you are not working you are not earning a wage.

No access to wages means running the risk of starving to death and since self-worth in capitalism is associated with ownership of property and possession of wealth, most attempts to do East-West Marxist comparative thought with Buddhist infused philosophy synthesizes this with "stuff" and the lack of ownership means "propertylessness"-of-being is viewed as less than human. The presumption is that "humanity" is the veridical norm into which the alienated subject returns. In other words, most of this work rarely engages with Marx in a serious way, and typically does so from the perspective of the early Marx who was still positing the "communal by nature" essentialist view of human nature.

Marx argued that wages are dished out in such a way that labor never has a chance to suddenly become capital. Instead of paying people in a lump sum, wages are dished out in small increments over the course of a lifetime. And, labor is different from capital because labor has only a body or mind to sell, whereas capital owns much more and can obtain liquidity or fixed capital to obtain more wealth. Hence, capital's position is always improving, whereas laborers (workers, the proletarians) are perpetually stuck at the bottom until a revolution occurs.

The most lucid definitions of production are given by Marx in the *Introduction to the Grundrisse*. Hiroshi Uchida argued that the second section of his introduction is where Marx differentiates himself from Hegelian logic, and forward a thesis about production in particular.[39] Marx reduces production down to three categories, and he does this because he sees the bourgeois division of labor in mental and physical activities; whereas, Hegel did not inquire into specific modes of human life which vary on the basis of historical and material conditions.

Consumption and Production—The identity of what is produced is immediately consumed, consumption in the production process, immediate consumption of products without much production process changing the thing, the identity of the thing consumed is the identity of the thing as it is in nature, in its natural state, a thing without being changed through labor: "a garment becomes a real garment in the act of being worn."[40] It is the process of consuming the product that brings it into existence as such, the demand for it, and the fact that the thing wears out in the process of consumption means that it must be replaced. In saying, "consumption creates the need for new production."[41] Marx perhaps inadvertently slips into a realm of analyzing "tanha" (thirst, appetitive side of the soul). "Tanha" or thirst is the most immediate cause of "dukkha" (suffering) when thirst becomes a craving, wanting, and an all-pervading vision of the self. Another example is food. When human beings obtain the food they not only ingest calories but also generate and express their culture.[42]

> One of the aporias between Marx and Buddhists is the presumed passivity in Marx's analysis that "Production thus not only creates an object for the subject, but a subject for the object. Production produces consumption. 1. creating material for it. 2. determining the manner of consumption. 3. creating products posited as objects."[43] It is assumed that Marx paints a picture of the subject as a passive receptor of the objects produced for its consumption; there is no free-consciousness to develop mindful consumption practices insofar as how the product is consumed, what products to be consumed, and that the state must take overproduction to force its subjects into a "communist subjectivity."

This misses an especially important point. Consumption can only ever be experienced as singularity.

Consuming a product such as food, there is only ever the singularity of consuming that use value in its singularity. Bill Haver explains:

When I consume a use-value, whether as a means of production or as final product, I do not consume the thing in the abstraction of its generality. Hungry, I do not consume "potatoes" or "rice," for example, in the universality of their categories; I consume this plate of potatoes or this bowl of rice, here and now. Thirsty, I do not drink "wine" in general, I drink this bottle of Romanee-Conti '08 (fat chance, that) here and now.[44]

Distribution and Production—"distribution determines the relation in which products fall to individuals (in amount)"[45] and production is the general form from which the particular can be chosen. The one from the same. If a class society allows more wealth to accrue among a particular class, more wealth accumulated means more purchasing power, and more control over wielding the products to "fall" to those individuals, production will distribute more to what it can sell, and what sells is not always what is consumed, but what is most likely demanded because it is thought to be potential consumption. More "wealth" means more demand and more potential consumption-power, which means more production-power will be directed toward that class. More products "fall" into the hands of individuals in that particular class. Hence, the subjectivity in that particular class becomes the hegemonic subject. Wealth is accrued through control of capital and capital is controlled through "protection of acquisitions . . . every form of production creates its own legal relations, form of government, etc."[46]

Exchange and Circulation—Exchange is an act comprised within production and can only be understood as outside of production when the product is directly exchanged for consumption (i.e., singularity).[47]

REIFICATION: CAPITAL AND THE OBJECTIFICATION OF LABOR POWER

Capital volume 1, chapter 1, section 4: Fetishism of the Commodity and its Subject is Slavoj Žižek's favorite section of *Capital*, and it is where he draws his critique of ideology from Marx. Interestingly enough, this also happens to be one of the most influential aspects of Marx on the Kyoto School. Let me unpack this section of *Capital* so that we may better understand how the Kyoto School made use of this section of *Capital*. For example, Miki Kiyoshi and Tosaka Jun both accused Nishida Kitarō of lacking a theory of reification. After careful reading of this particular section, I find these criticisms of

Nishida to be unwarranted. Especially in the ways that Nishida wrote about "enveloping" rather than a sort of ping-ponging dialectics typically associated with the Hegel-Marx dyad, if anything, Nishida's "intelligibility" as enveloping consciousness is closer to what Marx had in mind with real subsumption and ideology, which is developed in the famous statement from Marx: "they are doing it, but they do not know that they are doing it" in the sense that the workers buy into a system of exploitation under the promise of making money, without knowing that they are negating their own self-interests in doing so. This self-negating ideological behavior is only possible when the working class buys into capitalism hook line and sinker (i.e., real subsumption occurs) because their consciousness is completely enveloped by capitalist ideologies.

What bourgeois economists and moral conservatives fail to truly understand is that capitalism must be morally permissive to placate the demand for consumer decadence, perhaps even exacerbating it through the unbridled free-market economy that caters to unfiltered "depraved human nature" to sustain its expanding reproduction, and ward off the inevitability of the falling rate of profit, capital has to create newer and newer demands, and thus sell-back to consumers the objectified dimensions of objectified labor power.

Marx so succinctly characterizes the contradictions of this objectifying process:

> the existence of money presupposes the objectification (*Versachlichung*) of the social bond; in so far, that is, as money appears in the form of collateral which one individual must leave with another in order to obtain a commodity from him.
>
> *Here, economists themselves say that people place in a thing (money) the faith which they do not place in each other. But why do they have faith in the thing? Obviously only because that thing is an objectified relation between persons. (emphasis is my own)*[48]
>
> because it is objectified exchange value, and exchange value is nothing more than a mutual relation between people's productive activities . . . it serves as such only because of its *social symbolic property; and it can have a social property only because individuals have alienated their own social relationship from themselves so that it takes the form of a thing.*[49]

Ideologically, the bourgeoisie endowed the individual with unprecedented importance, but at the same time, it was a reified subject created by commodity production that mirrored bourgeois virtues. Bourgeois power over life became possible as the bourgeois control over land stripped away free labor power.

GLIEDERUNG: WHO CAN SPEAK WITHIN ARTICULATED HIERARCHY

The problem that both Marx and Nishida (and Nishida's philosophical progeny) grapple with is the question of intelligibility and the question of sensibility. Marx is really not trying to prove a connection between "economics" and consciousness. His work was a *critique* of political economy; his philosophy of praxis sought to change the world, not merely interpret it. This included transforming all reified forms of economics. Rent, profit, wage labor, the commodity form, and money itself were all under the scrutiny of the critique. Deeper questions emerged such as who can speak within the articulated hierarchy (*Gliederung*) of structures of power. Autonomy outside of these articulated hierarchies appears as if it were independent, but the autonomy of articulation must make sense within the context of the whole; therefore, all power relies upon a certain type of dependence with respect to that which is circulated in regards to the whole of circulation.

To understand an economy, there has to be an understanding of time, of the economics of a particular subject emerging out of historical time, and that must mean that historical time emerges that gives false reality to a fictional narrative, whereby the compulsion to construct concepts, species, forms, purposes, laws, and economy of identical subjects is a compulsion to arrange the world narcissistically. A world in which one locus is the center and resonates outward which thereby creates an economy that is calculable, simplified, comprehensible, and falsely thought to be secure.[50] A Marxist understanding of an economy involves the workers maintaining control over the ends of production. Production always means control over poiesis, the creation and bringing forth of life into existence, of producing, making, and disclosing life into existence. Command over production means command over beings, it means giving life, and this interpretation means that command over life extends beyond working time.

Marx forward a view of the working day which says that capital exerts a power that extends beyond the closing of the factory doors at the end of the worker's shift. What little we do know about behavioral conditioning should absolutely prove this thesis to be correct. In other words, there is a particular type of "yoking" that occurs in capitalism that conditions the brains of workers to truly believe that the only way to live is the way that life has been structured in the past and as it is currently structured. This is because time spent in the spaces established for work shapes the way workers view the rest of their leisure time. Marx writes, in several places, that there is an extension of productive time that exceeds the boundaries of the working day: "Working time is always production time, i.e. time during which capital is confined to the production sphere. But it is not true, conversely, that the entire time for which capital exists in the production process is necessarily therefore working time"[51] and he continues: "The production period is longer than the working period."[52]

This means that if an economy is about sustaining and reproducing life and life cannot exist without the work necessary to reproduce itself, then the anchoring point of life outside of the factory is contingent upon access to money, commodities, and/or capital. To live one must spend. To have the resources to spend one must earn a wage or have commodities to trade, or capital to expend. Life outside of the economic base is anchored to the economic base.

This is completely different from forcing equality upon everyone through coercive mechanisms of state repression. A "dictatorship of the proletariat" means that the proletariat has control over the ends of production. The dictatorship of the proletariat does not mean a state dictatorship that uses military power to create a new bourgeoisie. To draw comparisons with disciplinary practices, the Sanskrit word "yoga" roughly translates into "yoking."

Yoking oneself to practice because being captive in a body and mind in the world you will be yoked to those things, so it is crucial to take command and discover yourself as you truly are, rather than let body and mind fall into the hands of the ways of the world. Production "yokes," as if to put a figurative yoke on oxen to plow a field. Yoking is not about working the animal any way; when you yoke an animal you care about the animal, you do not want to work the animal to death, you work the oxen to maintain a level of care within limits, utilizing the best practices.

Yoking to the state can take two forms: ideological (discursive) apparatuses that put phrases in dispute to win the hearts and minds of the masses and the "hard core of the state is its repressive apparatus" as Althusser called it indicating that the last bastion of the hegemonic class and its last resort is always the use of pure violence.

Social production of desiring-machines is within history, that is, the mechanization of desiring, its reproducibility, its predictability, its repetitions as the same are completely subsumed within the history of objectified labor. Historical time emerges from humans who understand their powers as tool-making beings. To think and act as creating beings who produce and reproduce only as tool-making beings puts humans into a position of mastery unlike any other species on the planet. Not that man makes tools, but that being human is substantiated by that which it makes through the utilization of the productive power of tools.

To produce the logos means that there already was the contingency of creating using tools. The Promethean compromise. Discovering what is already there, perhaps by accident and that accident changes everything. Humans do not have claws as the tiger does, but humans can utilize brainpower to create tools that simulate those features that at first appear unique to the tiger and not that there is some absurd notion of humans inventing "history," as if the logos (the written word, the utterance of thought as speech prior to that) was the metaphysical emergence of historical man.

If, as Aristotle once claimed, man is the animal (zoē)[53] who possesses logos (speech, not yet language, but utterances, thoughts spoken, verbal communication), then we can utilize that to solve problems for ourselves. There is also no guarantee that logos will only be used to philosophize and turn our lives into endless navel-gazing even at our own peril, we can pontificate about the end of the world utilizing the power of logos all the way up to and including mass extinction. The logos must culminate in active living.

In the current capitalistic understanding of production, economy is a process of creating products. Since labor is alienated (i.e., not "free-conscious-activity" that it could be, and not an extension of a fully active social consciousness), because it is estranged and externalized, whereas externalization does not necessarily entail estrangement, in capitalism labor power sends its product where capital sells it rather than where labor power can most benefit from its use.

Therefore, labor power must be solely motivated by earning a wage. A constriction that leaves the individual laborer twisting in the wind as an atomized individual who must fend for him or herself and by rescinding control of the ends of production must ingratiate him or herself to a capitalist to survive (i.e., sell either mind or body as a commodity, an object, by objectifying itself, one hands over one's spirit), and eventually the brutal contradictions in the system, the dialectic of objectifying that deepens dehumanization and thick-skinned brutal competition means that labor power is left to only consider objectifiable notions of truth, pleasure, sensation, and commodified forms as the source of those "needs"; by being thrust into the objectifying pool of labor competition one begins to believe that only objects can produce joyful sensations in life.

Generations and generations of parents raising their kids to think that way, where their lives are determined and motivated by money, the "dead pledge of society."[54] Using money as the source value of all that an economy declares virtuous (i.e., selling a product rather than considering whether or not the product is needed and useful) hollows out and deadens the social bonds that form true subjective relations between human beings. People become objectified and therefore only consider objects as sources of enjoyment, which, clearly Marx and Nishida would agree is unethical. But, forced equality, especially forced equal wages, is equally as dehumanizing, which is a conclusion Marx would later draw in his *Critique of the Gotha Program* later in his life where in 1875, perhaps at the height of his eco-socialist leanings, Marx writes: "insofar as man, from the beginning acts towards nature, the primary source of all instruments and subjects of labor, as an owner, treats her as belonging to him, his labor becomes the source of use-values and therefore also wealth."[55]

In defining capital, it is important to understand capital is not necessarily a thing, but a process. Capital is always a process. Capital at times is an insubstantial process and at other times a substantialized form depending on what point in the circulation process. Capital may manifest as material forms within the flow of value as a circulatory process. A process of circulation that at certain points takes the form of a thing, a commodity, labor power, investment, money, machinery, and so forth. The end of production leads to the gratification of the self. In capitalism, the economy is based on the production of commodities which are external objects that satisfy human needs. If this is the case then immediately human beings are within the realm of transcendental materialism where there is a world outside of the mind and we predominantly rely on objects outside of ourselves to produce commodities for the satisfaction of our basic needs, objects such as food, clothing, shelter; gratifying needs of the stomach or imagination are created by mechanized tools over which no single unique human being can exert complete mastery.

Hence, Nishida writes: "What we think of as an individual may be the determination of a universal . . . however, when the universal determines itself, it must have the contrary meaning of a self-determining individual."[56] An endless telos of becoming that never arrives, when time stretches out infinitely into the future and the past, then becoming thinks as though determined by an infinitely unattainable individual. An eternal recurrence of being and becoming can drive someone mad when there is no thought of being (satisfaction with oneself as a self), but then, the dialectic that swings too far in the direction of mere being without becoming reproduces the Aristotlean individual as merely a unique substantia and therefore "it would cease to be a changing and moving thing."[57]

Even our creative desires ("tanha") cause clinging toward and grasping of commodities which gives false hope of placating our desires. "I will be happy when I get X, or When Y happens, then I will be happy" is to live in a state of "dukkha," separation, alienation, and suffering based on the mindset that "I" must grasp a reified from beyond myself to eventually obtain happiness, when in fact, what the Buddha taught was that happiness is not an object that can be "possessed," happiness is not a possession but a mindset that associates happiness with the qualification of it as a thing to be possessed is a mind living in "dukkha," and acting through "tanha," grasping, clinging, possessing, striving to obtain power over an object is the surest way to live in misery. Boredom, suffering, infidelity, and cycling through relationships are consequences of a capitalist society that bases progress on a marketing strategy of "planned obsolescence," the novelty of new commodities gives a momentary surge of pleasure that eventually wears off when the infantile consumer mindset loses interest in the newest and latest toys.

Here too one must not look at affects that circulate as if they are "my feelings," or "my sensations," subjectively, because there is no singular "I" in any objective sense. Feelings and affects are a basic trait of life and feelings like anger, resentment, fear, and the surface levels of the "ego-mind" are the symptoms of capitalist circulation (and other economic systems as well) that circulate neurotic affects (in who? the proletariat) as a way of spurring "economic growth" (for who? the bourgeoisie). Lower classes tend to be the dumping ground; the refuse of affects dumped onto the classes that are least agile in deflecting; the powerless tend to absorb the worst affects that a society circulates. It is not personal to that particular "I" who identifies with those feelings and emotions.

Imagine other ways of life beyond capitalism with ideological constructs mass produced by the culture industry. Gaps between M . . . C . . . P . . . C' . . . M' (money invested in commodities i.e., labor power, fixed capital/overhead, cost of production . . . production process . . . and "capitalized" commodity, or a finished product, that is then a finished piece of both exchange and use value which is sold for a "profit"—surplus value M', more money than went into the C . . . P—commodities and production)—but, Marx begins volume two of *Capital* by saying "The formula for money capital" and then he gives his famous formula "M-C . . . P . . . C' . . . M' and the dots indicate that the circulation process is interrupted" then he says volume 1 was about the purchasing of labor power, the production and sale of commodities; however, volume two is about:

> the different forms with which capital clothes itself in its different stages, alternately assuming them and casting them aside, remained uninvestigated. These will now be the immediate object of our inquiry . . . to grasp these forms in their pure state, we must first of all abstract from all aspects that have nothing to do with the change and constitution of the forms as such.[58]

Surplus value is the trick of the bourgeoisie in its concealment value as a form is a formless form "the different forms with which capital clothes itself" are empty and conceal the hidden abode of production. Monetary values do not just represent things, but are also coded surplus value signs and there is plenty of locked-up surplus value. What Marx shows is that behind every product there is work and stored up surplus value and the shakiness of the continuity of discontinuity in the circuit of productive time keeps the economy in recurring and perpetual crises and the corruption of the ground/ the Pure Land appropriates into the identity of the nation-state.

Echoes of Althusser would resonate with the same point: "the individual always has the significance of being determined by the universal."[59] Interpellation beckons the subject into subjection at the level of flippant, novel, fashionable individuation. Atomistic differentiation from the universe is what gives the universal class its hegemony. Asserting individuality is what allows the call of interpellation to seep into the psyche of the subjugated subject. In other words, freedom is merely ignorance of the forces that determine the illusion of "personal will." A theme that Nishida develops throughout his life, calling it transcendental will, active intuition, and then personal will in his last published essay *Nothingness and the Religious Worldview*.

Each commodity may differ in its use value, the *form of its value* (Wertform) is the same in every commodity, that is, the commodity form contains value based on its magnitude of value. Marx defines this as the average socially necessary labor time consumed to produce a commodity, and as a matter of fact, the kind, type, and time of labor power necessary to produce different commodities varies, but the very form under which value creation itself takes place is precisely the same for all commodities (i.e., within the mode of production). Marx says, "What exclusively determines the magnitude of the value of any article is therefore the amount of labor socially necessary, or the labor-time socially necessary for its production."[60]

While it is necessary for the capitalist to produce products that are of some use to a consumer, it appears to Marx that for the capitalist this is a necessary nuisance that may impede the real "aim of producing capital (which) is never use value, but rather the general form of wealth as wealth."[61] Use is not as important as a value in a commodity-producing society; therein lies the rub! The only thing that matters is whether the product sells. Not whether the product is useful or practical solves a problem. Marx notices this tendency even in the early stages of his writings.

> *Capital is not a thing*, it is a definite social relation of production pertaining to a particular historical social formation, which simply takes the form of a thing and gives this thing a specific social character. Capital is not the sum of the material and produced means of production. Capital is the means of production as transformed into capital, these being no more capital in themselves than gold or silver are money. It is the means of production monopolized by a particular section of society, the products and conditions of activity of labor power, which are rendered autonomous vis-à-vis this living labor power and are personified in capital through this antithesis.[62]

Marx and Engels were also correct in asserting that

> The bourgeoisie, historically, has played a most revolutionary part. The bourgeoisie, wherever it has got the upper hand, has put an end to all feudal,

patriarchal, idyllic relations. It has pitilessly torn asunder the motley feudal ties that bound man to his "natural superiors," and has left remaining no other nexus between man and man than naked self-interest, than callous cash-payment.[63]

THE WORLD MARKET, AN INTELLIGIBLE WORLD THAT TRANSCENDS OUR THINKING

An economy is a body we cannot see; there are elements of production, distribution, and circulation that are always concealed from the realm of what appears to the consumer. The intelligible world transcends our thinking.[64] Objects are immanent in their materiality within the world. Commodities are transcendent in the "hidden abode of production," the production, distribution, and circulation of the commodity beyond the sacrosanct domain of the individuated self who consumes it as a singularity. Consumption is required for the enjoyment of commodities. Consumption consists of taking the external commodity into the body, welcoming it in, there is a sense of hospitality at play in consumption; the consumer has a choice which products to put inside of itself; but this is trickier than it seems at first glance; not quite sure if consumers make rational choices by weighing pros and cons about which products to consume prior to consuming them; much more subconscious based on desiring-production/social production that pushes and pulls which are valued due to their usefulness; and it means that life is always already social in nature. There is no getting away from the community.

A commodity is valued based on its usefulness, which is based on the physical attributes of the commodity as an object. Hunger is a need, and a raw piece of animal flesh is an object that cannot necessarily satisfy this need. On the other hand, a seasoned piece of steak tartare is a commodity because it can be used to satisfy a bodily need, the need to eat. Therefore, labor is necessary to turn the raw piece of flesh into a finished good that is useful and once this finished good can be used to satisfy a need, according to Marx, it becomes a commodity, and commodities are the most abundant in a capitalist economy, most commodities are overproduced and go to waste, even though people are starving, food goes unused on grocery store shelves.

Money is the equalization of commodities so that values become interchangeable when the commodities are sold at the same price; use-value is valuable because human labor is objectified or materialized in it—*vergegenständlicht* is the German word Marx uses to describe this experience of human labor. The word is somewhere between *verstandlich*—which means understood, to make understood—*gegenstand*—to objectify—and *wertgegenstand*—the masculine noun for describing an object of value and in this sense *vergegenständlicht* is described as "A use-value or useful article, therefore, has value only because abstract human labor is objectified (vergegenständlicht) or materialized in it."[65] This word functions on these three registers and the commodity is the final result, the representative telos of labor power, which is why the commodity would have a fetishized or mystical aura. The proletariat who make the products are proud of what has been created by the sweat of their brow. Marx continues to say that "As exchange-values, all commodities are merely definite quantities of congealed labor-time."[66]

The value of a commodity is not pulled out of thin air; it is based on the value of the labor power that created the commodity. The value of labor power is then determined by time; the average degree of skill put in by labor, science, and its technological application; the social organization of the process of production; the effectiveness of the means of production; and the conditions found in the natural environment whereby the raw materials were procured. All of these factors weigh into the value of the commodity when it hits the market. It is essential to the Marxist analysis of capital to reveal the reality that all commodities are use-values for others; use value for yourself is not a commodity, and therefore agrarian subsistence farming is excluded from the commodity form and from the capitalist mode of production. Commodities are always social values. Bartering raw corn that can be traded among peasants without the use of an equalizing form of currency like coins and paper money is not a capitalist form of exchange. Peasants tithing to lords and vassals is not capitalism because tithing does not involve commodities. A commodity is worked on and refined so it has a utility, it must be consumed in a particular way to fulfill a particular need. Raw corn can still be transformed into other products. A commodity is a finished good that satiates a very narrow specific need. Due to this subtle distinction, a commodity is no longer a raw material and therefore the whole economy becomes interested in procuring values that satiate very instrumental needs. All knowledge is circumscribed by production which narrows its focus in capitalism, with scholars working within a division of labor that rewards specialized work in narrower sub-fields where more finely tuned focus is needed to appreciate the value of that work, and must produce instrumental value that solves problems and fix aporias.

The commodity is the congealed labor time. The substance of value is labor, the one unifying substance that links capitalist existence is not money or the commodity, it is labor, either workers produce or workers starve to death; production is being. Labor is the point de capiton or unifying button point that sews up all of the loose ends in the economic search for the metaphysics of value. After Marx one can conclude that labor power is the hidden abode of production that creates wealth for the bourgeoisie. With material ontology, God is no longer in the material world as an expression of its modes. God is immanent in the machinations of the modes of production on a physical plane of existence. This is why I believe that Marx is very patient in his subtle deconstruction of the way that the protestant work ethic weaves its way into capitalism whereby commodity fetishism draws on the metaphysics of Christian theology.

Again and again, the carryover from Christian ethics into Marxism is the presumption of servitude on behalf of the humble meek working class lambs who work over and over, producing and serving a purpose for someone else, the social component of value. The social value is appropriated from the working class to those who own the modes of production. Appropriation of value upward in the economic hierarchy constitutes the violence of the exploitation of labor who work, work, and work more while experiencing less and less share in the accumulation of wealth. This expropriation of wealth away from the working class into the hands of the ownership class enhances exploitation, alienation, and violence exerted toward the impoverished workers.

The revolutionary subject that Marx hinges his theory on is best described by Antonio Negri in his pathbreaking work *Marx Beyond Marx*:

> The expansive, imperialistic process of capital and its tension toward the constitution of average terms of world exploitation are then simultaneously the result and the premise for the conditions of revolutionary subjectivity. The imperialistic expansion of capital also represents its attempts to escape the resented opposition inherent in its determination as capital. Contradictions and antagonisms are motors which move capital toward ever higher levels of contradiction and antagonism. Every result is a premise, a new basis. Every regulative "limit" that capital poses to itself in this historical pursuit is the basis for the insurgence of new obstacles.[67]

Engulfed within its own expansive power, capital is consolidated through and upon circulation as "social capital" becomes the form in which the revolutionary subject is the subject of development. Positing itself as the subject of development, "in an ever-more determined manner,"[68] as the market forces that determine consciousness become less and less visible as the market forces of capital totalize as the only globalizing economic power.

If Karl Marx is correct, and I believe he is, then money is the predominant social relation in capitalism. It is a social relation defined by antagonism and it forms the basis of our social relations. As money is expropriated out of the hands of workers, the antagonism is exacerbated. The way to ward off a proletarian revolution, to prevent the potential energy from boiling over into the kinetic energy of full-blown class warfare, is to bombard the workers with mysticism and the Christian metaphysics of value as if circulation is grounded in the eschatology of the Christian notion of time. Circular-time of the as-yet-to-come arrival of the impending economic-collapse (apocalypse) when the revolution can then somehow begin since the Messiah (Marx) has already arrived, and inscribed into that notion of eschatology is the arrival and eventual return of the Messiah to judge, destroy, and sort out believers and non-believers. I do not think this is what Marx has in mind in describing the problems with capitalism. His foretelling of communism "yet-to-come" is an open-ended futurity, not a closed vicious circle of a set form of what communism would be (beyond the *withering away of the state*, one can presume that since the state, every state prints currency, that money, capital, debt, property, everything that the state uses to hypnotize will wither away as well).

A commodity has a metaphysics as a mystified fetishized object, and Manna from heaven reigns down on those who procure more and more of these fetish objects, more power, prestige, a greater aura of invincibility; these are all the sign values that accompany the metaphysics of accumulation that is inextricably linked to the Christian metaphysics of commodity fetishism, which valorizes those with wealth as if a class is a moral category. The etymological genealogy of "Werstein" (to be worth) is linked to the romance verb Valere or Valoir or Valorize, which is linked to chivalry and knights and the Christian metaphysics of valor, honesty, integrity, and it weaves its way through feudalism, paying tithes to lords and vassals who were protectors. And so, the bourgeoisie in a dialectical synthesis with the state become the lords and vassals of capitalism where the working class gives hard-earned value to these "trustworthy" and "honest" protectors who are valorized as if their position in capitalism is due to moral virtues.

Nothing is backing the value of money except the mystical illusions that cast spells over most people in capitalism that claim more wealth will guarantee greater satisfaction, greater security, and salvation either in this life or a paradise of wealth and consumption here on earth. Eventually, the orgy of consumption will end, and as Jean Baudrillard famously questioned, what will happen after the orgy? Can we think of social problems in terms of moral categories?

This is where Marx is a pathbreaking social philosopher because he overturns the notion that class is a moral category. In his work class is always a social and economic category. For him and most Marxists, it is more important to realize that class inequality and the accumulation of wealth have more to do with the circuitry of circulation whereby the money–commodity–money (C-M-C) circuit always expropriates wealth out of the poor communities where there is no money, taking wealth out of the hands of those excluded from ownership and into the hands of those who already have money. This means that at some point if Marx's analysis is correct, the division between the rich and the poor will become so immense that the poor will be so extremely destitute that the only option will be to overthrow capitalism and turn to C-M-C as the circulatory norm in the body politic, which is what is most importantly called communism. This is where something like hermeneutical communism is completely wrong because for the most part Vattimo and Zabala, as fascinating as their work can be, turn to Nietzsche more often than Marx. Communism is not a dialectical synthesis of discursive theses where the best ideas win out in the court of public opinion. Discourses have nothing to do with changing the capitalist process of circulation to a communist process of circulation.

The commodity form is always already a social value; it is the ontology of sociality; and it embodies the end result of the circuit of money capital. M-C-P-C'-M' was the visual aid that Marx uses to describe the circuitry of capitalist circulation and there is a temporal component to this circuitry as well. Money is transformed into commodities, raw, unfinished goods, become use-values—then the ". . ." is exemplary of a short circuit. These ellipses represent a break in the continuity of circulation, a friction, an antagonism whereby commodities are transformed through the process of production. The ". . ." posits friction and this friction is the exploitation of labor power utilized by capital in the production process, then there is another ". . ." and C'-M' is the end result whereby capital earns a profit that "signifies an increase in value that carries over to the capitalist, now this is fascinating, what happens to labor?"

The "..." is the violence of coercion of labor into factories, corporations, and the service economy ". . ." is primitive accumulation obtained by real subsumption where the working class is forced into exploitation out of the fear of starving to death, or falling into the poor destitute communities where wealth is expropriated elsewhere.

M-L is the visual aide that Marx uses to show how capital uses the money to purchase labor. Money is the glue of the social bond that forces capital into a relation with labor. But, if money is an antagonistic relation, then this relation becomes precarious and rife with potential energy that could burst into class warfare—the wage becomes the terrain where antagonism and revolution can occur, the place where the capitalist and labor meet socially.

The working class is the revolutionary subject and the spark that ignites the revolution is the antagonism of class-conflict that emerges when capital encounters labor over the wage. Wages are the point of relation and since this relation is mediated by money, which is an antagonistic relation the reason most strikes occur, most friction occurs due to the battle over higher wages. Marx was correct to posit,

> wage labor appears as the dissolution, the annihilation of relations in which labor was fixed on all sides, in its income, its content, its location, its scope, etc. Hence as negation of the stability of labor and of its remuneration.[69]

The condition of wages is non-fixity; wages are constantly in flux rising and falling with market forces that are outside of the worker's control, more than any moral integrity of wage laborers. Labor is always circumscribed by historical conditions that we have not chosen, but as if caught in a swirling vortex. Those conditions are constantly changing through the network of "production, distribution, and consumption" that Marx calls circulation.

VORTEX OF CHANGING FORMS AND MATTER IN CIRCULATION

"Change of form and of matter in the circulation of capital C-M-C and M-C-M"[70]

If we take circulation as the "groundless ground" of the ontology of capitalism, then it is much easier to indicate that there is no being in general. There is no horizon of being, beyond which nothingness is that has yet to be territorialized into being. Nothing is not a thing that can be subject to an apparatus of capture.

A change in form *formwechsel and a change of matter *Stoffwechsel take place simultaneously in the circulation of capital. We must begin here not with the presupposition of M, but with the production process. In production, as regards the material side, the instrument is used up and the raw material is worked up. The result is the product—a newly created use value, different from its elemental presuppositions. As regards the material side, a product is created only in the production process.

This is the first and essential material change. On the market, in the exchange for money the product is expelled from the circulation of capital and falls prey to consumption, becomes the object of consumption, whether for the final satisfaction of an individual need or as raw material for capital. In the exchange of the commodity for money, the material and the formal changes coincide; for, in money, precisely the content itself is part of the economic form. The retransformation of money into commodities is here; however, at the same time present in the retransformation of capital into the material conditions of production.

The reproduction of a specific use value takes place, just as well as of value. But, just as the material element here was posited, from the outset, at its entry into circulation, as a product, so the commodity in turn was posited as a condition of production at the end of it. To the extent that money figures here as the medium of circulation, it does so indeed only as mediation of production on one side with consumption, in the exchange where capital discharges value in the form of the product, and as mediation, on the other side, between production and production, where capital discharges itself in the form of money and draws the commodity in the form of the condition of production into its circulation.

Regarded from the material side of the capital, money appears as a medium of circulation; from the formal side, as the nominal measure of its realization, and, for a specific, phase, as value-for-itself; capital is therefore C-M-M-C just as much as it is M-C-C-M, and this in such a way, specifically, that both forms simple circulation here continue to be determinants, since M-M is money, which creates money, and C-C a commodity whose usevalue is both reproduced and increased. Concerning money circulation, which appears here as being absorbed into and determined by the circulation of capital, we want only to remark in passing—for the matter can be thoroughly treated only after many capitals have been examined in their action and reaction upon one another—that money is obviously posited in different aspects here.

AUTONOMY: THE LIMBS OF THE SOCIAL SYSTEM ARE DISLOCATED

The problem is that there are useful kinds of labor and exchange where the purpose is to "satisfy a definite social need," and

> satisfy the manifold needs of the individual producer himself only in so far as every particular kind of useful private labor can be exchanged with, i.e. counts as the equal of, every other kind of useful private labor. Equality in the full sense between different kinds of labor can be arrived at only if we abstract from their real inequality, if we reduce them to the characteristic they have in common, that of being the expenditure of human labor power, of human labor in the abstract.[71]

However, value and price can differ and do not depend on how the market values this abstract category that Marx refers to as "human labor in the abstract."

Hierarchy is reproduced based on autonomy. Interpellation calls the subject as an individual, as Marx writes:

> In constructing the edifice of an ideological system by means of the categories of political economy, *the limbs of the social system are dislocated.*[72]

To lump all of these together is absurd. Price does not differ, for Marx, due to the different values placed on the labor power that goes into the production of a product, but the labor time and the appropriation of surplus value by those who exploit labor and take the externalized/estranged products of labor power and basically steal more effectively. If in capitalism property is defined as theft, then the power goes to those who steal most effectively. One of the innumerable problems that keep the capitalist economy in a perennial crisis is that the value of a thing may differ from the price at which the thing is sold, that gap is necessary for the existence of surplus value.

Since there is a surplus that is appropriated (i.e., stolen) by the bourgeoisie, then there will be classes of consumers who only buy and do not produce commodities. For a class to organize an entire society around its interests, it must link the behaviors of the class as if they are virtues rather than decadent vices, apathy, wanton-excess, slothfulness as something to aspire to rather than as the vices of a society overwrought with the hierarchies that occur due to surplus value. Rotting away from the inside, all morals that were once solid melt into air, but not as if there was once a stable object one could identify as intuition and its representation in consciousness. Surplus means that there are people who only exist as consumers.

Surplus value poses the problem that Hegel completely missed, and that Louis Althusser was correct to reveal as the difference in the Marxist dialectic from the Hegelian dialectic: the problem of *reconversion.*

In other words, how to waste the surplus?

Gradually over time, capitalism tends to emphasize exchange value over use-value; this problem takes care of itself as exchange value becomes the productive consumption of wasteful expenditure.

MARX BEYOND THE COMMODITY: MONEY, CIRCULATION, AND LAND

During the banking crisis of 1857, Marx wrote a series of loosely compiled notebooks later collected under the title *Grundrisse* (or "Groundwork"), which were not published until the 1930s by David Riazanov, who would sadly become a victim of one of Stalin's purges in 1938. These notebooks were not available in English until the early 1970s.

Sadly, most of the people in the English-speaking world have little or no familiarity with the writings of Karl Marx, and rely on anti-socialist propaganda to fill in the gaps. What little is read typically derives from the *Communist Manifesto*, which was a pamphlet written as an attempt to propagate revolution during popular uprisings that occurred in 1848. If anything else is read by Marx, it is a reduction of his work to the first chapter of *Capital* where we read about his thesis on "commodity fetishism" which then serves to turn Marx into merely a critic of consumerism and the commodity. The notebooks titled *Grundrisse* are rarely read, except perhaps by graduate students. Yet, these notebooks turn the popular view of Marx upside down.

Grundrisse was rapidly written in a flurry of writing in 1857, over the span of a few months during a monetary crisis where the banking industry failed to inspire confidence. There was a run on the banks and people were withdrawing their life savings from the bank and hiding it under their mattresses. Why did they cling to money rather than burn it? More importantly, there were these strange debates at the time that seemed to pin the lack of confidence in the economy on the use of paper money rather than specie money (coinage), as if the use of paper that was backed by gold was less inspiring of confidence than using pieces of copper, silver, and gold as currency.

As the rush on the banks was at its peak in December of 1857, the American president at the time, James Buchanon, makes a statement to this effect, something that seems completely absurd in hindsight:

> Thanks to the independent treasury, the government has not suspended [specie] payments, as it was compelled to do by the failure of the banks in 1837. It will continue to discharge its liabilities to the people in gold and silver. Its disbursements in coin pass into circulation and materially assist in restoring a sound currency.[73]

Therefore, you have a lengthy section of the chapter on money where Marx deals with the gold supply and tries to debunk the notion that switching to gold-based currency gives currency intrinsic value. As Marx says later on in other places, no scientist has ever discovered the intrinsic value of a pearl under a microscope, and clearly the same can be said regarding the alleged intrinsic value of precious metals.

Rather than starting with the commodity, Marx begins with deconstructing the metaphysics of value by demystifying the value of money. He starts with money and then moves into capital, with almost no mention of "commodity forms"—and lengthy excursus on production, distribution, exchange value, and so forth.

It is because at that point Marx began working on the issues of the "syllogism of production, distribution, and consumption"—the problem of reconversion as an ideological auto-drive had begun. Since the workers were driven off the land and into factories, a long process of deskilling had occurred.

Most of the framing of "Marx" did not take these several hundred pages of writing into consideration until deep into the mistakes of the Russian and Chinese Revolutions and there were flimsy accounts of what "Marxism" meant including a rather shallow understanding of Marx as a serious philosopher. With the publication of the *Grundrisse*, there was a renewed sense that a new depth had been discovered. A leading British scholar at the time David Mclellan had published excerpts from the *Grundrisse* in 1971 and wrote in his introduction that the book should be considered the "centerpiece" of Marx's work. Some digressions contain the most illuminating aspects of Marx's entire oeuvre.

One of the most important exegeses on the *Grundrisse* was written by the Italian Communist Antonio Negri, who in 1978 upon the request of Louis Althusser fled felony charges in Italy to present a series of seminars on the *Grundrisse* in Paris. These are published under the title *Marx Beyond Marx*. At the time the text was understudied in any scholarly way, and in seizing an opportunity, Negri turned to what is most revolutionary about the unearthing of this new substantial body of work from Marx. What we find in these notebooks dating from 1857 and roughly thereafter is that Marx was working on different focal points within his critique. Money and circulation were the most important points of weakness that revolutionary praxis could attack; whereas, commodity fetishism had yet to be fully conceptualized. These notebooks were written during a run on the banks, when people were stuffing money under their mattresses the *Grundrisse* shows Marx disdainfully deconstructing an obvious aporia: Why do they still believe in money when they know the system is failing?

In other words, it is the Spinozian problem of why do they desire their slavery as if it were their salvation? In typical fashion, Marx in keeping the texts driven by these questions keeps the subtext of "they are doing it, without knowing they are doing it," the questions initially raised in the *German Ideology* and then again in *Capital*, the questions of ideology alive, through a simple, yet revolutionary question: Why do they believe in money when it is so clearly fake? Even those who fully realize that it is fake still behave as if money were real?

To understand this, you have to see what was at work in the notebooks titled "Pre-Capitalist Formations," which reveals a mythical pre-history of the present, when a series of social contradictions were set in motion. Is the nature of the distinction between pre-capitalist modes of production (Asiatic, ancient, feudal, etc.) and the capitalist mode of production in terms of grounding the consequences of making such a distinction in the first place. The notebooks on the pre-capitalist modes of production, like many notebooks in the *Grundrisse*, emphasizes the force of sociality and subjectivity in creating and transforming a mode of production, and I think it is important that one cannot emphasize enough the fact that perhaps in thinking of oneself as a passive-docile subject, many people have mistakenly thought of this problem of "agency" the other way around, as if workers are passive receptacles who take in the consciousness produced for them by the modes of production. It is in fact construed in quite the opposite terms in many places throughout the *Grundrisse*.

Regardless, the thesis that Marx forward in approaching pre-capitalist modes of production is that all of the precapitalist economic formations (Asiatic, ancient, feudal, etc.) have as their historical a priori not the separation of the worker from the means of production or the distinction between money and wealth but the integration of these resources within a particular community. Marx writes:

> This naturally arisen clan community, or, if one will, pastoral society, is the first presupposition—the communality (*Gemeinschaftlichkeit*) of blood, language, customs—for the appropriation of the objective conditions of their life, and of their life's reproducing and objectifying activity (activity as herdsmen, hunters, tillers, etc.) The earth is the great workshop, the arsenal which furnishes both means and material of labor, as well as the seat, the base of the community. They relate naively to it as the property of the community (*Eigentum des Gemeinwesens*), of the community producing and reproducing itself in living labor (*lebendigen Arbeit*).[74]

The thinking of the mode of production from the standpoint of its presuppositions entails thinking the mode of production from the perspective of the moment when these presuppositions emerged as contingencies, the moments of the encounter between the relations of free laborers and the wage. Once these elements of the economy encounter one another where the class that accumulates an excess of money encounters a population with only its labor power to sell, that is the emergence of a particular capitalist mode of production.

As Marx repeatedly points out, capital is constantly threatened by the unhinging of its two constitutive elements: the flow of workers that might dry up and the capital that could be wasted rather than invested with a profitable return on the investment. Rather than increasing freedom through the development of the spirit, capitalism entraps and encloses the free movement of labor.

One clear example of this is the way he opens that portion of the *Grundrisse*:

> A presupposition of wage-labor, and one of the historic preconditions for capital, is free labor and the exchange of free labor for money, in order to reproduce and realize money, to consume the use value of labor, not for individual consumption, but as use value for money.[75]

Free labor becomes separated from the objective conditions of its realization; in other words, labor power becomes restricted as labor power falls further and further into the hands of capital, mediating the valorization process by exchanging labor power for a wage. In precapitalist formations, this economic arrangement where capital holds all the wealth accruing apparatuses and the working class acts as the sorcerer's apprentice to the idiocy of the capitalist is a massive reduction of highly intricate relations. In the pre-capitalist formations, labor power has the soil as its natural workshop.

Communal property relations, tacit as these relations were because uncodified in any bureaucratic sense of being inscribed into written law, allowed the worker to directly and immediately relate to the objective conditions of his labor as to the product of labor. The highest intensity of difference is the highest approach to communism, and the transition to communism is not the dialectical reversal of capitalist power (where the workers are "tops" and the bourgeois are "bottoms"); not even in form, however, communism is the explosion of those forms completely.[76]

Marx assumes that "pastoralism, or more generally a migratory form of life, was the first form of the mode of existence."[77] Because of the nomadic way of life in the early communal pre-capitalist modes of production, gradually over time, what you have is the grounding of labor power into settlements, as capital entraps free labor power, the proletariat becomes stuck in place.

Marx, however, writes in much darker terms: "If money, according to Augier, 'comes into this world with a congenital blood-stain on one cheek,' capital comes dripping from head to toe, from every pore, with blood and dirt."[78] Hence, a communist subject would not reproduce such violence in its social production. However, the communist project seems to become less visible as the global market of capitalism eclipses any sense of non-capitalist difference.

Earlier in *Capital*, Marx evokes a sense that capitalism provokes a pseudo-revolutionary sense that things are changing, but in a chaotic, topsy turvy kind of way:

"Modern industry never views or treats the existing form of a production process as the definitive one. Its technical basis is therefore revolutionary, whereas all earlier modes of production were essentially conservative." In the creation of "new machinery, chemical processes and such" here one might also include the profit-motive incentivizing stronger illicit drugs under the category of "chemical processes," not just the transition from say steam engine to combustion engine to electric engines that no longer rely on burning oil, because Marx then specifies that modern industry continually transforms not only the technical basis of production but also the functions of the worker and the social combinations of the labor process.[79]

What occurs is that the "capitalist produces the old divisions in ossified ways," as the guilds become the trade unions and entire branches of production become riddles, not only to the outsiders but even to the initiated, as technology transforms so rapidly, "as far as the worker's life-situation is concerned; it constantly threatens, by taking away the instruments of labor, to snatch from his hands the means of subsistence, and, by suppressing his specialized function, to make him superfluous, creating an industrial reserve army," an excess of unused labor power resulting in the "reckless squandering of labor-powers, and in the devastating effects of social anarchy."[80] In yearning to hold back the hands of time, the worker today may feel misaligned with reactionary, even fascist forces that offer a nostalgic return to the greatness of yesteryear, when this technological "revolution" was not happening quite as rapidly, while unwittingly voting in favor of accelerating this "social anarchy" in the process.

All of these distract from an obvious contradiction that the bourgeoisie has to toe the line carefully, which is a simple question that is not asked on an individual basis, by individual "owners" but gets calculated impersonally on a mass-scale: If we pay workers more, they will buy more crap, but profits will be lower because we pay workers by cutting into profits. On the other hand, if we do not pay workers well, we accumulate greater surplus value, which is not always directly calculable in terms of monetary value, but then the workers grow agitated and may overthrow the wealthy.

While writing the *Grundrisse*, Marx discovered that in capitalism power means the "separation" of workers from land, leaving the only commodity available to sell which is their labor power.

The themes of the *Grundrisse* can be summarized in the following way:

For Marx, Hegel's logic is "the money of the spirit," the speculative "thought-value of man and nature." This means that in bourgeois society "man" and nature, and body and mind, are separated and reconnected through the relation of private exchange. Their relation is alienated from the persons who form the relation, which is mediated by value. They become "value-subjects," and those who possess enough value also rule the society. The logic in fact describes the value-subject abstractly.

In bourgeois society, the value-subject also rules nature, the indispensable condition of life, because the subject monopolizes physical as well as mental labor, so the non-possessor of nature is forced to engage in physical work. This coercion is seemingly non-violent and is legally mediated through the value-relation on which modern property is founded. In modern society, there is widespread acceptance of the legitimacy of one person controlling the product of another's labor, and the other's labor itself, to appropriate a surplus product. This approval is founded on the value-relation and the "form" of the commodity. Value is abstract and imagined in the mind, and also embodied in money. Hegel's logic implicitly ascribes a sort of power to money, and Marx presents money as the *demiurgos* of bourgeois society. That is why he characterizes the logic as "the money of the spirit." His task in the *Grundrisse* therefore consisted in demonstrating that the genesis of value and its development into capital are described in the logic, albeit in a seemingly closed system that reproduces itself, and overall, his work is directed toward transcending capitalism in practice.[81]

Rather than equality of force inflicted by the apparatuses of the state, an a priori being of beings as deriving life from the metabolism of nature. Marx wrote critiques of political economy, so there is a way that "communist ontology" is not to be understood as a political-economic equality, equality in the eyes of the state, or equality of wages, but equality as derived from the land as commons. In other words, even in a so-called private property system, what others do with the land has a ripple effect on "us" over here. This is more present in the modern era where complex logistical supply chains can ship products around the world.

MARX BEYOND WAGE-LABOR: THE AUTOMATIC FACTORY

This is one of the last pieces of writing we have from Karl Marx and which went unpublished during his lifetime. There you see him differentiating between "socialism" and "communism" substantively. Prior to that, except perhaps in areas of the Communist Manifesto, he categorizes socialism as a necessary stage of development along a gradual social evolution into a communist society. Distinguishing between these two stages of socialist and then communist society: in the early transitional phase, the laborer is still paid and buys consumer goods, the exchange still exists, and this is hotly debated today as the government may be forced to pay those wages in the form of what is today referred to as universal living wages. The second phase is the "communism," where each person contributes to society according to ability and draws from the common stock according to needs.

It is necessary for these stages to occur because of an immediate change to communism where there is no longer exchange, sale of goods, wage-labor, and markets. This can only occur to its full realization through what Marx called the "automatic factory."[82] The falling rate of profit places a burden on the capitalist to invest in the development of evermore efficient technologies to produce more in less time without having to pay a human worker a wage. While the capitalist system, according to Marx's calculations, cannot outpace the eventual demise of the system with the development of newer technologies, one possibility before the big collapse is that a fully automated factory may become a necessity, where all work is done by machines. Marx, a bit wiser at this stage in his life, realizes that capitalists may have more tricks up their sleeves. With full automation, there is not a utopia, but a new division between "a superior class of workers, in part scientifically educated, in part trained in handicraft; they stand outside the realm of factory workers." And, those who work directly with the machines, whose consciousness has been conditioned "from childhood upwards, in order that he may learn to adapt his own movements to the uniform and unceasing motion of an automaton."[83] The promise of the utopia of automated factory production only serves to subsume the workers further into the matrices of the machine, further and further into subsumption.

MARX BEYOND KANT: CONCEPTUAL TO FORMAL AND REAL SUBSUMPTION

Exchange value puts commodities into circulation and the necessity for the capitalist is to sell those commodities, which means, forcing to open new markets, creating desires in consumers to feel compelled to purchase new commodities (creating needs rather than merely responding to a priori needs), this inherently stretches out the subject into something malleable, flexible, compassionate, open-minded to ever new and changing experiences to the world. Not that this subjectivity is inherently bad, but that in a capitalist economy, consumers that are pan-theistic, open-minded to anything and everything will soon find that they are opening themselves up to some horrible, violent, self-destructive things as if they are freely, consciously, and rationally selecting those decisions. The market forces that determine their lives are concealed to them, they are not free, their freedom is living in ignorance of the determining factors that produce their consciousness. That is "false consciousness"; when as Immanuel Kant writes in *Critique of Pure Reason*, in one of the most difficult sections of the entire book, the section on schematism. A section that is notoriously misread and misappropriated, he makes a very simple point that Marx makes much clearer in his understanding of false consciousness, money, and the theory of value.

Kant says:

> In all subsumption of an object under a concept the representation of the object must be homogeneous with the concept; in other words, the concept must contain something which is represented in the object that is to be subsumed under it. This, in fact, is what is meant by the expression, "an object is contained under a concept." Thus, the empirical concept of a plate is homogeneous with the pure geometrical concept of a circle. The roundness which is thought in the latter can be intuited in the former.[84]

The question appears Platonic, but one has to think about where the "pure geometric" concept originates? Is it from the Gods? Or, from ideological modes of production (as Althusser may have later discovered in closely reading Marx). It is put into the minds of the subject through the "subsumption of intuitions under pure concepts, the application of a category to appearances."[85] To do that, it is not that the subject has a direct experience of the thing and then accurately understands the thing through direct experience.

The thing must be mediated. Kant continues: "This mediating representation must be pure, that is, void of all empirical content, and yet at the same time, while it must in one respect be intellectual, it must in another sense be sensible. Such a representation is the transcendental schema."[86] It is as if Marx had a copy of *Critique of Pure Reason* while writing his chapters on money in the *Grundrisse* where he writes:

> As regards the pure form, the economic side of this relation—the content, outside this form, here still falls entirely outside economics, or is posited as a natural content distinct from the economic, a content about which it may be said that it is still entirely separated from the economic relation because it still directly coincides with it—then only three moments emerge as formally distinct: the subjects of the relation, the exchangers (posited in the same character); the objects of their exchange, exchange values, equivalents, which not only are equal but are expressly supposed to be equal, and are posited as equal; and finally the act of exchange itself, the mediation by which the subjects are posited as exchangers, equals, and their objects as equivalents, equal. The equivalents are the objectification [*Vergegenständlichung*] of one subject for another; i.e., they themselves are of equal worth, and assert themselves in the act of exchange as equally worthy, and at the same time as mutually indifferent.[87]

The moment we understand is the moment we enter the realm of pure concepts that are metaphysically outside of our material life, the object registers within a prior existing schematism and must have a mediating object to convey that prior knowledge to the subject. This is puzzling because Kant immediately says right after the start of this thesis that "the pure concepts of understanding being quite heterogeneous from empirical intuitions, and indeed from all sensible intuitions, can never be met with any intuition." There is a metaphysics of the schematism that is outside of what is immediately available to our direct sensory experience of the thing, and yet, of course, this metaphysics, this perhaps sublime-experience that cannot be the direct experience of the thing, but is more in the thing than itself, occurs during exchange value (as indicated by Marx here) with the mediating object being "money" and the "commodity," of which the commodity takes a magnitude value, an implacable fetish-value beyond its mere usefulness. There is a mystification of the commodity that is irreducible to the thing-in-itself as an object. It is as if the moment when exchange occurs is the moment when the subject is most likely to escape and ideologically fantasize, by being close, but not realizing the schemata that animate meaning in the exchange itself.

However, at the same time Marx wants to appropriate this Kantian notion of the conceptual subsumption into "formal and real subsumption," concepts developed in the *Grundrisse* and in the three volumes of Capital, at length.

Conceptual subsumption becomes a non-metaphysical but a materialist conception where the subject is subsumed by the totalization of social relations that surround the subject. It is when the subject not only believes in the capital as the objective truth but cannot imagine any other way of life, a totalization of creative forces of imagination. Labor has no escape and is therefore objectified, for Marx, when the illusion becomes real is when the sum total of all social relations appears to the subject as a transcendent universal historical fact that enumerates a truth for all of history and all of the future, that is when the subject is subsumed into false consciousness. Precisely when the schematism of power (capital as a sort of incorporeal concept of power), as mediated by the instruments of power (money and the desire to consume provoked by the commodity in its fetish qualities), matches perfectly with the mediating representations that register as both intellectual and sensible in their truths are the product of a transcendental schema. The transcendental schema, Kant would claim, register with an always already existing innate intuition in the subject; these are analytic judgments rather than synthetic (or, combined). The intuitions that are not a priori or transcendental or universal, but are for Marx, socially constructed as a result of the changeable, groundless ground of social relations, and as Althusser would later develop further, ideologically constructed through repressive and discursive apparatuses of power.

All these powers are intended to conceal the varied nature of bourgeois economics, which is the class-conflict.

"Within bourgeois society, the society that rests on exchange value, there arise relations of circulation and production which are so many mines that threaten to explode it."[88]

MARX BEYOND HEGEL: DIFFERENCE NOT DIALECTICS?

Rather than take Marx as a reader of Hegel, casting Marx as a dialectical synthesizer and a soft, compassionate liberal multicultural subjectivist there is a way that Marx can be read as one of the greatest thinkers of difference and antagonism. My reading may work well in combination with the specific understanding of Mu offered by Zen philosophers as well.

Antagonism tends to be an affect associated with a pathological problem within an individual. Something to be mollified, softened, made-polite, the harshness of which is codified into a docile body. This has a long history at least going back as far as the Platonic dialogues and I will not delve too deeply into that here, but antagonism does not necessarily get its fair due as a political emotion and is commonly dismissed as irrational and therefore unrepresented as an emotion befitting of a political subject. Antagonism is commonly cast in a dyad with agonism or the playful, athletic, sporting sense of dialectical competition between friends. The goal of the agonistic competition, the "love of wisdom" shared between friends in a jovial debate on the issues, is to form a synthesis where the best ideas are combined and the debate resolves into oneness. I think that this is wrong not only because it never happens in real life but because in all situations where antagonism occurs there must be an object toward which the antagonism is mobilized. Antagonism does not fall from the sky as if out of thin air, as if the subject has been afflicted by demon-possession (demens/demented and therefore irrational were common terms denoting the conflation between this kind of moralizing at the early stages of the "psy"-sciences).

Antagonism implies a didactic rather than dialectical discourse that gives it much more confrontational rhetoric and that alone makes it a bit more controversial in the eyes of the guardians who do not want the people to imitate madness, and yet antagonism, grounded in a differential rather than an integral social logic, holds no end, or telos in mind as necessary to bring the subject to its resolution in synthesis with its other. Since antagonism has an object initiating its provocation, antagonism falls into a category closer to "fear." Rather than "dread" which is more of an existential feeling provoked by the awareness of the nothingness of being (closer to what the Zen traditions call "mu!"), and yet, in the politics of dread it may seem as though "dread" that is not provoked by an object and has no telos in mind, if synthesized with anger can adapt into something I would call "blind-rage," which is anger with no direction and blind to that which has provoked it (because on some occasions there is nothing provoking the rage); a trauma that persists without a stimuli, a noumenal rather than phenomenal stimulus to the affect.

This may or may not differ from antagonism because there is no grand synthesis of everything at the end of antagonism and yet the antagonistic subject would be resistant to synthesis. In many ways, Antonio Negri's positing of the "antagonism" of the constitution of the proletarian class in *Marx Beyond Marx* reproduces a kind of "monadology" of this sort, except on the level of class in the form of the proletariat rather than as atomized individuals living in the dream world that they are intangible islands beyond dukkha (suffering). Communist ontology is unlike any "Marxist state" that existed in the twentieth century. Even I wonder, as Antonio Negri did in his analysis of the *Grundrisse*:

> I cannot refrain from adding how much I like to imagine what Lenin or Mao would have done had they had the Grundrisse in their hands, just as Marx had, at a certain moment, the *Logic of Hegel*. I am certain that they would have drawn from the Grundrisse, with considerable relish, exceptional food for practice. Just like the bees with flowers. This is the path "beyond Marx" that I love.[89]

Grundrisse, is still not as widely read as the first volume of *Capital*, and it is often left unread as an unfinished draft of the work that would later become polished into the superior work of *Capital*. Nevertheless, it is precisely the unfinished aspects of the *Grundrisse* that gives us revolutionary possibilities as a deterritorialized text. Marx was still working out possibilities and the categories of his methodology were not yet concretized, not yet stable, they are fluid categories, you see how "money" and "capital" and so forth are connected. Hurriedly, Marx published this, and it was written hastily, albeit with brilliant analysis, in the midst of a banking crisis.

In the *Grundrisse*, there is a communist ontology that is approached in an anticipatory manner. Marx writes the famous line about the "anatomy of the human holds the key to the anatomy of the ape," in that the more developed form retroactively gives us the key to understanding the prior, less developed form, unlocking all of the truncated, potential power in the nucleic versions of communist modes of production that actually exist, but are kept in a repressed form due to their subsumption surrounded by capitalist productions.

Communism in methodology in the *Grundrisse* can perhaps be described as "determinate abstraction" by attempting to fetishize the object. Analysis strips it of its historical temporal nature as a shifting subject by rendering it a powerless, captured, and stable substance. As Marx sketches out his method of analysis in the *Introduction to the Grundrisse*, he starts from the base of the bourgeois economy: class-conflict and the appropriation of surplus value from labor to the bourgeoisie. Most political economies at that time, and perhaps even still to this day, start from the wealth of nations and move from top to the bottom of the economy. If the wealth of the nation is strong, then it is presumed that the wealth of the people is strong. Thus, this sort of bourgeois economics is laden with ideological aporias that are concealed from the economist. Aporias such as the essentializing and naturalizing of an entity called "the nation" or "England" and in this case "Japan," as if these are actual existing entities rather than after-effects, epiphenomenal results of labor power, class-conflict, and the hierarchies of power that result from the hierarchies of wealth inherent in class-conflict. In Marxist analysis, militaries and police exist to protect the interests of private property and the interests of collective capital, whereas in bourgeois "analysis" these are essentialized as human nature and our primal tendency toward violence and the need for security to protect "good" folks from violent "bad" folks. All of these are the product of class-conflict rather than any essential substantial form of human nature.

With the global market of capital becoming predominant, the problem posed by readers of Marx is that of being forced into a binary position. In the eyes of the dominant discourses "marxism" is on the losing side and therefore one must have recourse to the dominant discourses or provide testimony as if one is defending a guilty party.[90] Communism is not something to be propagated. It is the a priori, in the sense that community always already is, whether there is an awareness of community or not, *"pratitya-samutpada"*—conditioned co-production entails a kind of a priori of the commons. We are always already within the commons; even when there is vast disagreement, there is still common use of land, air, water; if someone dumps chemical waste into a river, the people, plants, and animals downstream will be affected. Whether or not there is or is not private property as the established norm, the river is still shared, the delusion that private property creates a monadic sense of existence is the delusion. The reality is that pollution has a nomadic contaminative effect on surrounding areas and perhaps beyond. Private property is the a posteriori condition. The use of "force" seems consistent with the apparatuses of primitive accumulation that thrust workers into exploitative factory modes of production, and henceforth mirrors such repression.

COMMUNISM AS LIVING UTOPIA

On communism as a living utopia Marx has this to say in the *German Ideology*:

> Communism is for us not a state of affairs which is to be established, an ideal to which reality will have to adjust itself. We call communism the real movement which abolishes the present state of things. The conditions of this movement result from the now existing premise.[91]

This fragment was written by Marx in his *German Ideology* notebooks in a free space above the lined area of his notebooks designated for writing. In a way, the stanza provides an afterthought on "communism" an epigram, after the fact, in an area above the original thought in the space where Marx had previously written about *estrangement*, the thought that one might say always catapults the mind into the metaphysics of non-place, of escape, of daydreaming, of casting our imagination toward other worlds, into u-topos, or non-place. Marx characterizes this *estrangement* as the movement to "propertyless" mass and universal competition. To be above and beyond the communist gaze casts its perspective from a place (or, rather a non-existing space) of world-historical, universal individuals. Up above the observant self looks down on creation in place of its local and immanent ones.

Marx went back to give a more direct description of "communism" to concretize the emblem of liberation, after the fact, to return from the future to what was once a dead end. He must concretize because he jumps into the non-place of that which is not yet here, that which has not yet arrived, and to wear the moniker of a materialist, to leap out above and beyond what is already here is to commit the taboo and paradox of experiential-metaphysics, and when all experience must, as we are told, refer back to production, there is no time for toiling in the positivity of unproductive nous (i.e., "common sense"). The fact is, however, that this unproductive nous forms the basis of the love of wisdom (philo sophia, philosophy). Thales was the man who was transfixed with the stars and fell into a well, crashing down to earth. In some way, Marx wanted to drag the earth up to the cosmos through the process of producing enhanced consciousness—material labor power metabolized through consumption, all use-value must be singularity. We consume not, "wine" but this particular bottle of wine when we drink.

A general intellect at the level of development upward into a global/cosmopolitics, Marx takes a gamble on the side of revolutionary spontaneity by claiming that "communism is only possible as the act of dominant peoples 'all at once' and simultaneously,"[92] clearly banking on the premise that the revolutionary subject is pervasive at the time of revolution. If we look at this from a perspective of "*Pratītyasamutpāda*" (interdependent arising, or conditioned co-production) we can apply inclusionary dialectics to this and see that there are theoretical tools that can enhance the ways we look at revolutionary subject formation. These are concepts from eastern philosophy that after the Kyoto School can better enhance our understanding of communism.

Previously, Marx points out that in his conceptualization of communism there is no specialization of labor writing that

in communist society, where nobody has one exclusive sphere of activity, but each can become accomplished in any branch he wishes, society regulates the general production and thus makes it possible for me to do one thing today and another tomorrow, to hunt in the morning, fish in the afternoon, rear cattle in the evening, criticize after dinner, just as I have a mind, without ever becoming a hunter, fisherman, shepherd or critic.[93]

This multifaceted subject is rich with a myriad of experiences through various leisure-time activities such as writing, fishing, and finding human development. Capitalism does the opposite. It reifies labor, and all human activities, under the "cash nexus"; hence, it is an over-determinism of the capitalist ideology that mirrors what Marx is saying as economic determinism, when in fact it is bourgeois economics that forward a determinist ideology, it is a failure of the "mirror of production" to misstep in this direction. The working day subsumes all experiences of time and with it the accumulation of capital and the payment of a wage become the sole motivation to human activity. Marx persistently argues that the opposite of this will be the pathway to human liberation. Up to and including this is the *Critique of the Gotha Program* where he says of this form of change: "It is as if, among slaves who have at last got behind the secret of slavery and broken out in rebellion, a slave still in thrall to obsolete notions were to inscribe on the program of the rebellion."[94] Fighting for higher wages while keeping the same system of wage-labor and capital in tact rearranges the content of capitalism while continuing its form.

Yet, Marx is adamant in maintaining his thesis that communism is something that develops out of capitalism rather than through a concocted sense of conceptual definitions pulled out of thin air. How can this dialectical dichotomy, which seems like a contradiction, be the basis of a new and freer communist society? By the time Marx was writing in his early 1844 notebooks during his time in Paris, he had already begun to adapt his theory of human nature. Adapting it from his earlier conception from the belief that humans are "communal by nature" implying that all we would need to do is strip away the alienating forces of machinery, alienation, and private property to return to our natural a priori as noble savages. His new philosophy changed into the understanding that humans were "social by necessity."[95]

After living in Paris while writing in his notebooks in 1844, this transition emerged in his work as he observed life in a cosmopolitan city. Experiencing life in a world-historical city connected to the global markets made him realize that the networking of social life necessary to develop a complex economy such as that of Paris at that time required the highly developed importing and exporting of goods into the emerging world market: a topic that he would later write about as the stage necessary for a global-historical revolutionary subject to emerge when all the economies of the world develop to such a point that there is mutual reliance. If one economy collapses there is mutually assured destruction of sorts, which then motivates all of the workers and traders to realize that it is not in mutual self-interest to destroy others. In this global marketplace, a new cosmopolitan world-consciousness would also emerge, which would make petty nationalism appear archaic.

It seems strange that this is even considered a controversial point in hindsight of how interconnected the global markets have become in the internet era, and in an era of logistical supply chains connecting the syllogism of "production, distribution, and consumption"[96] around the entire globe. There seems to be a consensus as interconnected markets are widely considered a good thing, perhaps beside the most trenchant miser, there is now no avoiding the interconnection of world markets. Whether or not this world market constitutes a "system" or a systematic way of unfolding this syllogism of production, distribution, and consumption insofar as the necessity of our social existence creates conditions where material needs are being met. The only way to do meet material needs on a worldwide level is to move from a general to a restricted economy through the regulation of production. To scale down consumption is one way of doing that, and this seems to be the task taken on by most social theories of the twentieth century. Focusing on the psychology of consumption and the trappings of its libidinal desires, how consumers (who are also workers of course) are directed to the desired products that are contrary to a collective self-interest. Or, the idea that the finitude of resources necessary for sustaining the production process will run out, compounded by gradual ecological crises, the patterns of this capitalist trifecta, it is presumed have already begun to break down, or will disintegrate under the sheer inertia of pervasive contradictions.

This inertial understanding of Marx is a rampant misreading of this subtle shift in his work. Readers who take a fatalistic determinist view of Marx elide the basic shift from "communal by nature" to "social by necessity." The subtle shift in terms reveals a monumental shift in methodology. Communal by nature implies a reliance on classical metaphysics from Aristotle up through at least Newtonian physics and his first law of motion: a body in motion will stay in motion unless another force acts upon it. If you take the inverse of this statement, a body at rest will stay at rest unless another force acts upon it, you see a determinist metaphysics of causality in this methodology. Marx was drawing on this early on in his writing, and the statement that there is an a priori "communal human nature" means that the historical a priori[97] with capitalism throwing human nature into an alienated, unnatural form, whereby a return to the natural tendency to live in communities will be reinstated once a primal naturalist lifestyle is implemented. In other words, rephrasing the Newtonian hypothesis: human nature is communal and will return to a communal a priori when alienation is removed. Remove the barriers between people and therefore communism will emerge. In a way, the statements from the *German Ideology* about hunting in the morning, fishing in the afternoon, are remnants of this reversion to the primitivism mindset of the early Marx, still indebted to a naturalist view of human nature informed by Newtonian physics. With "regulation of general production" life will revert to a natural "noble savage" form of existence. The good-natured human, the likes of which were common among his era, and the trends in philosophy and literature toward romanticizing primitivism.

The shift to "social by necessity" emerges when Marx starts to live in Paris and experiences life in a cosmopolitan city. He sees what life is like when a culture develops access to the world market, and this indicates a shift to a thesis that rings similar to one that Socrates makes in Plato's Republic.[98] His thesis is that cities are based on mutual needs, the concentration of population offered by life in cities makes life easier in many ways. Yet, the problem of specialization emerges where life in a cosmopolitan city offers the opportunity for many more people to engage in much more diverse kinds of labor and thereby the products that are offered in cities far surpasses those that could ever be available in small villages. Consequently, Marx's comments in the *Communist Manifesto*, readily seized upon by conservatives

What Is Communism? 153

in anti-communist propaganda speeches, that Marx and Engels loathed the "idiocy of rural life" perhaps ring true. The idea is that the social metabolism of life in a big city will enable more diverse social and cultural interactions, a process that is made possible only by the emergence of the world market, and this social evolution is enhanced by the development of cosmopolitan cities. Plato called these "luxurious cities" and they create highly specialized labor, which then makes the use of money rather than barter the dominant form of exchange value. This is because life in cities cuts off a direct connection with "production" via the connection to agricultural forms of production one must exchange on the basis of a highly specialized skill, craft, or service. The economics of life in a world-class city like Paris connected the people with products from all over the world, a point that many historians, including Marx, would later rescind as being patently and naively "good." See, for example, the chapters in the latter portion of the first volume of *Capital*, on *Primitive Accumulation*, where he writes, "If money, according to Augier, 'comes into the world with a congenital blood-stain on one cheek,' capital comes dripping from head to toe, from every pore, with blood and dirt."[99] Clearly, Marx understood the depth of the violence and also wrote that "force is the midwife of every old society which is pregnant with a new one. It is itself an economic power."[100] Every vital force takes a violent form, which replicates the violence inflicted on subjects.[101]

"Communism" has stood as an emblem of something other than a discursive concept, a theory, or an idea. Communism stands for an emblem of the desire to discover or rediscover a place of community at once beyond social divisions and subordination and techno-political domination, and thereby beyond the wasting of liberty, speech, and happiness.[102]

Most philosophers of money in the history of philosophy, starting with Aristotle in the *Nicomachean Ethics* up to and including Marx's first volume of *Capital*, conceptualize money as a system of equalities structured by equivalences. We must remember that much of what Marx says about money poses a modernist response to classical analysis. Early chapters in *Capital* argue things like ten linens are equal to forty bushels of grain, and that money is the exchange value representing equality of a vague notion of something of a qualitative relation between things that cannot be quantified, which Marx calls "magnitude value"—commodities with comparative value in relation to other commodities. A form of level value must exist to set magnitude values and have a functioning economy. A stable standard of exchange must exist. No such stable standard of value actually exists, as was made apparent in the early pages of *Grundrisse*, where Marx exposes the absurdity of bourgeois economics that claims an intrinsic value to gold rather than paper money. Therefore, money must be essentialized into any modern economic system, and a majority of mainstream interpretations of Marx start from the bizarre first principle: money is essential to exchange. This is clearly a wrong interpretation of Marx driven by "economic determinist" ideologies that unreflectively pose Marx as a mirror of capitalist ideology and production. No transcendental signifier exists and thus capitalism as an economy is a value-system with a center elsewhere to cite the Chan Buddhists whose work derive from the citing of the Heart Sutra: form is void, void is form. Value is a form without content.

The standard view of Marx casts him as an economic determinist. This position overlooks statements hidden in plain sight, such as Marx's brief all too brief mention of Peruvian and Slavic moneyless societies in the *Introduction to the Grundrisse* where he mentions in passing that Peruvian and Slavic societies had moneyless economies. Labor without wages can still occur and he says "It is simply wrong to place exchange at the center of communal-society as its constituent element."[103] Meaning that "communism" if can signify something, an ontology, is not determined by exchange value, use value perhaps, but not necessarily equality of wages as the monetary value of exchange between labor and capital. A point that Marx stays with all up to his final publication of the *Critique of the Gotha Program* is that "the exchange of equivalents in commodity exchange exists on the average and not in the individual case."[104] In other words, bourgeois economics that reifies labor power into commodified exchange value for a wage sees human beings on an aggregate basis as general, universal, interchangeable parts, standing reserve of labor. Consistent with the fact that our awareness is always our own, human life is always "a life" lived as a singular presence. Consciousness is always tethered to a particular perspective from a particular brain, even if that consciousness is a product of material conditions and constructed via interdependence.

In this sense, Marx may have an affinity with Nishida where equality is an equivalence of qualia or the qualities of a thing of which no transcendental signifier exists, no substantive magnitude value, no messianic God at the center of it all, no quilting point at which the entire narrative sutures together into a comprehensive meaning. I use the term "regime" specifically as currency, as money form the basis of regicide, or state power in the hands of a monarchical sense of sovereignty. Again, on this point, Marx also writes that Roman and Greek societies only introduced coinage and currency toward the end of their civilizations, with the point being shown that bourgeois economics cannot be seen as the only and "best" way to form an economy. Slavs, for example, used money only in relation to other external groups; money was used only with outsiders; it was necessary through inter-exchanges outside of the community because it was simply the way that foreign trade was conducted at the time; it formed a boundary between inside and outside communities.

Also, Inca economies used what is referred to as the Minka System (Mit'a, it is sometimes pronounced, as we know, archaic words slip through into modern usage in numerous ways, laced through with several significant resonances with other words, etc.) there was a wage-less system of voluntarism among the people that lasted for a very long time. Money was not involved in the way one would connote it with labor power today, in the sense of being the only motivating force.

While almost everyone is entirely pessimistic about any sort of project that would proceed from a sort of "workers of the world, unite!" unification of the working class and to be honest, that is not necessarily the purpose of this project, who wants to reunify the "volk/valkyries" and give the roots back to those who were most prone to fall for exploitation and oppression in the first place. Considering there are numerous fires to be put out if the human race were to survive, the communist hypothesis should have some consideration, even if at the level of a hypothetical contingency, the likelihood of an actual communist revolution in a world where one of the largest capitalist economies on the face of the earth wears the banner of the Chinese Communist Party, we are not likely to see much progress on this in any serious way. My concluding remarks in this chapter are as follows:

What communism must open up are the spaces (i.e., pure lands/u-topos) of innovative ontological production and sustainable constitutive ethical planes of conscious development. A living utopia that imparts the basic human demand for congruence between feeling and will, the subject finding itself, not necessarily as a return to essence, nor that an entire representation must emerge prior to analysis, but that transitions into that which real subsumption would not allow to arise as difference.

Communism is a social network where ontological innovation is socially and productively integrated, rather than wasted in the novelty of atomization and the plethora of isolated dead-ends (i.e., aporias). Individualism and communalism are spoken of as if they are unique and distinct social ends. But, the society that creates conditions where "individuals in society fully engage in action and express their natural talents"[105] will have the greatest progress.

NOTES

1. Marx. *A Contribution to the Critique of Hegel's Philosophy of Right*.
2. Marcello Musto. "Marx in Paris: Manuscripts and Notebooks of 1844." *Science and Society* 73, no. 3 (July 2009). Pg. 386–402.
3. Jean-Francois Lyotard. *Libidinal Economy*. Pg. 100.
4. Herbert Marcuse. *Eros and Civilization*. Beacon Press, 1966.
5. Georges Bataille. *The Accursed Share*, volumes 1–3.

6. Jacques Derrida. "From Restricted to General Economy." *Writing and Difference*.

7. *The Accursed Share*, volume 1. Pg. 58.

8. Mark Fisher. *Capitalist Realism: Is There No Alternative?* Zero Books, 2008.

9. Slavoj Žižek. *For They Know Not What They Do*. Verso, 1991.

10. Marx. *Economic and Philosophic Manuscripts of 1844*. Pg. 135.

11. Ibid. Pg. 146.

12. Aaron Bastani's *Fully Automated Luxury Communism* and the work of Nick Srnicek on Post-Work societies are some of the most exhilarating thought processes on what automated production may have in store for humans in the next few decades or centuries.

13. It makes sense to add to this, rather than "privileges"—birth-rights, we now have a system of wealth inequality that distributes wealth on the basis of birth-right, not ability, it seems optimistic to say ability.

14. *Capital Volume 1*. Pg. 544–546.

15. Especially see Marx's work on the famous "Fragment on Machines" in the *Grundrisse* notebooks where this thesis becomes clear. These are commonly understood to be the pages 690–712 Penguin Classics edition.

16. Marx. *The Economic and Philosophical Manuscripts of 1844*. Pg. 135.

17. Ibid.

18. Ibid.

19. Nishida. *Intelligibility and the Philosophy of Nothingness*.

20. Ibid. *Unity of Opposites*.

21. William Leogrande. "An Investigation into the 'Young Marx' Controversy." *Science and Society* Xli (1977). Pg. 137.

22. *German Ideology*. Pg. 176–183.

23. *German Ideology*. Pg. 57.

24. No one has argued this clearer than William Leogrande, 1977.

25. *1844 Manuscripts*. Pg. 135.

26. Marx. *German Ideology*.

27. Ibid. Pg. 89–89. Prometheus Books. 1989.

28. *Capital, Volume 3*, this is his thesis throughout.

29. Georg Lukács. *The Ontology of Social Being. Volume 2: Marx*. Merlin Press: London, 1978.

30. Ibid. Pg. 5.

31. Quid and the Quale as the basis of Western Ontological Logic goes back at least as far as Plato's *Meno* dialogue.

32. Buddhist scholar Red Pine dates the earliest written form of the Heart Sutra somewhere in the vicinity of 660 CE and is widely considered one of the most important texts in early Medieval Tibetan Buddhism and many strands of Mahayana Buddhism regardless of subsect.

33. A good starting point for understanding pervasion is S. Bhattacharya's "Danial H.H. Ingalls on Indian Logic" published in *Philosophy East and West*, volume 5, no. 2, July 1955. Pg. 155–162. An introduction to Daniel H.H. Ingalls "Materials for the Study of Navya-Nyaya Logic" from Harvard University Press,

1911, which was one of the first full length books to address the comparisons between Greek Logic that utilizes Propositional Logic and Indian Logic that grounds truth in Pervasion.

34. Form is void, void is form—in my context, juxtaposing Chan Buddhism in this case with Marxist thought, the commodity-form conceals the exploited labor power and/or the use of slaves that produce the fetishized product. Hence, the "form" of the commodity has as its counterpoint the "void" of labor power trapped behind various mediations such as the wage, or no wage at all, or lack of visibility to the consumer as an appearance that matters in the minds of those consuming the product, to know where the thing originates.

35. Enrique Dussel, *The Invention of the Americas: Eclipse of the "Other" and the Myth of Modernity*. Continuum: New York, 1995. Pg. 20–21.

36. *Karl Marx, Capital Volume 1*. Pg. 916.

37. Ibid. Pg. 926.

38. Ibid. Pg. 899.

39. Hiroshi Uhida. *Marx's Grundrisse and Hegel's Logic*.

40. *Grundrisse*. Pg. 91.

41. Ibid.

42. Uhida, chapter 1.

43. *Grundrisse*. Pg. 93.

44. William Haver. "Labor Process and the Genesis of Historical Time." In *Confronting Capital and Empire: Rethinking Kyoto School Philosophy*. Leiden: Brill, 2017. Pg. 66.

45. *Grundrisse*. Pg. 89.

46. Ibid. Pg. 88.

47. Ibid. Pg. 99.

48. Karl Marx. *Grundrisse*. Pg. 160.

49. Karl Marx. *Grundrisse*. Pg. 160.

50. Luigi Pirandello's theatre of the absurd makes this point in the play *Henry IV*, where the anti-hero truly believes himself to be the Roman Emperor Henry the Fourth, and yet, he is surrounded by actors who construct a fictional set around him, and each perform roles to feed into this massive delusion. The provocation raised during this massive "absurdist" stage play is one of presentation of self in everyday life. Who is king and who is mad? All the world is merely a stage, those who are deluded enough to believe they are actually "king" and convince the world that they "are" kings are the most deluded and dangerous.

51. *Capital. Volume 2*, chapter 13: "Productive Time." Pg. 316.

52. Ibid. Pg. 317.

53. Giorgio Agamben has made a career out of this distinction between zoe and bios, confined life and vital life, disposable and bare life. Zoe being the root of zoo (caging animals) and Eve that which must be confined, controlled.

54. Karl Marx. *Grundrisse*. Pg. 160; here, it should be noted, Marx turns to Aristotle's *Nicomachean Ethics* book V, chap. 5, paragraph 14 to make his point clear that he is trying to evoke Aristotle as a means of deepening his views on money, as a means to enjoyment rather than as eudaimonia in and of itself. Money can never

be pure eudaimonia, pure happiness, because it brings you things, it is a means of exchange rather than a thing in and of itself that is intrinsically enjoyable.

55. Marx. *Critique of the Gotha Program*. Tucker, 526.
56. Nishida Kitarō. *A Preface to Metaphysics*. Fundamental Problems of Philosophy. Pg. 4. Translated by David A. Dilworth. Monumenta Nipponica Press. Tokyo.
57. Ibid. Pg. 5.
58. *Capital Volume 2*. Pg. 109.
59. Nishida Kitarō. *Preface to Metaphysics*. Pg. 7.
60. Marx. *Capital, Volume 1*. Pg. 129.
61. Marx. *Grundrisse*. Translated and intro. by Martin Nicolaus. Penguin: London, 1973. Pg. 600.
62. Karl Marx. *Capital Volume 3*. Chapter 48. Pg. 953. Italics are my own emphasis.
63. Marx and Engels. *The Communist Manifesto*. Pg. 2.
64. Nishida Kitarō. *The Intelligible World*. Pg. 38.
65. *Capital Volume 1*. Pg. 129.
66. ibid. Pg. 130.
67. Antonio Negri. *Marx Beyond Marx*. Autonomedia Press. Pg. 121.
68. Ibid. Pg. 121.
69. Grundrisse. Pg. 891.
70. Grundrisse. Pg. 667–668.
71. *Capital Volume 1*. Pg. 166.
72. Karl Marx. *The Poverty of Philosophy*. Pg. 110–111.
73. James Buchanon. *State of the Union Address*. December 7, 1857.
74. *Grunrdisse*. Pg. 472/385.
75. *Grundrisse*. Pg. 471.
76. *Marx Beyond Marx*. Pg. 149–150.
77. *Grundrisse*. Pg. 472.
78. *Capital Volume 1*. So-Called Primitive Accumulation. Pg. 925–926.
79. Ibid. pg. 617.
80. Ibid. pg. 618.
81. Hiroshi Uchida. *Marx's Grundrisse and Hegel's Logic*. chapter 1. Routledge. 1988.
82. *Capital Volume 1*. Pg. 544–556.
83. Ibid.
84. Kant. *Critique of Pure Reason*. Transcendental Doctrine of Judgment: The Schematism of the Pure Concepts of Understanding. Pg. 180.
85. Ibid.
86. Ibid.
87. *Grundrisse*. Pg. 160.
88. *Grundrisse*. Pg. 159.
89. Antonio Negri. *Marx Beyond Marx*. Pg. 19.
90. Jacques Derrida. *Spectres of Marx*. Pg. 52.
91. *German Ideology*. Pg. 57.

92. Ibid. Statements like these have been hastily read as signs of economic determinism as the basis upon which the "communist" subject emerges, that economics overdetermines the consciousness behind the revolutionary subject.

93. Ibid. pg. 54.

94. Karl Marx. *Critique of the Gotha Program.* Part 3.

95. William Leogrande. "An Investigation into the 'Young Marx' Controversy." *Science and Society* Xli (1977).

96. *Introduction to the Grundrisse.*

97. Michel Foucault. *Archaeology of Knowledge.* Pg. 126–134. Foucault is important here because his thesis is that there is a myth of origins thesis that creeps into naturalist readings of historical texts. Marx was making this mistake early on in his writings.

98. Plato. *The Republic.* "Origin and Composition of the State: Its Ruling Class." Lines 368–434.

99. Marx. Chapter 31: The Genesis of the Industrial Capitalist. *Capital Volume 1.* Pg. 926.

100. Ibid. Pg. 916.

101. Georges Bataille. *Oeuvres Completes,* volume 1. Paris: Gallimard, 1970. Pg. 332. Bataille's observations are important comparisons with the Kyoto School.

102. Jean-Luc Nancy. *Inoperative Community.* Minnesota University Press: Minneapolis.

103. *Grundrisse.* Pg. 103.

104. Marxists.org—Marx Archive, *Critique of the Gotha Program,* part 1.

105. *Zen no Kenkyu.* Pg. 137–138.

Chapter 4

Kokka Minzoku (State Nation) ~ Minzoku Kokka (Nation State)

"Communism is Soviet power plus electrification."—Vladimir Lenin[1]

"The state is an abstraction. The people alone is what is concrete."—Karl Marx[2]

"The nation is the mirror of the Pure Land in this world."—Nishida Kitarō[3]

"The state, therefore, has not existed from all eternity. There have been societies which have managed without it, which had no notion of the state or state power. At a definite stage of economic development the state became a necessity because of the cleavage of society into classes, the state became a necessity because of this cleavage. We are now rapidly approaching a stage in the development of production at which the existence of these classes has not only ceased to be a necessity, but become a positive hindrance to production. They will fall as inevitably as they once arose. The state inevitably falls with them. The society which organizes production anew on the basis of free and equal association of the producers will put the whole state machinery where it will then belong—into the museum of antiquities, next to the spinning wheel and the bronze ax."—Frederich Engels.[4]

OWL OF MINERVA: DISINTEGRATING EPOCH OF NOW

> When philosophy paints its grey in grey, then it has a shape of life grown old. By philosophy's grey in grey it cannot be rejuvenated but only understood. The Owl of Minerva spreads its wings only with the falling of the dusk.[5]

In a way, Hegel has been misread as a philosopher of the future. Projecting universal categories cast hasty generalizations upon the world, which were taken up as manifestoes for colonial empires with modernizing, civilizing projects on their minds, knowledge/power linked in the most dangerous ways. The penultimate example of this being the rise of fascism in the twentieth century as an outgrowth of the ethos of universality, generalization, homogeneity, and the power of the state wielding violence behind the soft mechanisms of "freedoms" that dialectically synthesize with prior apperceptions toward a totalizing absolute mind. In the aforementioned famous passage, Marx tries to turn this around by looking toward the future, rather than the Owl of Minerva (philosophical thought) taking off in the evening, in hindsight, in the a posteriori, to paint grey on grey, means that philosophy cannot see into the future. It can only bring out the conceptual social structure that is imminent and already slowly disintegrating.

If Marx is to be taken seriously, then this warning from Hegel must also factor into his writings, and we should also count the twentieth-century attempts toward communist revolutions (Lenin and Mao being the two most successful movements, and also the two biggest failures), as attempting to push the dialectic of history forward perhaps too soon. The failures of twentieth-century communist state revolutions were a product of not yet fully understanding that the epoch was approaching its end. Hegel was describing social orders that were disintegrating. By extension, Marx's inversion of Hegel as a philosophy of the future is a philosophy of a future that is completely open-ended, as it is not posited as a return to essence. By saying that history is a nightmare, Marx, not yet knowing that the twentieth century would carry all these psychoanalytical developments, would imply that there are latent traumas carried in the psyche of the exploited that are residual effects carried into the present, traces of which have to be dealt with to move forward by looking into the future.

KOKKA MINZOKU (STATE NATION) ~ MINZOKU KOKKA (NATION STATE)

After his retirement, Nishida's writings took a political turn. Nishida's pivot toward addressing a more openly political set of topics can be explained by his freedom from teaching and institutional responsibilities, along with the looming exigencies of Japan's war with China in Manchuria, and the colonial nationalist ideologies that gained traction as a result of social, political, and forces in the marketplace. Historical conditions set in motion during the Meiji Restoration arrived at a devastating apogee when Japan sealed its alliance with the Axis Powers in a tripartite pact on September 27, 1940. Political policies of the Taishō Period, as liberal as it was, gave momentum to the closing of intellectual openness. As early as April of 1925, the Japanese government issued a peace ordinance (chian ijihō) to suppress socialist and Marxist movements that were gaining momentum on college campuses. It was also in 1925 that the government suggested to the imperial universities that "if the university so wishes, a military officer may be dispatched to each campus to conduct military training."[6] On March 15, 1928, the government arrested more than 1,600 people in a single day in the first "large-scale organized application of the Peace Preservation Law,"[7] including steps over the next several months to remove leftist professors, including Marxist economist Kawakami Hajime, author of *Tales of Poverty*, who agreed to resign voluntarily. Nishida's writing turned political after his retirement in 1929, but the political shift from "Taishō democracy" to the militarism of the Shōwa years placed political issues at the forefront of his work.

Some have argued that Nishida's later political writings were informed by social constructivism, a popular philosophical movement among scholars of the early twentieth century, and by over-emphasizing the cultural aspects of world history and the perception of subjectivity contradiction, his political resistance toward colonialism ultimately failed.[8]

Yet, what is interesting, again, is the way most of this analysis "reifies" the economics of colonialism in ways that shield it from a full Marxist deconstruction of the metaphysics of value. Nishida perhaps talks about power in "culturalist" terms because he was offering a reading of state power as reified "culture" or "social relations" and therefore his reading did include Marxist categories of analysis, albeit concealed in the subtext. As John Maraldo offers a thesis that in part I agree with, we must start to understand Nishida's political writings as laden with subtext because there were many political pressures at the time, including direct censorship under Japanese fascism that forced Nishida and many other philosophers of that era to conceal the more direct assaults on expansionist colonial ideologies. Two of the clearest examples within the Kyoto School were Miki Kiyoshi and Tosaka Jun. Both took more overtly Marxist views during the rise of fascism and both died in prison. Kiyoshi died in Toyotama Prison on September 26, 1945, forty days after the Japanese surrender on August 15th. MaCarthur did not order the release of political prisoners until October 4th, at which point many communists were released from prison. Tosaka Jun died in Nagano Prison on August 9, 1945, after being arrested under Japan's Peace Preservation Laws in 1938.

More to the point about Nishida's writing, his tactical concealment of critiques of the state are alluded to in his specific wording of "Kokka Minzoku" (state nation) rather than "Minzoku Kokka" (nation state) indicating that "state" is focalizing the disbursement of "logic of place" ("bashoteki ronri") called into a "dialectic of place" ("bashoteki benshōhō"), which Nishida uses to imply not just a dialogical, discursive interlocutory discussion, as in the sense of the Socratic Dialogues where Socrates debates Crito, Euthyphro, and so on through predicate logic and discursive, and spirited philosophical debates, but a material dialectic (a social relation, a metabolism of nature, etc.) that is always already happening. Our awareness of the dialectic of place is concealed or unconcealed depending on factors of alienation, atomism, and market forces that push consciousness into reified forms of egoism, rather than representing subjectivity accurately. Bashoteki literally means place-view or space-target, and it indicates a focalizing process that occurs through political closures as harnessed by religious "heilige"/yoking transmuting an expansive consciousness of interconnectedness, gradually harnessed into a myopic world/political view.

Focusing of the "ego"-self into one particular atomized viewpoint alienates the self from the fact of the "I" as existing in open space. The "I" is fissured by space and no-thingness that calls it forth, and makes it what "it is" and in many senses the "being of beings" as Heidegger referred to it can only be understood in lieu of its non-substantialist relation to this movement of the openness of the "nothing" as Basho. Nishida's political theses were informed by non-Western metaphysics of samsara, basho, pervasion, and *pratitya-samutpāda* (interdependent arising/origination or conditioned coproduction), and were conversant with modern and premodern Western philosophy. Although not published until after Nishida's death, I speculate that his "bashoteki" might have a lot in common with a deconstructive reading of the power/knowledge of "the Archimedean Point" in the sense of a focalized telescopic worldview, where a man reaches out to seek knowledge and only finds himself, "the Archimedean wish for a point outside the earth from which to unhinge the world," and yet, the metaphysics of the human condition attempting to extend its power into the vast expanse of limitless cosmic space, in seeking moral laws, and natural laws, humans must confront laws beyond the reach of direct human sense experience.[9]

The discovery that there is much more depth than what merely appears forces the production of a wildly unsettling metaphysics in that there are layers of depth, and expanses of infinitio (unfinished) vistas to the cosmos that stretch to unbridgeable gaps beyond what is immediately and directly accessible to human sense perception that the only authentic emotional response would have to be a nihilistic malaise.

However, I urgently and emphatically argue that "nihilism" and "political theory" are not two separate philosophical categories. "The state" if anything is not only policing property in the sense of shifting materials created by workers into the hands of "capital" and throwing people in jail and collecting taxes. It is a surge protector against the revolutionary nihilistic malaise of seeing the reality of nothing.

Bashoteki ronri, being the "logic of place" of the atomized subject that has yet entered into the "bashō no benshōhō," "dialectic of place" the metabolism of social relations of a world-historical-subject, only possible after the world market has developed. In describing forms of social intercourse in this passage from the *German Ideology*, Marx was also concerned with a "social epistemology" and my argument is that Nishida also worked through the dialectics of place in the same way that Marx hinged his view of communism on a materialist dialectic:

> Communism differs from all previous movements in that it overturns the basis of all earlier relations of production and intercourse, and for the first time consciously treats all-natural premises as the creatures of hitherto existing men, strips them of their natural character and subjugates them to the power of the united individuals. Its organization is, therefore, essentially economic, the material production of the conditions of this unity; it turns existing conditions into conditions of unity.
>
> The reality, which communism is creating, is precisely the true basis for rendering it impossible that anything should exist independently of individuals, insofar as reality is only a product of the preceding intercourse of individuals themselves. Thus, the communists in practice treat the conditions created up to now by production and intercourse as inorganic conditions, without, however, imagining that it was the plan or the destiny of previous generations to give them material, and without believing that these conditions were inorganic for the individuals creating them.[10]

NISHIDA'S DIRECTION OF NOTHING, VISIBILITY IS A TRAP

This is very similar to the way Nishida says that when we speak of today's consciousness, yesterday's consciousness has disappeared, and yet it still acts in the present consciousness, "what has become nothing must be thought to be acting,"[11] what is thought to be the transcendental will is the image of the self within itself. To be clear, a self can be a human being, a nation, a political entity, an economic body, and so forth. Nishida, in my opinion, takes an expansive definition of self beyond the corporeality of a flesh and blood, the body of an atomized individual. In his anti-substantialist view of reality, Nishida claims that this is the "direction of nothing," which is inextricable with the unity of consciousness. Rather than pieces of matter, monads are separated by empty inert space, the nothing is what unifies the material of what it is.

His "uncreating and uncreated" appropriated from Scotus Erigena is that which cannot be manipulated through poiesis and therefore may have frustrated a materialist such as Marx. Showing your entire hand is improper; it gives too much power away through the form of honesty. Power also forms in the gaps, crevasses, fissures, and possibilities of emplacement that allow for the free imagination of u-topos, that is, the pure land. The state cannot surveil what the panopticon cannot bring forth to see: the no-thing. Michel Foucault's famous line "visibility is a trap"[12] in a way expresses this point although without recourse to Nishida philosophy. Freedom exists in avoiding, rebuking, rejecting, apparatuses of representation; however, there are vast expanses of spatial and temporal emptiness (sunyata) that dwarf the miniscule realm of political agency in the cosmos.

Marx makes a similar conclusion, albeit in a different direction when he writes in *The German Ideology:* "It is a question of spirit which creates itself out of nothing, hence it is a question of nothing, which out of nothing makes itself spirit."[13]

POLITICS IS WHAT ENTERS INTO THE "INTELLIGIBLE WORLD"

In Marx's writings, the state should never be understood as a permanent fixture in political life. In Nishida's writings, contrary to reading him as an (ultra)-nationalist, his "individualistic" approach can be seen as a response to the social and political momentum of the post-Meiji era. Nishida forwarded "self-contradictory-self"-subjectivity when "Japan" was identifying itself as a homogeneous political entity.

All states are temporary measures toward an ultimate telos—a good end, which is the production of a stateless society and a society free of class conflict. Interestingly enough, the move toward a more explicit political theme in Nishida's work coincides with gradual removal of the conceptualization of a "transcendental will," and that is where Nishida becomes exciting as a unique political philosopher because politics was not conceptualized as immanent or transcendent will, pushing and pulling corporeal material around. Politics has to do with what enters into the "intelligible world"[14]—a theme he explores all the way up to and including his final essay on the world of different peoples ("minzoku"), who have not yet entered into a temporal order with respect to one another and are not yet historical on a world scale.

People must form a "world-principle"[15] when entering into the field of temporal-spatial intelligibility one encounters in the differential dynamics of social life. Nishida moves away from a "pure"-experience of Kantian inflected categories of ethics in his earlier works such as *An Inquiry into the Good* toward a difference-infused thesis that claims: "A truly global spirit must be one in which unity incorporates diversity, and absolute includes relative."[16]

Nishida's writing style could lead some readers aghast because these seem like hyperbolic discursive propositions pulled out of thin air. For those who hang in there, his work reveals a rich philosophical oeuvre upon multiple readings.

Remember, "We call the case where a certain phenomenon necessarily accompanies another phenomenon, with absolutely no end or telos whatsoever, mechanical activity."[17] In the subtext of Nishida's view of mechanical activity changed, as years later he would refer to "will" as an abstraction. Later on in his life, he describes the transcendental will as something that individuals neither cause nor originate. One can presume a similar definition to the state. For those who are nativists to the existence of the state, the mere existence of the state is presumed to be necessary as a condition of its status as transcendental will. Marx typically writes about the state as a tool rather than a machine. In the sense that machinic consciousness has no telos, whereas the state must have a telos: the liberation of the people, and if the state has outlived its usefulness, in somewhat thanotic terms it must disintegrate, because it has become an apparatus used to trap rather than free.

In this analysis is a view espoused by Marx, a subtle difference between a "tool" and a "machine," insofar that, "the tool makes the worker independent—posits him as the proprietor. Machinery—as fixed capital, posits (workers) as dependent, as appropriated."[18] The thesis forwarded here is simple: the state is the machinery of capital. State power appropriates and territorializes land, situates labor, controls its flow, and creates monads rather than nomads. The ways that the state exists in capitalism prevents the emergence of the kind of difference-inflected worldview that Nishida describes.

STATE, CAPITAL, VIOLENCE

One of the key aspects of reification is the false consciousness that confuses a thing that is a product of social relations as if it were an objective fact. The state, property rights, ownership of land, ground rent, and private cultivation of land are symptoms of a very narrow set of property relations overseen by a particular kind of governance and should not be mistaken for a factual thing, vaguely referred to as "human nature." In fact, the many ways that Marx refers to our relations toward nature are as an ever-changing metabolism, rather than a set of ready-made objects to be discovered, known, and mastered.

As you see in the examples from Mao and Lenin, the failures were in negative-negation and negative association with behaviors and attitudes that their states did not want the people to exhibit. It is like the opening scene in Michel Foucault's *Discipline and Punish*, where the enemy of the state, as punishment for regicide is tortured, "flesh torn from his breasts," wounds "poured with molten lead, boiling oil, burning resin," and his "body drawn and quartered by four horses and his limbs and body consumed by fire,"[19] basically, the Ling Chi' torture in medieval European context, and the absurd tendencies toward cultural relativism make "Orientalist"-otherness seem so exotic that analysis of the state as such becomes obscured.

As Deleuze and Guattari write: "Marx made the observation in the case of capitalism: there is a violence that necessarily operates through the state, precedes the capitalist mode of production, constitutes the 'primitive accumulation' and makes possible the capitalist mode of production. It is difficult to see who is the thief, who is the victim, or where the violence resides."[20] This is again a problem in the "anti-essentialist" reading of a world where capital takes all that is solid and melts it into the air, the "bashoteki"/open worldview must confront the limitations of apperception. All that is solid melts into air, ethically, politically, and synthesizes with the "good" virtues of capital, as if that is all there is.

There is a famous line from Michel Foucault that says: "Marxism exists in the nineteenth-century like a fish in water; that is, it is unable to breathe anywhere else."[21] Foucault was certainly a bit polemical by writing that but may have echoed the point that we are still fully in the midst of the historical epiphenomena from the "Enlightenment" era and certainty of "historical induction" from those eras can bias our perspectives of what is possible in the future. Historical induction is the statement of the belief that what happened in the past will inevitably persist into the future. A point might remain that the failure of "Marxist" revolutions in the twentieth century might have to do with the appropriation of an "egoist"/individualized view of rights, political subjectivity, and representational governance, all stemming from a "cogito"-focal point to subjectivity.

This is why many political theorists who have turned to Marx have tried to rethink what is living and what is dead in Marx. Yet, there is a dreadless way that reification gives the appearance of solidified, settled truth, when "capital is not a thing, it is a definite social relation of production pertaining to a particular social formation, which takes the form of a thing and gives this thing a specific social character."[22] One question is the underdeveloped theory of the state in Marxist thought. Is the state to be viewed as a contingency? Or, as a means to an end to protect the worker-controlled modes of production?

Depending on what people believe about this, a view similar to structuralists may emerge, in the sense that the way "Marxist" political movements have seized the state as a method of gaining worker hegemony (a "dictatorship of the proletariat") has almost always ended in terror, violence, and politically motivated murders at the hands of the "Marxist state" because the structures of liberation replicate the forms of oppression they claim to resist, precisely because for structuralists "liberation" can only come from within the structures of power that oppress in the first place. Hence, it has been presumed, even in some aspects of the writings from Marx, that communism exists within capitalism as a germinal substance. This may be a remnant of Hegelian dialectics. Clearly, this thesis needs serious rethinking because the "communist hypothesis" could only work within what was available to it at that time, which was the view that "cultural progress" in politics meant epistemologically binding subject to the metaphysics of the "Archimedean Point."

PLACE, DOMINION, AND THE STATE

The use of the land for cultivation and improvement as the basis with which ownership is determined was a newer idea in the social contract theory of law. Even John Locke wrote that labor had the right to claim ownership of what it improved upon. A radical idea for a time when feudalism had only recently fallen out of use and the democratizing revolutions of the enlightenment period had not yet occurred. Hegel conceptualized that the state actualized itself in world history as an already existing national-Geist and that a universal world spirit would eventually emerge. A theme that the younger Marx took upon himself to more fully develop was that the communism took a shape as the becoming of world spirit in *The German Ideology*, which took a sort of fatalistic, one might say even reflexive path to communism.

This view would require a conception of the world as related to the state in terms of place or basho, and the state must be purely functional. Once its function is no longer needed, it is best for the state to wither away, rather than reproduce itself in the service of itself as its own end.

This is striking considering the Western legacy of the state and international law goes back to the Treaty of Westphalia in 1684. It is fascinating how easy it is to forget that people were nomads prior to the invention of the state which serves as a mechanism that keeps people penned in like human livestock.[23] Law is not eternal but a zone of intensification that short-circuits assemblages between a larger family beyond merely the nuclear family. State power has three characteristics of sovereignty, according to Michel Foucault, and mind you, he is not merely talking about "state power" in a literal governmental sense, but governmentality within the subject as well.

Firstly, an asymmetrical relationship has to be established through a levy or a deduction on one side and an expenditure on the other (i.e., taxes taken from subjects). Secondly, sovereignty bears the mark of founding precedence—something like a divine right, a conquest, a victory, and a submission, something like birth or rights of blood, so that sovereignty has the power/knowledge of history "on its side" so to speak where it can look back and point to something it considers as a definitive foundation that constitutes its power. Thirdly, these relations are not isotopic in the sense that each of these power relations is tangled up and intertwined with one another so that it is not so simple to point to one single thing, one single reason, and say "voila! this is the origin of the power that sovereignty holds!"[24]

Even though the mechanisms of disciplinary power are often concealed from the subjects it works upon, it does not mean that the implementation of power cannot be exposed. It can be made apparent that disciplinary power, the power the sovereign exerts over life itself, the biopolitics of the sovereign who is given the power to give and take life is also the power to "anomize," to normalize the normal, to tell its subjects what is and what ought to be the normal way to live, and to isolate those whose lives do not fit squarely into the defined categories of what is normal. State sovereignty also tries to promote the notion that the categories of normal and abnormal, even though they are temporary methods of pragmatically obtaining hegemony over its subjects, the state endows itself and casts a deluded cloud over its subjects which gives it the presence to feel as if these laws are created unhistorically in a bizarrely universal of timeless duration.

The biggest trick the state plays on its subjects is getting us/them to truly believe that it is a permanent fixture in our lives, when the state is a temporary construction, a mobile theatre-stage in a world where everything is but a stage and we are all merely players, performers, and portrayers. The sovereign is merely the most deluded to not only convince him, her, itself that he, she, it is actually a king, queen, prince, princess, or president but that the deluded are deluded enough to convince everyone else to continue with this charade. The truth is that no emperors have any clothes.[25] The struggle today is that cynicism about structures of power is common, the people are often aware that the emperor has no clothes, and yet there is so much fear of revolutionary, radical change that there seems to be a political paralysis on issues that if they are left to remain unchanged could perhaps lead to the extinction of life. The worst mistake would be to continue the political paralysis that presumes the state is a timeless fixture, a perennial dimension of human life, rather than a novelty that has faded in its purpose.

The state is a stasis-machine. It confines, incarcerates, stops the flows along the plane of immanence that differentiate subjectivities and pin beings down to particular territories, spaces, areas, there can be no "workers of the world" to unite when there are territories that imagine spaces as human-livestock-pens and nature as a standing reserve merely as resource potential. The state slows down the natural tendency of life which is nomadism and the free-traversion of labor, productive-creation, and represses perverts the natural desire to give without expecting anything in return: as the literal son of God does and has done since the absolute-zero[26] spark of life.

A major mistake that the twentieth-century communists made was utilizing the state as a permanent fixture of life. To experience an awakening at all times is impossible. If that is the logos of ideology, then the experience of political fatigue can seem unsettling, unless there is a practice of active forgetting. Some nocturnal dreams are necessary; sleep is necessary for all organic life to continue. To force an animal to deprive itself of sleep is to force it into schizophrenia. Always "woke" is a crazy-making recipe. There is a degree of sleeplessness that is fatal to life, ruminating in sleep and forgetfulness is necessary for any life to continue. Periods of sleep are regenerative.

To propose a communist ontology of the state is to emphasize that this is not realist ontology of the state. An ontology based historically on what is and what was is to return to the past like a Hegelian "Owl of Minerva" as if historical knowledge weighs upon living as something other than a nightmare. To reify knowledge as the Owl of Minerva flying overhead, flying at night, and looking retroactively at the success or failure of the ideas of the previous works and days. If you base communist ontology on history, then clearly communism would be an erroneous failure. However, to take a cue from the early Marx and the Marx of the *Grundrisse*, there are still other immature communisms in the process of becoming that can only be examined after the fact of their actualization, the human unlocks the anatomy of the ape only after the human actually exists. You can argue that Stalinism and Maoism had some successes, but overall were not the full development of actual communism, but were truncated versions of communism that could only exist in lieu of a partial transformation of small spheres of the world economy, amidst a capitalist society that ran parallel to it, and therefore, the communists had to have an increased sense of paranoia in order to compete with the real external threats, the specter of capitalism looming outside the walls of their nations. Communism had yet to be a fully worldwide revolution; nations, boundaries, and "others" still existed.

It is crucial to think about the state as assisting in the annulment of private property, rather than aiding and abetting in its propagation. As a propagator of man's relation to himself as mirrored back through the representative channels of governance, the state can be the temporary mirror of man's consciousness as "species being." Species being is the special way that man understands himself as a social being, not merely as an individual in relation to all other beings, but as a being that is fundamentally and inextricably linked to other beings within its species. Labor power, with its necessary social dimensions, will always develop the consciousness of the worker as a species being. This social consciousness will develop as a result of having to engage with others through trade.

The exchange of goods always means that there is a social exchange. If the state is the facilitator of the economics of human life then there is a way that the state can play a role in facilitating social relations with one another, since, in every economy, there is no human that is an island. Remember, Marx gives many clear definitions of what communism is (not that these have to be taken as gospel but to be clear about what that term means) that it is "crude communism" that is merely mirroring capitalist wage-labor power when one thinks of communism as equality of wages. If you think that equal wages constitute "communism" then you are still operating within the dysfunctional consciousness of capitalism because you are defining it within the wage-labor system.

A clearer definition that is perhaps more useful in the context of talking about the state, Marx says

> Communism as the positive transcendence of private property as human self-estrangement, and therefore as the real appropriation of the human essence through and for man; communism therefore as the complete return of man to himself as a social (i.e., human) being—a return become conscious, and accomplished within the entire wealth of previous development.[27]

In order for this to happen the state must wither away, and the problem is that in the interim, if there were to be a heavy-handed bureaucracy to set everyone's papers in order, there has to be a way to push through the bureaucratic stasis the inertia that enables the state to sit, squat, and maintain its hegemony as if it were a permanent, eternal entity.

While Nishida's philosophy, and Buddhist philosophy in general,[28] is largely a-political there are ways that the precariousness of his language indicates a temporal flow to the being of beings that makes it easier to think of the temporariness of the state, because all ontological entities are temporary. Just as any society divided against itself in competition and in class conflict among its members in most Buddhist writings, sincerity is equated with wholeheartedness. Both Marxist critiques of class-based political economy and Buddhist teachers point to the conditions of non-alienating life (be it social life or life within oneself), nobody divided within, nor a society that divides people against one another can act from the intentions of sincerity. Therefore, true and honest compassion becomes completely impossible in societies where there are forms of political and social exclusion. Where people feel that they have no voice within the society they live, they tend to become aggressive and ferocious toward one another, because their needs are not met.

NISHIDA: "THE NATION OUGHT TO BE THE MIRROR IMAGE OF THE PURE LAND IN THIS WORLD"[29]

"Each state and each people live their individual and historical lives, and at the same time, due to their particular world-historical missions, they unify and form a world-of-worlds."[30] Reality as dialectic (benshōhō) by its very nature is not static but dynamic, involving the self in self-contradictory, oppositional processes. A theme that weaves its way throughout Nishida's work is the theme of contradictory self-identity (mujunteki jikodōitsu). Life is a contradictory paradox; for example, he writes, "We both must and cannot think that in the world there is a beginning."[31]

What Nishida calls "religion" (shūkyō) had been a concern in his philosophy since his writings on pure experience, epistemology, and the historical world; however, his later writings indicate his attempts to view the concerns of the religious worldview in dialectical terms. Nishida's appropriation takes religious ideas from both the East and the West and so the dialectical method has elements of Hegelian, Marxist, as well as Taoist, Buddhist, and Confucian philosophies while developing his own unique perspectives.

In specific ways, there were earlier engagements with existential philosophy through eastern thought that thematize "religion" as the sense of the individual in confrontation with the facticity of impermanence. One must feel the depth of self-awareness in the tension between life and death; in the earlier essays Nishida is clearly grappling with religion as "being-toward-death." As John Krummel explains: "What people call 'God,' or 'absolute,' is what the finite self immediately faces in those depths of self-awareness, that is, the alterity of the source of being and knowing, the wherein in which we find ourselves always already, always in excess of our attempts at conceptual reduction."[32]

In the last few paragraphs in that final essay, he veers from discussing Christianity and God and then makes a statement that "This corrupt world reflects the pure land. Pure land reflects this corrupt world" in a dialectical statement, and then he remarks that "this points to the interconnectedness, or oneness of the pure land." He may be making his intentions clear that in understanding the state there is always a metaphysics of interdependent arising that forms the basis of all that exists. The state is no exception. Obviously, the swerve from Christianity and God to the state is not accidental. Remember, toward the later era in his life Nishida critiqued his own early writings as putting a naive emphasis on "pure experience" and therefore one might forward the thesis that toward the end of his oeuvre he had moved away from emphasizing a kind of analytical conception of the good as self-evident on the basis of a priori intuition.

In the last line, "The nation is the mirror image of the Pure Land in this world," what is interesting is that "pure land" is, as many know, a type of Buddhist religion as well as an idea in some strands of Buddhist thought that indicates a sort of "u-topos" or a metaphysics of salvation, "heaven" so to speak. So, the link I am trying to draw is that Nishida is imagining the state as the manifestation of the interconnected "geist" (as Hegel would call it); but in a very Marxist sense "in this world" the hopes and dreams of the people, the fears and paranoid ideas of the people, made manifest "in this world" as he adds at the end to make it clear that he means a "historical materialist" interpretation of the state, but not in the sense of consciousness as traditionally understood by those inspired by Marx.

An earlier incarnation of this thoughtful line of flight was written by Hakuin (1686–1768) and is supposed to be meditatively chanted in his "Chant in Praise of Zazen" with the last line recognizing the immediacy of the "pure land":

What is there outside of us, what is there we lack?
Nirvana is openly shown to our eyes.
This earth where we stand is the Pure Lotus Land.
And this very body, the body of the Buddha.[33]

There are many other examples of this immanence of the pure land, even the journey has to escape the restlessness of venturing elsewhere, when the palace of awakening is within oneself: "before you take a step, you are already there."[34] Hakuin again echoes this sentiment of wherever you go, that is where you are by saying: "How sad that people ignore the near, and search for truth afar."[35]

As inner consciousness is activated by the external world, cogitated by inner consciousness, we find ourselves confronting each other and nature in mutual determination, while also having freedom. A paradox that he grappled with throughout his life and in his last essay, he lays out his Nishidean dialectical view of the world. "The self exists as the absolute's own self-negation."[36] In many ways, this can be viewed as Nishida forwarding an existentialist thesis and in some respects, this is how there should bridge a gap between existential and Marxist strategies on the utilization of organized praxis. Nishida continues: "The religious question is always a question of the volitional self, of the consciously active individual. But this has nothing to do with the usual conception of religion as giving one peace of mind. Peace of mind is not a religious matter."[37]

Nishida views the concrete world as neither reducible to its material-mechanistic nor biological-teleological physical, nor purely ideal explanations. Bios, as Nishida tells us, serves the purpose in ancient eastern philosophy (of say, the natural flow and the three types of power described in the Tao te Ching), as he explains gives a sense of a "historical-natural" inevitability to the world;[38] as a self-negating power of fatalist inevitability to the way of the world, rather than the religious worldview which is not primarily interested in comforting and producing docile useful bodies, but self-individual expression as the negation of the absolute.

In turning to Zen, the religious worldview cannot be understood based on unwrinkling every contradiction into a categorical kingdom that ends in a Kantian sense of ethics, whereby the categorical imperative "commands" subject to obey the non-contradictory universalizability of ethical behaviors. Zen's principle of the absurd must be grasped as a paradox. This presentation of paradoxes, known as the kōan, has nothing to do with mystical experiences as many may think. A kōan is merely a means of bringing to awareness the paradoxes in existence itself. A self-awakening that produces kenshō (seeing one's nature)[39] brings awareness of aporias that appear to be irresolvable contradictions if simply understood through the lens of logic that demands non-contradictory statements. Nishida's example to exemplify this:

> One day Shuzan, taking up a bamboo stick, said: "When you call this a bamboo stick, you are wrong, and when you do not, you are also wrong. What, then, do you call it?"[40]

Nishida is not utilizing flippant irrationalism to form our awareness of the "contradictory identity of universal and particular."[41] The tension between the particular and the abstract universal no longer resorts to sense-certainty as the alpha and omega of thought. What Hegel brazenly calls "dialectics" begins from sense-certainty of the "this" which is immediately present, and which carries "meaning" (*meinen*) to ultimately return to terra firma once again in the form of a universal spiritual subject. In the *kōan/kenshō* dialectic, the process of self-seeing opens into sunyata, an emptiness of all intrinsic nature.

BLUT AND BODEN ("BLOOD AND SOIL"): THE FASCIST ETHOS

Carl Schmitt, whose writings were the basis of the fascist ethos, had this to say in his book *Land and Sea*:

> The order of the firm land consists in its division into state dominions; the high sea is free, i.e., state-free and subject to the authority of no state dominion. These are the basic spatial facts, out of which the Christian-European law of peoples developed in the last three hundred years. This is the basic law, the nomos of the earth in this epoch.

Schmitt, whose work focused on the politics of *Blut and Boden*, "blood and soil," summarized his work as such: "I leave it to the attentive reader to find in my exertions the beginning of an attempt to bring to fulfillment this §247 in a way similar to that in which §§243-246 was brought to fulfillment in Marxism."[42]

The passages referenced by Carl Schmitt, the philosophy of which he would like to bring into fulfillment via fascism, was the Hegelian *Philosophy of Right*, and the penultimate passage §247 deals with the "terra firma" or the power to control land. Hegel's passage begins as:

> "The principle of family life is dependence on the soil, on land, *terra firma*."[43]

Hence, the battle to control the earth, the soil, and territorial power is purely fascist! Thus, the way to read the third volume of *Capital* is as a deconstruction of "ground rent" and what would later become appropriated into the fascist ethos of *Blut and Boden*. Connecting volk on the same soil is believed to connect one family with the same bloodline, and the volk are called to shed blood to protect territory. Hence, Marx and Engels call for workers of the world to unite should not be conflated with any sort of fascist nationalism. Terra firma also takes a psychological sense of evoking a conservative certainty about what is true and correct, epistemologically speaking, and yet Schmitt's point is that the modern development of advanced technology and trade must be accompanied by a political power that projects state power out into the open seas. Echoing Hegel who examines the development of European colonial powers as compared with societies who had not embraced sea-faring trade.

While the *Grundrisse* shows us the gradual process of capital taking ownership of land and pushing farmers and workers from land to subsume all aspects of "ground rent," volumes two and three of *Capital* are really interesting, albeit much much less optimistic. Marx goes full throttle into a critique that he could not finish because the depths were too deep! He was digging deeply into "falling rate of profit" and "ground rent" and the capitalist labyrinth, in my mind, becomes something that is inescapable and yet terrifyingly doomed to fail! There are only two ways to spend "profit" (surplus-value)—by putting it back into circulation and production or by consumption (food, clothing, "fun," etc.). Hence, production is extremely, extremely wasteful and forms a kind of black hole that eventually tears down everything.

KENOSIS AND THE STATE

As a temporary apparatus of mediation, the state can temporarily enact a process of "kenosis" or God's self-emptying. In understanding the religious signifiers of a given society, the religious beliefs, from a Marxist perspective, offer an ideological escape from real suffering on earth. Karl Marx's best analysis of how the state functions as a sort of ideologically driven political theology is offered in the now oft-ignored essay "the Jewish Question" and in my opinion, there are some semblances and some provocative differences in the way Nishida writes about religion and the state in his last published work "*Bashoteki ronri to shukyoteki sekaikan*" (*the Logic of the Place of Nothingness and the Religious Worldview*).

Nishida's last lines in his final essay can possibly be seen as a last homage to Pure Land (*Jōdo*) Buddhism synthesized with Mahayana and Zen. In some regards, this interpretation has evoked a sense that Nishida was defining his philosophy in much broader terms. In 1944, he began to characterize his work in much wider terms as "Buddhistic."[44] This later turn to Pure Land has been ignored by critics who would like to pose Nishida as the Zen philosopher in juxtaposition to Tanabe Hajime who is cast as the True Pure Land philosopher within the Kyoto School. However, what if in taking into account the historical circumstances right after World War II, with Nishida being such a close reader of Marx. Nishida still is the penultimate Zen philosopher and utilizes Pure Land to construct a radical critique of the State. In a post-fascist Japan immediately following the war, his last writings give an eerily critical, perhaps even antagonistic, approach to the state and the notion that Buddhist philosophy had been appropriated into violence because the state (in being a static homogenizing entity, unable to admit the contingency of its own existence) tramples on "personal will" much like the numerous descriptions throughout his last essays of particular types of homogenizing religious institutions.

The last several lines of the concluding paragraphs in Nishida's final essay read:

合は容易に考へられるが、仏教は、従来非国家的とも考へ

translated as "Buddhism has traditionally been considered apolitical."

"A fusion of the Christianity of God as Lord with the nation may easily be contemplated; but this is less easily contemplated with respect to Buddhism, which in the past has even been regarded as apolitical."

He continues by citing a passage from his colleague D. T. Suzuki on the assembled throngs in this world, who venerate the Buddha as the center of their religious life, and

> see the Pure Land, so too this world is seen by the assembled throngs who have already attained the Pure Land. This corrupt world reflects the Pure Land, and the Pure Land reflects this corrupt world. They are mutually reflecting mirrors. This points to the interconnectedness, or oneness, of the Pure Land and this corrupt world. I think I am able to conceive of the nation in these terms. The nation is the mirror image of the Pure Land in this world.

Let me be clear about my reading of this: this is not a resounding endorsement of Pure Land Buddhism. Let me repeat, anywhere there is a state, the state serves the sole purpose of penning people in on the land, the state is nothing more than an apparatus of capture, a war machine. When Nishida penned these lines, he was living through the last days of World War II. Given that historical context, it would be too bizarre to think that Nishida, having seen such devastation, death, and destruction as a result of nationalism, would then make a pro-nation-state declaration as his last publication. When the nation is the mirror image of the pure land in the world, it is precisely this principle of identity, the principle of equality that produces the sort of non-reflective citizens that are amenable to fascism.

Pure land is oneness with land and the "utopian" vision of heaven, and let us consider Nishitani Keiji's assertion about Nishida's views on the state as an accurate description of Nishida's beliefs. Then, perhaps this final statement is not an assertion that the nation is the mirror image of the Pure Land in this world, and that this is a positive assertion about Pure Land. If the "Pure Land reflects this corrupt world" then there is an antagonism inherent in the pure land that a simplistic-oneness with the state resolves into fascist-identity. When the state ascends to the role of the religious identity for the people, which happened under State-Shintoism, then there are fascist ideologies afoot. Therefore, some separation between self and state must be preserved so that the personal will is not completely destroyed. Perhaps consider Nishida's distinction between "life" and "bios" where he claims:

> Each pulsation of life, each formation of life, perishes, while the organism or the biological world endures. In this fashion the biological world is always moving,

from the formed to the forming, within the structure of the contradictory identity of the many and the one. It is an infinite process of transformation. Living beings are dynamically formative, organic. That is why the biological world is conceivable in teleological terms.

STATE WILL AS ALIEN WILL

"Freedom consists in converting the state from an organ superimposed upon society into one completely subordinate to it; and today, too, the forms of state are more free or less free to the extent that they restrict the freedom of the state."[45]

Why do many among the working class resent the government? Why are the working classes so easily manipulated into anti-state laissez-faire capitalism? Marx puts forward two rather straightforward theses: "State will = alien will to my will"[46] and "Private property = egotistical property"[47] and within a society whose sole experience is with private-egotistical property, communism is quite incomprehensible. "Communists do not oppose egoism to selflessness or selflessness to egoism. . . . (communists) rather demonstrate (egoism's) material source, with which it disappears of itself."[48] Change the material source of property and egoism withers away. Since the "private individual" and private property are the historical and contemporary a priori conditions, then: what is called the "general interest" is constantly being produced by the other side, "private interest."[49]

NOTES

1. Vladimir Lenin. *State and Revolution.*
2. Karl Marx. *Contribution to the Critique of Hegel's Philosophy of Right.*
3. Nishida Kitarō. *Nothingness and the Religious Worldview.* John Krummel translates the title of Nishida's last published work "Bashoteki ronri to shūkyōteki sekaikan" as *The Logic of Place and the Religious Worldview*, so the translation of the title is a bit slippery in English. Clearly, it harkens back to his work on basho and the nothingness of place.
4. Frederich Engels. *The Origin of the Family, Private Property, and the State.* Chapter IX—Barbarism and Civilization. Pg. 158.
5. Georg Wilhelm Hegel. *Preface to Philosophy of Right.* Oxford: London, 1962. Pg. 13.
6. Michiko Yusa. *Zen and Philosophy: An Intellectual Biography of Nishida Kitarō.* Pg. 210.
7. Elise Tipton. *The Japanese Police State: Tokkō in Interwar Japan.* Bloomsbury Academic: London, 2012.

8. Kosuke Shimizu. "Nishida Kitaro and Japan's Interwar Foreign Policy: War Involvement and Culturalist Political Discourse." *International Relations of the Asia-Pacific* 11, no. 1 (2011).

9. For the condensed version of this western epistemological tendency to gravitate power/knowledge toward a metaphysical focalized point, see: Pg. 257–268. "The Discovery of the Archimedean Point" in Hannah Arendt's *The Human Condition*.

10. Marx. *The German Ideology*. Pg. 54.

11. Nishida Kitarō. *Expressive Activity*. Pg. 41.

12. Michel Foucault. *Discipline and Punish*. Pg. 200.

13. Karl Marx. *The German Ideology*. Prometheus Books, 1998. Pg. 161.

14. Nishida Kitarō. *Intelligibility and the Philosophy of Nothingness*. 1927.

15. An appropriation from the *German Ideology*, a World-Historical-Consciousness.

16. NKZ 11:457.

17. Nishida Kitarō. "Expressive Activity." In *Ontology of Production: Three Essays*. Pg. 39.

18. *Grundrisse*. Pg. 702.

19. Michel Foucault. *Discipline and Punish*. Pg. 3.

20. Gilles Deleuze and Felix Guattari. "7,000 B.C. Apparatus of Capture." *A Thousand Plateaus*. Pg. 497.

21. Michel Foucault. *The Order of Things*. Pg. 262.

22. Karl Marx. *Capital Volume 3*, Chapter 48, the Trinity Formula. Translated by David Fernbach, Penguin: New York, 1981. Pg. 953.

23. Not my term. Felix Guattari utilizes this concept in his *Anti-Oedipus Notebooks*.

24. For a discussion of this see Michel Foucault's lectures on Psychiatric Power at the College de France in 1973–74. the lectures on November 21, 1973, in specific even though this methodology is introjected throughout the lectures and Foucault's oeuvre of collected publications.

25. See my "Politics is an Illusion We Have Forgotten is an Illusion." In *Fast Capitalism*. 9.1 2012 Special Issue on Occupy.

26. Dharma Chakra, Ashoka Chakra on the flag of India that went from a spinning wheel to a pulsing wheel that effervesces life out of an eternal source, the center of which is emptiness, twenty-four spokes share one hub, and the concept of which is based on the twelve stages of dependent origination and the two sides to each stage.

27. Marx. *Economic Philosophical Manuscripts of 1844*. Private Property and Communism. Pg. 135. This is obviously taken from the early Marx whereas Louis Althusser correctly points out, he had yet to form his "epistemological break" from humanism. Marx is a bit of a romantic here positing a fully human "essence" and giving a description of communism as a return to some prelapsarian utopia, a primal state where perhaps we forget that the horrors of modernity ever occurred.

28. Not that Nishida is categorically Buddhist, nor that it is possible to categorize Buddhism in such narrow terms, yet, some have argued that Buddhism can be cultivated so as to be amenable to fascist ideologies. The book *Zen at War* by Daizen Victoria makes a similar thesis.

29. Last line to the last work written by Nishida Kitarō.

30. Nishida Kitarō, *Sekai shin chitsujo no genri, Nishidan Kikkotekki*, volume 8.
31. Nishida Kitarō, *Ningenteki Sonzai*, 1938.
32. John Krummel. *Nishida Kitarō's: Chiasmatic Chorology: Place of Dialectic, Dialectic of Place*. Indiana University Press: Indianapolis. Pg. 119.
33. Hakuin. *Chant in Praise of Zazen* (sometimes translated as "Song" however, the choice to translate that as chant provides the meditational overtones of solemnity, reverence, and seriousness with which Hakuin wants us to attune ourselves to being fully present in the world, now, in order to see the pure land in its immediacy.
34. Wu-Men's response to Koan #48 in the *Gateless Barrier*, compiled by Robert Aitken.
35. Hakuin. *Song of Zazen*.
36. Nishida Kitarō. *Last Writings: Nothingness and the Religious Worldview*. Pg. 92. There are problems with the David Dilworth translation, but these lines are easier to track down for the lay reader as the translation is more widely available than the text in the original pre-World War II Kanji.
37. Ibid. Pg.92.
38. Ibid. Pg. 92.
39. Ibid. Pg. 108.
40. Ibid.
41. Ibid.
42. Carl Schmitt. *Land and Sea*.
43. Hegel. *Philosophy of Right*. §247.
44. Nishida Kitarō *zenshu*, volume 10. Pg.59.
45. Karl Marx. *Critique of the Gotha Program*. Part 4.
46. Ibid. Pg. 350.
47. Ibid. Pg.370.
48. Ibid. Pg. 264.
49. Ibid. Pg. 264.

Chapter 5

Nishida Kitarō and the Later Marx
Ground Rent, Utopia, and the Pure Land

I am not the first to forward this thesis. Kobayashi Toshiaki concluded that the formulation of the central concepts in Nishida's philosophy of history—"dialectics," "poiesis," and "active intuition,"—would not be thinkable without understanding Nishida's profound engagement with the writings of the later Marx.[1]

William Haver writes in the introduction to his translation of three key essays from Nishida Kitarō:

> Nishida's most explicit engagement with Marx is in *Human Being*. Although he could not name Marx, it is clear that he was reading volume one of *Capital*, the *1844 Manuscripts*, and the *Theses on Feuerbach* . . . in Nishida's later work there are sustained rigorous engagements with Marx's problematic, and that there are profound agreements with Marx, who never abandoned philosophy, least of all in *Capital*.[2]

How did concepts derived from Marx influence Nishida's philosophy of basho, Zettai Mu, Mu No Jikakuteki Gentei, and the Pure Land? It is clear that if Nishida had been reading the *1844 Manuscripts*, then he was aware of the notes on Rent of Land, and the five types of communism that Marx outlines in those notebooks. I tried to give readers a context for the theses on communism in chapter 3: "What Is Communism? Mu!" These topics are analyzed in much greater detail by Marx in the three volumes of *Capital*, especially the unfinished third volume where there Marx's concerted attention is given over almost entirely to the use of land. This chapter attempts to look at the later Marx and the pure land as it occurs in the work of Nishida, again, this is more of a hermeneutical exercise, a speculative fiction rather than an objective veridical correction of sorts. Marx and Nishida differ on several points, each with their own style and brilliance; however, there is a way in which, throughout this book, I attempt to insert my own thinking into these hypothetical "round table"[3] discussions as Michel Foucault called it.

In a way, the idea is again one part detective work and one part science fiction narrative. Snooping around to figure out if the concept of "ground rent" influenced Nishida's last lines that the nation amounts to "corrupting the pure land" in one of the last lines that Nishida ever wrote in bashoteki ronri to shukyoteki sekaikan (*Nothingness and the Religious Worldview*, 1945). David Dilworth's translation might be a little misleading in that it reads, "The nation is the mirror image of the Pure Land in this world."[4] But in the Japanese original, this is a prescription, not a description, reading: "The nation ought to be the mirror image of the Pure Land in this world." A Marxist reading might make sense if you look at the Japanese original. It reads more Marxist than Hegelian. Rather than the nation already being the embodiment of the Absolute Geist, it ought to be what realizes our hopes and dreams. I think Nishida recognized that it's not necessarily so but that it should be so. The nation ought to realize the Pure Land in this world; therefore, the normative aspects of Marx's work on the Ground Rent in the third volume of *Capital* may give us supple ground, if I may, to find affinities between the utopian vision of the pure land, as described by Nishida and the Marxist project of freeing property relations to make that a reality on earth, especially the land.

"It is because of Marx, that sleep comes hard to me."—Nishida Kitaro

"Control: Giving your sheep a limitless pasture to roam is the way to control them."—an old Zen saying.

NISHIDA KITARŌ AND THE LATER MARX

The metaphysics of "interdependent arising" implies a level of give-and-take, trust, and compassion. In earlier chapters, I looked at the ways to understand interdependent arising through the syllogism of production, distribution, and consumption, and then a detailed analysis of the state. If we are connected, then what happens on the production side if a supply chain is affected by demands on the other side, and vice versa. States are formations of "ego" in trying to claim territory out of a fear-based set of intentions. Why must a group carve out a territory for themselves unless that group feared that it could be lost? The whole basis of countries is to keep what you think is yours and to cling to the false idea that militarism can keep people safe by protecting property from theft. What states cannot understand is that all property is theft. Compassion cannot develop ethical edicts based on territorial imperatives. This is the thesis in the "state" chapter of this book, which will be furthered here in a close reading of ground rent and pure land.

Later in life after retiring from his professorship at Kyoto Imperial University, the fully mature philosophy of Nishida Kitarō emerged. In retirement, he had a clearing of time, a stipend, and no other professional obligations to distract him. His wife recently passed, and he spent many nights alone or debating with students and colleagues into the dark night. Nishida immersed himself in his deepest period of philosophical meditation. His close friend Nishitani Keiji wrote that Nishida was experiencing a "great turning point" and "the undiminished enthusiasm he showed for carrying on research after being freed from academic obligations"[5] had long abated. There he sat, in deep contemplation, donning a morose calm about his way.

According to the recollections of his student Nishitani Keiji, Nishida often sat quietly while guests at his home conversed deep into the night. Ruminating on the trajectory of world history and the impending wars, seeing his name smeared in a leftist magazine called *Senki* (War Banner) that ran a lead article that proclaimed the time was finally right to pulverize "Nishida's philosophy theoretically and practically."[6] Nishida grappled deeply with questions concerning the problem of thoughtless-Marxist-praxis. Keyword "thoughtless" happened to latch onto an authoritarian view of communism missed the opportunities for mindfulness in meditating on to expand upon the insightful critiques of capitalism offered by the philosophy of Karl Marx.

For example, earlier in the introduction to this book, I pointed out that this may have been a major mistake made by revolutionaries. Particularly, Mao Tse Tung missed an opportunity for engagement with neo-Confucian philosophies such as those by Mencius' *Niu Mountain* that may have provided mindfulness practices amenable to an eco-communist project.

To show his care toward these writings and the draconian tactics used by those claiming to be inspired by Marx, he composed a haiku that reads: "It is because of Marx, that sleep comes hard to me."[7] As Nishitani Keiji tells us in the biography of his teacher, Nishida was serious when he wrote that haiku. Nishida still invited students and colleagues to his home and the discussions would stretch deep into the night, and because of the rapidly changing politics in Japan, it forced his attention onto the philosophy of Marx. In *"Zen No Kenkyu"* there are glimmers of engagement with Marx. As I show in earlier chapters, however, those engagements always seemed to resolve into a sort of phenomenology and psychological explanation of pure experience. Whereas, in his later writings Nishida shifts to an overt materialist methodology. Although often concealed and insinuated rather than explicitly stated, the influence is clear. Some have argued that the reason why Nishida could not be forthright about the influence of Marx on his work was that he was under careful scrutiny from censors.

With the work of the Young Marx widely published in 1932 and the later works of Marx, such as the second and third volumes of *Capital*, and the *Critique of the Gotha Program* not yet widely circulated in Kanji, it is tough to make the case that Nishida had read Marx in translation. Nishida was definitely fluent in German and read Heidegger, Nietzsche, and many other works in German. With the recent translations of three key essays from the 1920s to 1930s, you can see that throughout his 1935 essay, *The Standpoint of Active Intuition*, he utilizes words like "space-time" and "external qua internal, internal qua external"; clearly, an attempt is made to provoke a challenge to a common understanding of what the philosophy of Marx ought to be and well into the Japanese occupation of Manchuria which began in 1931, and with Nishida himself being remarried in 1931 he began to move away from the psychologism of his earlier works into a new era in his work.

This was to critically engage the false binary between being and nothingness. Some of his attempts to move beyond the positions staked out in his 1911 work *An Inquiry into the Good*, which he later admitted relied too heavily on William James' conceptions of "pure experience." Do we attune to the historical or the philosophical methods offered by the juxtaposition of Marx and Nishida? Due to the limitations of the space allotted this has to be understood as an opening salvo rather than a conclusive statement on the matter, but as Slavoj Žižek's famous joke goes: "We have a choice between postmodernism and class consciousness. The answer is yes please!" The choice between historical materialist and philosophical readings is actually a non-choice. We can have both. As I tried to show in the earlier sections on "Marx Beyond Kant," "Marx Beyond Hegel," historical materialism does not need to rely upon Kantian pure apperception and a linear, teleological understanding of historical cause and effect as moving like dominoes in historical succession from one stage to the next until something resembling a "communist utopia" emerges. In the earlier writings from Marx, *the 1844 Notebooks*, there is definitely a categorical way that Marx plots out five stages of communism.[8] Engels has a horrifying pamphlet[9] that should raise eyebrows for its xenophobic statements, echoed in the *Communist Manifesto* that communism would require the confiscation of the property of emigrants and enemies of the majority, and of course his *Socialism: Utopian and Scientific*. Of course, by the 1930s Lenin had died, and the rise of communism has transitioned into Stalinism. Japan and the Soviet Union were embroiled in many border conflicts throughout the 1930s. "Marxism" is not this theoretical hypothesis for Nishida and his colleagues at the time. Communists are looming adversaries—yet, the thought of Marx is still something that Nishida and his students Tosaka Jun and Miki Kiyoshi took very seriously.

By virtue of his Zen background, Nishida holds a completely different metaphysical approach to the being of beings, not as anticipation of some *"futur anterieur*" as "communism will be here, after late capitalism" as-yet-to-come of the communist idea; however, as the *sayō* activity not as a return to an essence but in the essence of what it is now. Mu! As the nothingness of unexpected truth that smacks the subject with the shock of the uncanny, because it opens awareness of a boundless open sea beyond apperception, beyond a return to the stable ground of what is already "known," let loose from the terra firma.

Perhaps this standard did not go far enough in the deconstruction of the metaphysics of value, due to placing nothingness as a subsidiary of the a priori of being. God is prior to the production of beings. God is allegedly omniscient, omnipresent, and omnipotent, and therefore always is, was, and will be forever. God is understood to be an eternal presence. Therefore, the timeless and eternal nature of being can be relied on because life sprung from an eternal source. Life comes from God and God will not let life end. In this way, there is no real sense of change, just the repetition of the same, because that would require a sense of place, spaciousness, and temporality. Awareness of change immanent within consciousness can only occur at the cusp of the perceptible, and yet, to truly know when a border exists, one would have to traverse both sides, which is impossible.

Temporally, things change, and yet we can never know for sure if there always already is being prior to nothingness. In substituting this logic of Being creating beings, you wind up with a metaphysics of money based on the same absurd metaphysics. As if money is an intrinsic purveyor of wealth rather than a symbol of social arrangements representing the inequality of exchange value.

Money cannot ground itself in value, as if money were valuable as a thing-in-itself, as if money were a value-conducting-being. In fact, it is the opposite. Money is not a cause of power. Rather it is an effect of power. Marx explains this throughout the third volume of *Capital*, which unfortunately he did not have a chance to finish before dying. He did claim that money is commonly understood as a form of exchange for wages from capital as a payment on labor power, and as a price placed on commodities, which constitute the two most common uses for money among the working class who, Marx explains correctly, are trapped in a kind of hamster wheel of possessing nothing of value to sell besides their labor power, commonly bound up in the body of the laborer (the mind or body, intellectual or kinetic power). However, the other use of money beyond means of payment on tangible commodities is the means of circulation and means of purchase for other forms of capital, in other words, methods of accumulating through investment, building stock portfolios, hedge-funds, ownership shares in corporations, and so forth.[10] Slavoj Zizek has been most outspoken against what he calls "frictionless capital"[11] where the accumulation of capital need no longer rely on the realization of production in a tangible product.[12]

In fact, in the Zen tradition nothingness is neither being nor nothingness, the dialectical pairing of being and presence, or basho rather than being, the place of the nothing (basho no mu) as Nishida developed this concept of nothingness. An egoless notion of the nothing. Nothing does not reflexively return back to "Me"; the "I"; nothingness is not the bothersome meddling onto which even God cannot cling.

No, the place (basho) of the nothing gives nothingness a groundless ground. The political ideologies presenting themselves as a true "communist ontology" never take this perspective into account. In other words, nothingness is grounded in the commons and the commons are groundless ground.

Nishida Kitarō describes the indescribable. Using terms like space, time, nothingness, being, his work has been viewed as influenced by Chan Buddhism which stems from the dialectic of "form is void, void is form" thesis as stated in the Heart Sutra.[13] As I tried to show in an earlier chapter, for Nishida the self is an epiphenomenal after effect formed from experience. Me-ontology of the subject is the study of nothingness with the being of beings as interdependent upon nothingness rather than dialectically opposed—you must understand the Buddhist view of conditioned coproduction to fully "get" the me-ontology that everything arises in connection with something else.

"Actually, existing space must be the mediation that mutually relates singularity and singularity together; it must be the mediation of the continuity of discontinuity."[14] Because of the temporal, changing nature of time, this definition of actually existing space gives us a perfect definition of conditioned coproduction—and in the definition of basho from Nishida, readers may see parallels with some continental philosophers "smooth and striated space" (ala Deleuze and Guattari)—"the singular-plural" (ala Jean Luc Nancy and Maurice Blanchot)—"continuity of discontinuity" (ala Bataille) Foucault's Nietzschean genealogy, and the definition of communism as written by Karl Marx in the *German Ideology* as "the flourishing of the individual as correlated to the flourishing of the community"; not that the community squashes the unique individuality of the "singularity" as in fascism, but that the community is established in such a way where individuality enhances the community, individuality is integral with non-alienating social relations, rather than differential, competitive, and violent (as in capitalism). Fascism is not only a thing but a social relation between persons mediated through the space between persons and things.

As Pierre Lavelle describes this in his article *The Political Thought of Nishida Kitarō*, there was a paranoia about those who might individuate from the official state-logos at the time. Under the imperial regime, 1868–1945, anyone involved in politics was obliged to position himself in relation to official doctrine, which itself formed a part of the imperial doctrine (*tennō ideorogii*), the official teaching combined a Shinto mythico-historical conception of legitimacy, a Confucian-based morality, and Western-type law.

Its central dogma was kokutai, which can be translated as national polity, national entity, or, even better, "national organism."[15] How might "nothingness" factor in as a political conception? In effect, nothingness is that which cannot be reified. Therefore, if the central dogma was building momentum toward the telos of a national entity, a oneness, and the fascist ontology necessitated a unified-objective (a unified-objectification of its subjects), then the nothingness described as "continuity of discontinuity" may perhaps indicate a social-political drift toward singularity, if singularity involves the becoming singular, the ontological movement of an exception to the general form laid out by the state as the national oneness of the time.

Obviously, not every individuating impulse is anti-fascist, because fascism often gives a home to loners, the anomic, by grounding the atomizing process of individuation in fascist unity. This sort of grounding is one of the most prominent features of fascist interpellation using race, "land and soil," and nationalist propaganda.

Nishida's last publication ends on a resounding note that affirms this point and brings an "idiocy of rural life" sort of criticism to Pure Land Buddhism:

> This corrupt world reflects the Pure Land, and the Pure Land reflects the corrupt world. They are mutually reflecting mirrors. This points to the interconnectedness, or oneness, of the Pure Land and this corrupt world. I think I am able to conceive of the nation in these terms. The nation is the mirror image of the Pure Land in this world.[16]

Obviously, there are connotations with consciousness as produced by material conditions; if material conditions are nature (i.e., the pure land) and consciousness is the general intellect as reflected back in the sovereignty of the nation. However, what is this "corrupt" that Nishida has to put in the sentence? Something is out of joint, alien, something is wrong, even in the Pure Land and its unreflective identification with state ideologies.

Nothingness is the gap between beings and therefore beings are constituted on the basis of their relation as mediated by nothingness (i.e., space between things), and not being and its "other" as an invisible void (which is true to some extent, but without the understanding of the invisible void of the other who is subjected to violence as mediated by a nothingness that becomes problematic, then this dialectic between being and nothingness remains overly simplistic. "I" and "You" have to be two separate entities as mediated by the spaces between us and that space is what mediates our mutual understanding of one another. There can be an intuition of space (not just an intuition of time)—and this space between beings is what mediates our relationship—to produce an enemy, and to mistake the spaces between beings as alienating is one way of perhaps interpreting the Buddha's first noble truth: "there is suffering" or, rather, there is *dukkha (a more literal rendering of dukkha is perhaps separation, suffering, being out of joint, alienated from)*, rather than as Nishida writes upon discovering his conclusions that time is circular: "what is called the actually existing world can be thought . . . as the world of the mediation of discontinuity, as the world of the dialectical universal."[17]

Dialectics can only ever be a thought of oneness, because dialectical methods rely on a representational method based on apperception, or the assimilation of new knowledge into what is already known by the subject; hence, the problem with taking a dialectical approach to Marx is precisely the assimilation of "communism" into what is allegedly known about "communism" (the horrors of the gulags, state repression, and so forth); the "other side" of the dialectic is constituted as an other that still relies on a shared sense of the Universality of nothingness and space—when space is the affirmation of the non-substantial consciousness of time (the external relation is dialectically antithetical to the internal intuition) and time is the affirmation of the non-substantial consciousness of space (the internal intuition is dialectically understood as antithetical to and yet, synthesized with the external world), then these ontological experiences are actually existing as internal qua external, external qua internal, space qua time, time qua space.

Space or basho is not merely the place in which things are laid out, the space between entity and entity. Basho is rather the means by which the arising of all things becomes possible. It is the Zen way of meditating on the problem of why there is something rather than nothing. Zen offers the solution that there is no distinguishing between something rather than nothing, because something and nothing are mutually binding. Existence not an either/or question.

If connections are understood to exist between two substantial, physical entities then there will always be an insurmountable gap, an epistemological gap between two separate entities. One entity cannot fully connect with another substantial entity without becoming a different entity, losing its uniqueness in the connection with another entity. Epistemologically there would be a gap because one entity can never fully know what it is to be another entity. For example, it is impossible to see behind someone else's eyes. However, if we understand connectedness as the nothingness between entities, that which connects us is insubstantial, non-physical, and immaterial.

Yet, in my understanding of Buddhist philosophy on this notion of emptiness and nothingness there are two different notions here, but both resort to an understanding of space as containing and connecting entities rather than driving objects apart. Even within the nothingness, there is a cosmic field that connects and unifies all things. Therefore, the notion of "detachment" (i.e., one of the most important of the Buddha's famous Four Noble Truths); you have a detachment from our flawed experience of ourselves as substantial, physical entities and meditating on this "detachment" brings the awareness of a deeper, more profound sense of connectedness deriving from our shared experience through space and time. That is, in other words, all beings are beings that must exist in space and time and there is a relief in finding full awareness of the temporal nature of existence as a substantial being.

As the Buddha surmised there are three marks of existence: the three characteristics that apply to everything in the natural order are impermanence (anicca), suffering (dukkha), and the absence of permanent identity or a soul (anatta). Buddha was not necessarily essentializing these facts of existence, but rather positing these experiences as pre-reflective forms of consciousness. Unless awareness is cultivated these facts of life will not even appear to the mind. Nothing in nature is identical to what it was the moment before, if there is repetition, it is the repetition of change, temporality, and difference. Form is void, void is form, because the form of a thing is empty, its content can differentiate as time passes. If a form changes content so drastically that it differentiates from itself, it may become unrecognizable as the prior form.

It is important to note that difference is understood as something other than "negation"; because negation would mean the death of one's ego rather than two entities at war with one another. Self-negation (jiko hitei) means the death of the ego. The only way to fully understand God.

Accordingly, when the Buddha says in the Heart Sutra: "Form is Void, Void is Form," and that the "Five Skandhas are empty," what he is revealing are the limitations of our sense perception. There are limitations in the five skandhas (the five senses are sight, sound, taste, smell, touch) in fully understanding the nature of reality because reality itself contains no intrinsic meaning, nor is nature contingent upon our subjective awareness of it.

Self-negation is not a dialectic of inner-conflict between self and true self where the Cartesian dualism is internalized to pit self against self. Rather, self-negation means that the self always arises from nothingness. Self-awareness means self-awareness of nothingness as the source of all. In a society that prioritizes being as the origin of everything (God exists eternally, gets bored, and creates more beings to torture), nothingness is the a priori in Zen metaphysics, so self-negation brings the self closer to self. "Being" is that which dances upon the prior zettai mu, a point developed further in the chapter on basho.

Nishida writes:

> In order to say that thing and thing relate mutually, there must be something called a mediation. Yet if that mediation is thought as continuity, there is no mutual interaction. What is mediated is mediated to the extent that it possesses

the characteristics of what it mediates . . . the fact that thing and thing are mediated spatially, they mutually interact; but we can say that thing and thing mutually interact . . . to the extent that the thing possesses the characteristics of space.[18]

An allusion to Zeno's Paradox: if thing and thing mutually interact to the extent that they are mediated by space, then interaction does not entail the implication of contact between two things; for two entities to interact there must be an inter-relation between two entities, but in order for there to be two entities there will always be a space (or spaces) between those two entities—for fascist ontology, that gap, that Otherness, is something that although impossible must be conquered, because that gap is what constitutes the limit of state power over its subjects and others, and provokes fear, worry, anxiety, dread.

In The space of nothing cannot be transformed because nothing has no form. Yet, the modus operandi of fascism in its reaction toward this "gap" is to oversee the nothing as something to conquer, and active intuition must be understood as an integral qua differential, universal qua singular aspect of the world as understood to be a dialectical universal.

"If we see things on the basis of intentional action; the thing determines the self, and the self-determines the thing. And that is active intuition."[19]

It is not a subject that creates itself in reaction to repression, or external power, where there is a subject with superior knowledge that can then condescend and tell the destitute subject how things truly are for them, but the subject is an active subject that creates a subject perspective on its object as it would like that object to be. Hence, the ontology of active intuition is never alienated from itself (ala Marxism). Nishida gives us something unique, trust in the subject to think actively, non-infantilizing the workers as needing the vanguard revolutionary to bring revolution to workers.

Nishida continues:

If force is conceived to be what moves the self from the outside, then what we call the self disappears. . . . If we think of impulsivity as the unconscious, or the self as something like an animal instinct, then there is no self. If we consider the self as what is unconscious, then we think it to mean merely the negation of consciousness, then there is no self. The self must be absolutely that which itself determines itself. The self must be free; therein is the significance of the fact that we act consciously.[20]

His rebuking of Marxism (as understood as consciousness passively, falsely constructed by material conditions) and psychoanalysis (as understood as consciousness as its negation in the unconscious at the driver's seat of human actions); and offering a different way, an autonomous way.

Nishida continues by critiquing the Western ontology of "self as something like a singularity construed as the determination of the universal,"[21] as a small part that must fit into a general form, the legacy of Plato. Time factors in because in that sense of ontology: "The acting thing is thought as the self-determination of temporal space in which instants are arrayed simultaneously"—instead, Nishida is thinking of "self-determination in a dialectical world." If action is grounded in prior conditions that condition and structure the acting self, then: "to say a thing acts is necessarily to say that the thing negates the thing itself."[22] Unless "the actually existing world is always singular . . . according to physics, simultaneous instants tend to be construed as an infinite number of points; that is, they tend to be construed spatially."[23]

I think this goes to a point that Eastern Metaphysics is starting from a completely different sense of nature than the West, and therefore, saying that "consciousness is conditioned by prior material conditions" means that truth can still have a touch of the mystical, a sense of chaotic uncertainty, unknown and the silent unnamed of the Tao, than post-Enlightenment Western philosophers who view nature as something to be mastered, penetrated (as the idealist philosopher George Berkeley said in an off the cuff remark somewhere), and in the West nature is understood only as something to be turned into "standing reserve," a resource to support human economics.

Hence, there are no round trips in time, yet time is not just a linear construct; if time is just a linear construct, then it would only march forward like an army conquering the future. Circular time (based much more on a Vedic, rather than Abrahamic understanding of time) provided by Nishida Kitarō gives us a new sense of anti-fascist ontology. Because of our experience of time, the phenomenology of time is as Nishida points out: "moving from past to future."[24]

Continually passing from instant to instant, restless, never completely sitting still, this provocation of the being of beings, this restlessness is indicative of something resembling the cusp of a fascist ontology, restlessness, never feeling at-home in the place where you are, constantly trying to improve and project into the future resisted through the stillness of (perhaps) the unspokenness of the Tao, the quiet of the Sitting-Yoga/meditation (the irony is that now, with computers, cellphones, tablets, and entertainment galore, folks project into the future and have all these amazing adventures while sitting in one place for most of their lives).

> Time is thought as the form of an internal experience; internal experience is thought to come into being on the basis of the unity of time. . . . the self is a dialectical being. There is neither the past without a future nor a future without

the past. We cannot conceive of the self without recollection, but neither is there any recollection without anticipation of the future.[25]

Since the self is a kind of dialectical being, the brain projects the kind of order that the self creates for it as a world-image, a spatial-time image, a world as a picture, as picturing, projecting, and mapping onto the future, but for Nishida, it is a discontinuity rather than merely an extension of the present, there is the possibility for rupture to occur, hence the nothingness of the future is presented as "mu"—an explosive nothing, a nothing that can, at any moment, transform into a satori/enlightenment moment. Politically this might be what some on the left have called an "event." This may be viewed as irrational based on state-ordered political action, but it is necessary to disrupt the continuity of the transcendental thrust of fascism in its occupational tendencies.

Time cannot be reified, only temporarily as fear ossified into an object, that is, ideology and resentment are always reactionary, on the defensive, and cannot eternally numb the anxiety of daily life by providing the nothing with an object to fear. Anxiety that projects onto an object will eventually return to anxiety once the object is removed (i.e., the boogey man of this or that enemy of the state). Fear may also solidify into paranoia and take on the ideology of a permanent state of being (which, look around, the US is there already in many regards, the constant surveillance). Yet, this is an almost completely Western construct based on metaphysics that provokes being into a state of worry when confronted with the nothing.

Zen is an assemblage that arises out of the context of Vedic philosophy and is a manifestation of Buddhist enlightenment practices specific to Japan. To understand and be comfortable with the nothing one has to understand the metaphysics of nothing as the Zen metaphysics understands nothing. Nothing is prior to being and non-being is different than nothingness as an existential non-entity. Hence there are dozens of words for nothing in Japanese and this shows a comfortability, commonality to the notion of the nothing, rather than anxiety-inducing terror.

If the Abrahamic religions (Judaism, Christianity, and Islam) build a metaphysics upon fear and nervous anxiety toward nothing, the nothing may not be an issue for Vedic religions (Hindu, Buddhist, Taoist, Confucianism, Shinto). Nirvana literally means the moment when the funeral pyre is extinguished upon the cremation of the dead body (the only true moment when desire can be completely extinguished). These are both (to some extent) self-negating, Nishida gives us a third way.

"Mu" as an explosive, revolutionary sense of the nothing, provokes radical change—that is, Satori, instant awakening! Total shift in ontology that explodes out of the nothingness, the stillness of time, and not as a recollection or representation of a prior memory (perhaps?!?) but a redirection of the flow of time to different-being of beings. Not merely the unveiling of what the subject always already knows, not a reaffirmation of what the subject told itself prior to the Satori moment, but the revelation of an Uncanny, throwing the subject into upheaval, the Zen masters slap to the face of the student who asks, "What is the meaning of life?"—"Mu!"

To think an ontology that presumes that in making there is being. To think of a communist ontology that is something other than a merely equal distribution. To settle for a thought of justice as simply a fair piece of the pie is to invalidate the revolutionary possibilities of this novel ontology. In other words, Nishida's novel ontology is not thought of distributive justice, in the sense of equally divvying up scarce commodities for consumption. It is rather thought of the common experiences that are not based on metaphysics of value. A share of the whole in common experiences such as language, space, and time.

Kantian subject-object distinctions are just that, distinctions without symbiotic connections. Subject passively observes and reflects objectively through synthesizing new information via combinations of recognizable forms. Kant writes: "There are two pure forms of sensuous intuition, as knowledge a priori, namely space and time . . . space is not a conception derived from outward experiences."[26] Space is intuitively understood as an inactive external intuition that everyone has a priori, or else there would be no movement, no knowledge, no awareness of anything around us in relation to our surroundings.

In an essay titled *The Standpoint of Active Intuition*, published in 1935, Nishida engages in a provocative critique of Kant by assuming that intuition is not inactive, as Kant posited. Intuition, if it is to be understood as an intuition of space and time, is anything but inactive. Eventually, even Immanuel Kant ceded the point that we learn a posteriori through combining the experience of this and that object through what Kant called synthetic understanding. A thing is added to another thing to make sense of the object. We learn the concept of a bird by combining birds and the concept of "flight" to understand that all birds fly (except penguins and ostriches).

Space and time are always temporal, and this is the basis of intuition, the vital concept of Nishida's ontology; you get not just the synthetic understanding of surroundings but a move further than that, where the subject and object are one and the same—the emptiness between the things is the illusion, the illusion of separation is what causes anxiety and worry, that empty-void nothing is what rearranged from the circular nature of time. An ontology that he hoped would change the world, not merely as decrepitude, but as a circular returning of the subject, where the circular return is not simply the return of the same, but a return that may open to radical contingency, material implications of time, a place that are particular and contingent in those conditions may occur once and never again—the consequence of action and inaction may have effects far beyond those particular material conditions.

The common conception of time is that it progresses in a linear fashion like a straight line. This conception of time is flawed because it lacks an ontological understanding of how time is experienced. Understanding time as linear also creates a faulty understanding of how historical epochs progress by assuming that teleology was akin to the linear progression of an organism growing more and more complex where the previous instant is thought to have vanished forever, never to be recollected at a future time.

What is intriguing about Nishida's ontology is that the trace of the past is always immanent within the being's comportment toward the present, comportment that ultimately influences a being's anticipation of the future. Experience is historical rather than universal to everyone. It is inextricably bound to the contingency of what has occurred and the possibility of what may become. The past, although the memory may become distorted, is never absent, but is co-terminus with an understanding of the present and future.

Time must, in one aspect, be circular. But to say that time is circular, linking past and future is to negate time—or to think of time as an existential contradiction. To think of the past as not yet passed, or the future, although not yet come, as already appearing is to think of time otherwise than as an existential qualifier of itself, that is, singular unto its own particular momentary conditions that manifest as singular material conditions, arising uniquely, perhaps this is what Nishida had in mind when describing "consciousness, as that which reflects, to be something like a mirror; but what reflects and what is reflected must differ absolutely."[27] This is the challenge before us here today. To think of time as a future that is heralded now.

The future has a shadow cast over the here and now, what is, and what will be, what we reflect upon the future, and what it will become may be totally unrecognizable from our previous memories of the future, the memories looking forward from younger, earlier ages, and yet, this looking-glass mirror gaze upon the future, blocked by the barrier of its own self-projection reflecting back in a transmogrified form is what prevents us from moving forward, the nostalgia of what we thought the future would be when we were younger, and that reality of what it is now. If one thinks of the past and future as linked, in one large coterminous circle, then this is the conception of time that we are used to in Western ontology, the future as a simple extrapolation from the present mapped onto the future.

Thinking of a series of instants is not necessarily the same as thinking of a novel characterization of beings at each moment; as we move into the future, we shift along with the objectification we create about what it is we collectively and individually experience in it. What remains true in both instances is the memory of some seemingly singular property that makes up a given essence of the thing from instant to instant. There are characteristics that remain from the previous instant into future instants and there are new characteristics that change yet there is no one property that remains obstinate from moment to moment that constitutes the individual's own-most identity. This perception of identity shifts as temporality fluctuates and changes over the course of the passage of time.

Memories are never completely gone and can resonate in the present into the future. Karmic and dharmic momentum, our habitual energy from the past as carried over into the future and projected onto the future, can be disrupted, and it is important to remember that karma and dharma in early Sanskrit usage, some have argued meant something akin to actions—that is, our moral actions carry consequences into the future, in this world and in a cosmic field perhaps beyond, the spiritual trauma to the soul, to the vanishing point known as the self, the form that is void and the void that is form that the Buddha described in the Heart Sutra.

Nishida thinks of a different, circular conception of time, not as a measure but a thought of the instant as a pure abstraction in the sense that if you cannot think of the instant you cannot think of time. Time is not necessarily made of a continuous series of instants linked together in a linear fashion. These instants are continuous and discontinuous, which is a contradiction people must be willing to live with if they are to understand the true nature of time and existence. For Nishida, the instant is ungraspable precisely because it is temporal.

If before and after are represented in time as linked, it is impossible to conceive of time without conceptualizing it as an instant stretching out into eternity, but that the instant can crystallize and as light refracts through crystals when shot through from different angles, the same is true of time and our experience of the past moving into the future. Now is always now, yet now is the unfolding of then and recoiling of the future. Recollection of the past is always an anticipation of the future and vice versa—and the future is "the thing and self as co-determinate on the basis of mediation of continuity of discontinuity."[28]

In this sense, time is always based on a circular experience with "I and thou" pushing back, reacting, recoiling, and pushing into one another. There can be no now without a then having occurred and there can be no future without our anticipation of it having already shaped the future from the beginning. One must have a recollection to provide the perspective on which to base anticipation of the future. Recollection and anticipation are always packaged together giving a circular nature to this novel ontology, where most analysis of Nishida assumes this was based on a unilateral critique of Kant.

> The subjective and objective are necessarily and in all respects mutually opposed; thing and consciousness differ utterly from each other. One might

conceive consciousness, as that which reflects, to be something like a mirror; but what reflects and what is reflected must differ absolutely; absolute negation must be interposed between them.[29]

Social-time must not mirror political-time, the subject as a social being must refuse subsumption within the realm of the political, time must be experienced as circular and reject mirroring state-intervention into daily life.

The circular nature of time does not forestall the possibility of revolution but presages a type of revolution that will interrupt the future through the co-immanence of poiesis and being. The tools utilized in the production process determine to large extent the consciousness of general intellect that is associated with the possibility of revolutionary subjectivity.

The circular nature of time is a contradiction to be dealt with, not overlooked;, however, the poiesis of production itself is where the truly revolutionary possibilities exist. New waves of technology designed to reduce the production process to zero and designed to increase productivity to an infinite speed are always reshaping the way the worker is subsumed within the production process. The essential component of production is the worker's relation to the tool in which the worker becomes the prosthesis of the production.

Nishida was an astute reader of Marx's "Fragment on Machines"[30] in the *Grundrisse*. The worker is defined by propertylessness and the fascism of capitalist production constitutes a perpetual restlessness and the infinite, unclosed time of exploitation. In the sense that the worker has been excluded from property ownership, but also in the sense that the worker's essence is always wrapped up in relation to the mechanization of the production process. Active intuition reflects production, and is production.

The subject creates and is created by the object. The worker is ultimately an appendage to the causa sui of the machines and yet the subject irreducible to the logistics of exploitation is perpetually exploited. That is capitalist machine is a cause that has no cause.

In Spinoza's era, he wrote of this causa sui as a conception of God. In Marx's era this causa sui of God was replaced by the machine. Nishida, a keen reader of Marx, sees poiesis "as subsumed by this interconnectedness and cannot be isolated from the world to the extent that it be thought to be actually existing, it must first be the temporal aspect of the temporal spatial world."[31] This is an attempt at materialist ontology and frankly, communist ontology, it echoes what Marx said in the introduction to *Capital*:

> For Hegel, the process of thinking, which he even transforms into an independent subject, under the name of "the Idea," is the creator of the real world, and the real world is only the external appearance of the idea. With me the reverse

is true: the ideal is nothing, but the material world reflected in the mind of man, and translated into forms of thought.[32]

The self must be free; therein is the significance of the fact that we act consciously. To think that there is something like an unconscious at the heart of the self's acting is to deny the freedom of the self.[33]

Once we move past pre-reflective consciousness where we are not necessarily strangers to ourselves, we can know our true intentions and act as agents.

Consciousness can be infinite, but not all-inclusive. This means that consciousness of the subject's other can be irretrievably unrecognizable as the object the subject wants to make it into, and yet, subject and object form a space co-constructive of one another, or perhaps it shall be said one and other. An explosive space to bring forth satori is always a condition of possibility. "What mirrors" and "what is therein mirrored" is what Nishida interprets as nothingness, and yet, he makes sure to clarify by saying "in absolute nothingness there is nothing that mirrors."[34]

This is a circularity based on determined contingencies of time, not to be confused with the common notion of history as a banal repetition of itself. Time is the unfolding of the unfamiliar. What is at stake is a thought of futurity informed by the possibility that instants are radically discontinuous while remaining continuous retroactively. After the fact, memory congeals contingencies that break the frame of reference, but not in the sense of objectifying or reducing the subject to an object.

To view even the subjective as objective constitutes a scientific method. Although, we can say, as in physiological psychology, that consciousness accompanies a certain physiological constitution of the living thing…experience must already be both internal cognition and external cognition, both external and internal cognition.[35]

Nishida repeats for emphasis. Continuing: "Experience is originally subjectivist/objective; it is in its temporality that our selves are determined, and it is in its immediacy that experience can be thought to be the ground of knowledge."[36] Experience as actively interpreted is an active intuition that shapes both our perspective and experience of the object and is shaped by the object as well because subject and object are actively coproductive even with the appearance and ontological separation of difference. This is how one must understand time. The past is gone but our memory is like the glass one looks through but cannot ever recognize what one sees in it, even though that thing shapes our experience.

Essentially this is a contradiction in terms. We should however accept that this ontology is closer to the truth about the human experience as determined by its poieses, the creation of singularly produced contradictions—illogical, yet ontological, self-negating perhaps, but intractably at one with the metaphysics of the puzzle of reality, riddled with contradictions that are illogical and make perfect sense that way, a perfect symmetry of imbalance, circularity of the yin and yang that balances in a topsy turvy flow of dark and light. It is not a contradiction in how we think about things but as existence itself being a contradiction, an existential and ontological contradiction.

Open up the future to the disclosure of an undisclosed possibility of telos in nothingness—nothingness without fear of stasis, to be present in the moment.

ZETTAI MU: ABSOLUTE NOTHING

Nishida is clear: "in absolute nothingness, there is nothing that mirrors,"[37] and this is because in absolute nothingness there is no consciousness and no being in any substantial sense. Absolute nothing (the nothing that is a priori to being—nothing that is prior to the being of beings) is an unconditional condition of being. Zettai mu is also the telos of being. Being exists within an ellipsis of nothingness that can perhaps be diagrammed as such:

Nothingness (being) Nothingness

Nishitani Keiji, in his biography on Nishida Kitarō, explains this aporia of absolute nothingness. The end of being in its total and absolute negation. True and absolute negation implies an impasse at which all praxis closes off, a Great Death in which the self-identity of the subject breaks down. If, basho no mu is the place of nothingness that "implacement" allows for the arising of being, then there one must also think of this experience is not merely a spatial sense, but also a temporal sense as well. Being is bookended by nothingness both prior to and after the fact of the arising of being.

What if we read Marx through Nishida's ontology of absolute nothing, rather than being (i.e., money) as the principle of presence that then conquers an "emptiness" that forebodes and somehow provokes dread to utilize a Heideggerian catchword. However, money (and commodities) i.e. the value-form is a Nishidan "formless form"—(the "economic structure" as the base of the economy, the mode of production—is rife with spaces, gaps, itself a cracked-ontology, spaces mediating gaps between thing and thing, to emphasize this point, in Volume 1 of *Capital*, in the last section of chapter one dealing with commodities and money, a section wrongly translated as "The Fetishism of the Commodity and its Secret"; when in fact the actual German written by Marx reads: "Der

Fetischcharakter der Ware und sein Geheimnis"—in English means—the fetish character of the commodity and its secret.

There is a subtle difference between *fetishism* as a finished, productive, perhaps already enclosed form of ideological production, and *fetish character*, a notion of the commodity, as indicative of an avatar of the commodity, value projected onto a use-value that is normalized as if to carry intrinsic value in itself.

An unbalanced "Grund as Ungrund" is revealed in this distinction due to dissatisfying instability and desire-provoking contradictions between the fetish and the fetish character. Perhaps prompting the sudden event of the active negation of the grund that arises from within the internal inconsistencies of the grundwerke. The cracks within the foundation of the Grund are the open spaces (the place of nothing), the clearing, the emptiness, the gaps within and out of which can burst forth something other than the ground itself. Mu! Is the clearing from which an immanent negation to the repetitive drives that emerge repetitiously in non-reproductive intuitions—hence, actively and without patiently waiting until the end of time for ideal conditions to arise. Hence, the foundations of the drives (in Marx's political ontology this is "labor power") the grundwerke, the base of the superstructure is not a solid, cohesive, unified ontological "being" of harmonious integrated natural energies and impulses, but a tangle of contradictions, habits, impulses, and fragmented contradictory drives.

Marx emphasizes this point in a footnote explaining his theory of base and superstructure that begins with bringing the historical dimensions of a specific myopic type of bourgeois economic analysis into clarity:

> Economists have a singular way of proceeding. For them, there are only two kinds of social institutions, artificial and natural. The institutions of feudalism are artificial institutions, those of the bourgeoisie are natural institutions, in this they resemble theologians, who likewise establish two kinds of religion. Every religion which is not theirs is an invention of men, while their own is an emanation of God."

And he continues,

> My view is that each particular mode of production, and the relations of production corresponding to it at each given moment, in short "the economic structure of society," is "the real foundation, on which arises a legal and political superstructure and to which correspond definite forms of social consciousness," and that "the mode of production of material life conditions the general process of social, political and intellectual life."
> Taken from a *Contribution to the Critique of Political Economy*.

Yet, in this chapter Marx makes this point clearly in emphasizing the empty form of value as differentiated from wealth. It is not the intrinsic value of a thing-in-itself that grounds the base of the economy, because the value is not a thing-in-itself, and money is not valuable as a thing-in-itself. Money is the form where exchange-value takes. Exchange-value is a continuity of discontinuity and particularly in "fiat currency" where the only thing grounding the value of a currency is the other currency, the exchange-value of money gives us a quintessential example of Zettai Mu (absolute nothing) that there is nothing prior to the value of money that grounds the value of money. Hence, this quote from Marx aptly describes the absurdity of hunting for essences to "exchange-value" as if "exchange-value" is discoverable as a thing-in-itself, and may reproduce exchanges within languages used within the economy. Language speaks us and not the other way around.

"So far no chemist has ever discovered exchange-value either in a pearl or a diamond"[38]—there is an emptiness, perhaps a formless form even to the value of a pearl or diamond. There is no concealed, deeper hidden form to value; there is nothing beneath the surface of the form of value. Form is void. Void is form.

"Economic structure" could be interpreted as "economic-being" that then splits time and space dividing each against other that would be the "being as a principle of presence" way of thinking of a very Marxist view of the economic structure of say, division of labor. But, if you take zettai mu as the ground of this "economic structure," the base of the economy rests upon nothing, then the division of labor is nothing splitting apart beings from beings—there is no superior being among beings that does the splitting, the nothingness of absolute nothing is the prior ontological principle of space between entities. Deconstruction of the metaphysics of value is necessary if Dasein (the principle of origination of all other beings) is being, but simply to return metaphysics into another being of beings (i.e., money is another being that can take the place of God—what we would be left with is, in the wake of the death of God, we have a new Holy Trinity, capital, money, and commodity fetishism).

However, if you start with zettai mu, or the absolute nothingness that is a priori to the substantialized somethingness of the being of beings, then the metaphysics is always already understood as standing upon a groundless ground and therefore need not be deconstructed; there is no taking apart if you begin with nothing to take apart.

If we read Marx to be saying that labor power is what grounds the metaphysics of value of the commodity, then we must beware of those who would enter into yet another metaphysics of beings of beings elucidating yet another Heideggerian view of communist ontology. Thus, labor power becomes the new being as a principle of presence, grounding the metaphysics of the economic structure of this or that political system, and in that reading, you may return to a state-communist ideology (perhaps?) where labor power then is the being of presence that is a priori to the structure of the state and the economic structure.

There is no "structure" to the form of money, money is the currency that extends into society, like tentacles on an octopus growing out, like Bashō as the frog's splash. The waves emanating from the being in point of contact with the water, the structures are created by human beings and perhaps take an architectural form that when militarized give the place a violent emanation; money is not "violence" but —the state is violence. The state extends its territory by its territorializing process by laying hold of the ground (as if it is graspable), for example, by setting up benevolent structures as a way to situate, transplant, cultivate British colonial power in India, ala the civil station in E. M. Forsters' *A Passage to India* which reads:

> The people have to be driven down to acquire disillusionment. As for the civil station itself, it provokes no emotion. It charms not, neither does it repel. It is sensibly planned, with a red-brick club on its brow, and farther back a grocer's and a cemetery, and the bungalows are disposed along roads that intersect at right angles. It has nothing hideous in it, and only the view is beautiful; it shares nothing with the city except the overarching sky.[39]

The civil station is rootless in that it is put near the city but holds a groundless space and shares nothing with the city except the overarching sky, implying a metaphysical unity from "above" that which is the perspective of metaphysics "from above"; the colonial perspective of power as if given by God, a universalizing mission to bring the natives into Christian metaphysics, protestant work ethic, so forth. Later on, in that novel we see Forster describe that the roads built as a "gift" of Western progress and modernizing are eventually named after famous British commanders, an emanating of British power deeper into the network of the architecture, the infrastructure of the Indian economy.

Money is not a purveyor of value as if it were a "thing-in-itself." Money must have a social component to it, and often, this social component must take a discursive or violent form. Win "hearts and minds" to the use of this or that currency open up this or that nation to trade, if not, there is a threat and/or use of violence to win oversight of a people.

Althusser articulates this if we take a deeply ontological view of the capitalist as true-believer in the rhetoric of its own oneness with itself,

> I'm the one who owns the means of production, and the legal consequence (have a look at the civil code) is that I also own its products; I'm free to concede a share of them to my workers in the form of wages—something that is moreover, quite "normal"—in exchange for their "labor."[40]

Althusser's entire analysis of the hamster wheel of capitalist reproduction is from a deconstructive perspective—he continues "But we say, so to speak, because there is a way of suggesting that all this is not true. We can show why." Simply having the bureaucratic paperwork, the proper oeuvre of ownership at your disposal does not mean that the capitalist proves that capitalist power is a legitimate form of power, that is a groundless ground, that only the megalomaniacal capitalist who holds itself up as "the One" would truly believe, because there is no appearance in the capitalists mind of different ontologies beyond itself; since capital sends out commodities, money, purchases labor power so as to beckon, interpellate, and gain profits that return back to itself.

Capital sets itself up as a principle of presence, the being that every other being yearns to be, bonded to desire as the basis of overcoming the nihilism of the Great Death.

As Marx eloquently writes in the *Grundrisse*:

> When it is made into a real activity through contact with capital—it (labor power) cannot do this by itself, since it is without object—then, it becomes a really value-positing, productive activity. In relation with capital, this activity can in general consist only of the reproduction of itself—of the preservation and increase itself as the real and effective value, not of the merely intended value, as with money as such.[41]

Labor power is affected by capital, capital narcissistically cares about the reproduction of itself as the preservation and increase (conatus—the hunger, the appetitive side of the tripartite soul, the drive for more and more) is imparted into the laborer who may identify "success" as capitalist-drive qua labor power, and not vice versa; labor power tries to be capital, capital never tries to be labor power (except in an election year).

A joke that perhaps Tosaka Jun's work on humor might illuminate, the backside being that capital does not care about labor unless it is necessary to grease the wheels of democracy to ensure the candidates that winning elections will serve the interests of collective capital over the long term. Capital imparts an objective sense of itself into the laborer, activating the intuitive sense of self the laborer has beckoned by capital, but there is also a subjective ethos that "discontinuity" can be a force for non-mimetic, reflective but non-identical presentation to that of the capitalist. The proletariat loses itself in the identity imposed upon it through the capital-labor relation, if there are constituent parts of a unique individuating identity in the working class. What eventually happens is that the working class subjects are stripped of some semblance of unique singularity, the subject is gradually hardened into the objective aspects of selfhood that the capitalist needs in its labor supply (i.e., as exploitation worsens, as the falling rate of profit worsens, as labor competition worsens)—and this is a result of what Marx called the "General Law of Accumulation"—uneven circulation of wealth tends to circulate back to the capitalist—as accumulation rapidly accelerates the growth of profits at the same time.[42]

The greater the absolute mass of the proletariat and the productivity of its labor, the greater is the industrial reserve army. The same causes that develop the expansive power of capital also develop the labor power at its disposal. "The relative mass of the industrial reserve army thus increases with the potential energy of wealth. But the greater this reserve army in proportion to the active labor-army, the greater is the mass of a consolidated surplus population, whose misery is in inverse ratio to the amount of torture it has to undergo in the form of labor . . . this is the absolute general law of capitalist accumulation." There is a correlation between rapidly expanding capitalist production and accumulation and the corresponding expansion of strata of "the active army of labor and the dead weight of pauperism."[43]

One can conclude all sorts of things from this, one important social problem that capitalism is always failing to deal with is this "dead weight of pauperism" the bodies that do not produce anything, the lumpenproletariat external to active labor—scooped up by prisons, hospitals, and mental health institutions. The major contribution of Michel Foucault to social theory in my opinion is to show the institutions that "modernity" invents to marginalize, conceal, and silence the "dead weight of pauperism."[44]

PROPERTYLESSNESS OF THE PROLETARIAT AND ANTI-ESSENTIALISM

In stripping the proletariat of "property" (ontological properties, selfhood), one is also stuck in destitution, one is constantly losing oneself. Being lost to oneself means in other words self-negation. The "negation of the self" implies the active erasure of the ego, a common emphasis in Zen Buddhism with its emphasis on meditative practices. There is overlap between this and what Marx calls "propertylessness" in that the humility of the working class, the selflessness, may manufacture docility that makes the working class malleable to the "lordship" of the capitalist (in a culture based on building the character of the protestant work ethic this is exactly what happens, except, in Zen there is also the notion that the "self" is itself an avatar cast upon the backdrop of absolute nothingness (zettai mu) which makes an enormous difference). The "detachment" of the nomad is not detached enough because the nomadic subject is still worried enough to play the games that capital needs from it in order to survive.

If there is a chapter in *Capital* where propertylessness and the "nothingness" of those who must navigate capitalism as the propertyless is best understood, it is the brief section buried deep in the bowels of chapter 25, a section that undoubtedly also had an immense influence on Gilles Deleuze: "the Nomadic Population."[45] Nomads constitute "the light infantry of capital, thrown from one point to another according to its (*capital's*) present needs."[46] Nomadic populations[47] do all sorts of menial work such as building drainage ditches, brick-making, lime-burning, railway-making, and may be used to improve towns and villages that lack sanitary arrangements.[48] Moving around so often doing dirty jobs makes the nomad into "A flying column of pestilence, it carries smallpox, typhus, cholera and scarlet fever into the places whose neighborhood it pitches its camp."[49]

Obviously not meant in a mocking tone toward menial laborers, the diseases are accrued in the body of the nomadic laborers due to the fact that their working conditions are disease prone. Working in sewers and diseased marshes anyone will eventually develop illnesses. In this description, Marx briefly ventures into what Michel Foucault called a "noso-politics": the politics of illness and disease. And, if there are shortened lifespans due to extreme cruel working conditions then there is also (to utilize a trendier word) biopolitics afoot, the politics of power over life. The diseases that threaten and horrify the capitalist are produced by the capitalist's need for dirty jobs due to the technologies capitalism creates and calls "progress"—a truly promethean compromise. Yet again, that which capital tries to hold at a distance is that which is produced by the dialectics of the material conditions of capitalism due to its need to open up new forms of labor power, produce new needs in the minds of consumers, and what will eventually amount to a failed attempt to ward off the inevitable falling rate of profit will wind up opening new avenues of labor to exploit.

If anything describes what William Spanos refers to the spectral nothingness of being (das Nichts) that must be transformed into a comforting and/or productive totalized Something a *Summun Ens* it would be the way that capital tries to turn this "nomadic" labor power into something productive yet capital perpetually deflects responsibility as existing in a dialectic with nomadism. It is capital's need for precarious, groundless, propertyless labor power in menial jobs that stir up diseases (like working in sewers, on railroad lines, in high-risk menial jobs) and the inequality of opportunities that puts nomadic labor in precarious material conditions where the lumpenproletariat will accept these tasks because the alternative is perhaps starvation. "Nomadism" is the discontinuous continuity of capital, it is discontinuous because capital disavows its role in exploiting the deterritorialized/displaced workers, and continuous because it is the relations of production; the relations between production, capital, and the nomads that make nomads "necessary." Even though economic conditions provoke desperate measures among those on the fringes of the economy "the economic" is never a priori transcendental given.

Not that Nishida is explicitly evoking images of destitute workers in shantytowns, however, one has to remember that there was incredible destitution going on in the interregnum between the two world wars. Perhaps there was an inertial winding down to post-Meiji Japan that is felt in Nishida's writing. My reading of Nishida is that his views on ontology are in a similar wheelhouse to Marx and Althusser, with clear differences, and some notable affinities. One notable gap in the literature on a Marxist reading of the Kyoto School is that most Marxists are unable to understand, or even attempt to understand, Zen conceptions of self, and therefore resolve Nishida's ontology into a sort of Cartesianism that is otherwise foreign to the Japanese philosophical tradition.

"With all that one lives on nothing but dust."—letter from Karl Marx to Frederick Engels, March 1, 1882.[50]

"If place exists, where is it? For everything that exists is in a place. Therefore, place is in a place. This goes on to infinity. Therefore, place does not exist."—Simplicius, Commentary on Aristotle's Physics[51]

"古池や
蛙飛び込む
水の音
ふるいけや
かわずとびこむ
みずのおと"

furu ike ya
kawazu tobikomu
mizu no oto
Ancient pond,
Frog jumps,
Splash!

Frog Haiku by Bashō[52]
(widely considered to be the first haiku)

BASHO: THE PLACE OF NOTHING

Obviously, there is a difference between the Matsuo Bashō (1644–1694), the inventor of the haiku, and the use of the term "basho" in the work of Nishida

Kitarō, but not by much. The first haiku, the frog-splash, is an imaginary silence where one might conceive of a monk meditating peacefully, only to be interrupted by the jumping frog whose splash at a concise point in the still waters of the peaceful pond makes a sound. Plop! Thus, the sound enters the mind of the monk and the sound of the frog *is* the mind of the awareness which hears. The frog enters the water at a specific point, yet the sound of its "Plop!" connects it with the ear that hears.

In his initial formulation of "basho" in the 1926 essay of the same name, Nishida Kitarō swiftly establishes the concept as vital to his work. At that stage in his career, the approach was mainly an epistemological response to subject-object dualism. With the phenomenological trends occurring at that time it was of paramount importance to say that we must consider "not only what sustains the system . . . but what sets it up . . . where it takes place, everything that is, is in something else."[53] In his later work, what Nishida initially referred to in a negative sense as the basho of nothingness, he would later refer to as *The Standpoint of Active Intuition*.[54]

On a deeper level one must consider, as Nishida urges us to do, "When we think of things, there must be a place to reflect them to us. To begin with, we can think in terms of a field of consciousness."[55] We must consider the space out of which the appearance of separate entities arises. It is the place that frames the field of consciousness. If the subject reflexively sees the appearance then the consciousness is shaped by its field. There is something behind this field of consciousness that transcends reality as a reified object that is appearing ready-made without any historical basis.

Bashō in its deepest sense is understood as the concrete situation, that is, the "placedness" or "implacement" of our lived experience vis-à-vis reality, in the whole of its dynamic structure, that grounds cognition and whence the bifurcation into subject-object derives. The attraction of Nishida's basho theory is in providing a philosophical glimpse into that concrete situatedness that we all live and experience "always already" (immer schon), hence, implacement/placidness, the gap into which being arises, the conditions of the space of which consciousness can be produced. Nothing surrounds the dwelling of being, and modern man is modern by sheltering itself from nothing, but this is an impermanent solace. Nishida is appropriating from an ancient Japanese philosopher, known as the greatest writer of haiku. Bashō's writings were instrumental to the earliest understanding of the Zen philosophy; however, in the modern period perhaps an updated theory of basho became necessary. A human being is always emplaced, as a frog entering water.

Consider one of Nishida Kitarō's brighter student's method of thinking and clarifying this in *The Study of the Human* in 1936, Miki Kiyoshi writes, while struggling with the way social scientists were trying to define "human being" as an objective category of logic or to define "human" in a categorical sense, it is to strip away humanity in a subjective sense, and view it as a collection of logical facts, "society in creating culture and expression cannot be referred to as something opposed to us and not so much as human interiority, but as a wider interiority that includes the human."[56]

Basho is an abstract characteristic all things must share; we must think of basho/splace as the universal power of connectedness. Without basho there is no awareness of arising, of thingness, of subject, of consciousness. Rather than a Cartesian subject where the self is a self-asserting, thinking being that knows it is real in lieu of itself as a reflexively self-positing being, the Zen conception of self relies on basho (and in the case of Nishida Kitarō the metaphysics of zettai mu) as its vital concept. Self-negation is not a dialectic of inner-conflict between self and true self where the Cartesian dualism is internalized to pit self against self. Rather, self-negation means that the self always arises from nothingness. Self-awareness means self-awareness of nothingness as the source of all. In a society that prioritizes being as the origin of everything (God exists eternally, gets bored, and creates more beings to torture), nothingness is a priori in Zen metaphysics, so self-negation brings the self closer to self. "Being" is that which dances upon the prior zettai mu. If as Marx tells us correctly, that history weighs upon the living like a nightmare, then the implication is easy enough to spot all around us. With the weight of the past so easily available to us, it makes it more difficult for the new to emerge in any transformative historical sense of a new indicative of a paradigmatic shift.

Capitalism is so diffused that even though the myth of a central-command casting power down upon people from above still holds a grip on the imagination of workers (perhaps, because people truly wish that someone is still in complete God-like control over their/our lives), there is no central structure to control. If there was a king in a castle sending orders out to the people then that is easier to rebel against, all you have to do is locate the king, drag him out of the castle, cut off his head, and move on with life. That would be the "immediatist" way of looking at, say, the Rinzai school of Zen. The Koan (which literally means the tables of justice and the balance of the law) is about immediate, swift, enlightened kenshō (i.e., self-knowledge). Nothing is terribly wrong, the object that causes oppression is removed, the peasants can live on knowing that the problem was solved and all is well and good. If, on the other hand, capitalism is not a single sovereign casting down power from above, then it outflanks the subject on all sides, as if to situate itself within the mind as a parasite of the mind. Relations of capital are invisible, "not a thing, but a set of social relations mediated through things," as Georgy Lukacs was apt to note.[57]

In Marx's dialectical methodology only the totality can give an explanation. "Human anatomy contains the key to understanding the anatomy of the ape."[58] The implications of the higher development can only be known once the higher form is already known, hence, communism as a higher development must be known as an actually existing ontological presence to know how communism would supply an understanding of capitalism, the way that capitalism supplies its understanding of ancient economies. Dialectical universalism, if understood as originating and culminating in zettai mu (absolute nothingness), cannot be understood as "substantial" oneness, because that would resolve the dialectic to an absolute somethingness. This would end in a kind of substantialism that Nishida Kitarō was trying to offer an alternative to and perhaps this makes sense in lieu of this aporia and the vital concept of bashō in Zen philosophy and the importance of place as a dialectic. Lenin once said "the fundamental thesis of the Marxist dialectic is that all limits in nature and society are conventional and mobile, there is no phenomenon that cannot, in certain conditions, be transformed into its opposite."[59]

Once basic material needs are met, the next thing that happens is the invention of new needs as humans then look around to satisfy more complex issues of desire—love, affection, purpose, and creative fulfillment. Human life is about both freedom and necessity or, to put it in Buddhist terms, rather than necessity, "yoking"—necessary needs are always a part of life, you will always be hungry if you are alive, you are yoked to your hunger, your body. However, there is also a class conditioned "unconscious" of one's particular consciousness within socio-historical and economic conditions. This class conditioned "unconscious" can be a yoke that one must thwart. To be clear, Zen differs in that it is not a religion. Linguistically, religion derives from the word "heilige" to bind oneself to something else. Religion means aligning your consciousness to God as if "God" were a central point, an Archimedean Point looking down from the cosmos.

Zen is not a religion, it is a process of self-discovery that denies yoking and binding to an ephemeral figure as the path to personal freedom. As developed elsewhere in the book, Zen in various forms, be it Rinzai or Sōtō, takes the path of liberation through cutting the yokes and ties that bind. One way that Nishida reveals this freedom is by allowing his readers to see what is hidden in plain sight—the mediating bonds between entities are synthetically produced from our narrow field of consciousness, a process that he writes about in almost scientific terms, but with the implication that deepening awareness will allow the subject to see through the clearing.

The clearing, the opening, the space, and the opening of time are allowed by the emergence of logos, but logos are the defining ontological capacity for creativity that is particular to human beings. Our creative-productive capacity as human beings to make things that constitute the emergence of logos, in other words, it is poiesis that is prior to logos. It is not that one is reflective and pondering and then forms an idea of the wheel and then develops this technology, as if out of thin air. The wheels are a technology in the sense of being a technique that enhances production. Labor power created the wheel through the spark of poiesis and logos (our creative, logical, and productive capacities as humans) during an era when wheels became necessary to supply the material needs of human beings. The creative spark of the subject provokes the logos and the logos can emerge through the opening of freedom. Therefore, technologies arise from production, production of material needs being the reaction to some sort of material need, however, the examples Marx often uses to characterize technological inventions as meeting the needs of enhanced production if and only if these technologies enhance profitability for the capitalist and meet a need for the consumer, are classical examples of technological production.

NEO-LIBERALISM

Western capitalism after World War II transitioned into what is now called "Neo-Liberalism." This was not something that Nishida Kitarō or Karl Marx lived through. Therefore, there are aspects of the "economism" of neo-liberalism that they could not have foreseen. This economic policy, associated with the Bretton Woods Organizations created after the war (World Trade Organization, World Bank, GATT) and presaged the completion of the world market, reached world hegemony for capital after the fall of the Soviet Union in the late twentieth century. Neo-Liberalism fused anti-state paranoia after the rise of fascism and the conflation of something called "Communism" in the common imaginary of the proletariat, with the unleashing of global capital synchronous with the deconstruction of state, and the rise of totalitarian levels of economic inequality.

The big takeaway is that the alienation of capitalism is subverted toward the state, and shielded away from global capital, through the frame of the ideological superstructures. Written about extensively in Marx's reaction of Stirner in *The German Ideology* ("Private Property = egotistical property, state property = collective power, which is cast as threatening to egotistical power, therefore, the paranoia of the egoist/private property consciousness, is easily cast upon the state).[60]

Neo-Liberalism is now the disintegration of imagination in the complete and utter lack of alternatives, therefore capitalism is effaced as a signifier because it is submersed in naturalism. Proving the point that there is a lack of alternative visions, not to mention a lack of alternative praxis, there is scant critical Marxism on the emergence of competing state-monopoly capitalisms, rather than alternatives, in the form of BRICS Organizations (Brazil, Russia, India, China, South Africa), renamed into the New Development Bank, as a capitalist alternative to the Western Hegemony over global capital.

Neo-liberalism is often used to refer to a new kind of market-driven capitalism that promotes deregulation, lowering trade barriers, minimal interference from the state by cutting bureaucracy, privatization, and austerity budgets. Neo-liberalism indicates a re-establishment or a return of market-driven economies as presenting capitalism as if it were the only choice left with which to define the political and social categories of freedom. Neo-liberalism is a new form of liberalism that has given up on structural alternatives to capitalism and has resigned itself to reforming capitalist policies, rather than a structural break from capitalism in and of itself.

Something like a minimum-wage increase rather than questioning "first principles of capitalist ideology" such as "why wage-labor at all?" is a retreat into neo-liberalism which is the basic form of leftism that remains in the west since the end of the cold war. Culturally it may be accompanied by nostalgia, retro-chic, cultural memories that are utilized as ready-made templates for contemporary cultural forms. Drawing from already existing cultural forms and appropriating them with slight modulations to appeal to the initiate and the connoisseur in the same way, so as to efface "high culture," and to mass-produce cultural commodities with the goal of reaching the widest audience possible, these are the trademarks of the ideological superstructure of neo-liberalism.

On a cultural level, the superstructures rely on mass-homogenization of subjectivity that draws from an aesthetic of the margins where the repetition of difference is enacted in the service of the mainstream. For example, a new band can create a song that sounds exactly like brit-pop, or a new wave from 1982, with slight modulations to make it subtly nostalgic. The other new form of neo-liberal market logic is the logic of globalization, whereby this homogenization process of cultural forms and the mass production of commodities throughout the world has now made a global market where the same cheeseburger can be consumed in a McDonald's New York City in exactly the same way as in Tokyo, Japan. The world market threatens to obliterate cultural differences in the name of "economic growth and progress."

This also has an effect on the importation of eastern thought to the west where typically one winds up with the most watered-down productivist form of Zen—the mindfulness practices that one might get at a corporate team-building retreat to make employees more productive and efficient at work. A mind-only form of consciousness is akin to telekinesis where people take meditation to mean something akin to "think and grow rich" where one can train the mind to magnetize wealth toward oneself, a most narcissistic form of neo-liberalist interpretations of enlightenment.

In this process of neo-liberalism, the reestablishment of capitalism as the only structure, and with it the retro-chic of prior forms and cultural nostalgia that goes along with it, gives consumers a sense of placelessness, of ungrounded-being, of nomadism, of being deterritorialized. Any codes, any rules, any laws that previously held a grip on social order are shredded and the only thing that seems to hold the system together is the nostalgic self-referentiality to prior cultural forms that feign nouveau-chic while the trap of nostalgia has been sprung upon consumers. With transnational corporations accumulating so much capital that their empires span the global economy, not bound by national loyalties or governmental strictures of law that would apply to the proletariat in a completely different way, the placelessness of capital as political power is represented to the proletariat in merely cultural consumption. Placelessness as a consumer product, where McDonald's can set up franchises in any corner of the planet, is not the kind of cosmological placelessness that evokes a sense of the Great Death and the Great Doubt. When we are awash at sea in the topsy turvy chaos of the cosmos, then we can feel our ineptitude while attempting to grasp and see the absolute nothingness that marks the fact that we are thrown into finitude. Place has no place, the ground cannot be mastered.

NECESSITY AND FREEDOM, DELIMITED BY PLACELESSNESS

Necessity is what is necessary for life, our material needs. Freedom is always limited by these necessities, in the sense that life can only be sustained by the recurrence of "tanha"; or thirst, desire, appetites, and so on. One might ask if someone is to live an examined life, where do the resources necessary to quench these thirsts, desires, and appetites come from?—the land, the earth, the ground. Therefore, in the third volume of *Capital*, Marx writes that the base of value is land and labor power, rather than the narrowly examining factories and mass production. He turned to an expansive view of production beyond the factory walls, to dig into deeper and deeper the totalities of subsumption and reification using land, and its payment as "ground rent"—a wasteful expenditure. It is crucial to notice that the rise of fascism was all about land and property, territorializing, and pinning down nomadic labor power through political theology, which has had a totalizing effect.

If all that exists as a historical actuality is that which has been produced, and production revolves around this dialectic of freedom and necessity, then there are aspects of being a human being that are bound by the limitations of the historical actuality of the present conjuncture of material conditions as these conditions have been historically produced as such.

Conditions of possibility to end alienation are contingent upon labor power placed within basho no benshōshō, the dialectics of place, that is, place in relation to other places with consciousness expanded in its universality to an indeterminate "nothing" (mu), encompassing determinate beings (yū). Nishida writes:

> The true a priori would have to be that which constitutes its own content within itself. Thus, we may conceive . . . a domain category beyond constitutive form. To see universal concepts determined in the object realm of our cognition is due to this place determining itself.[61]

Nishida is most concerned about passivity, especially as many critics of Marx have seized upon what appears to be the rather passive notion of consciousness in his 1859, *A Contribution to a Critique of Political Economy*, where he writes:

> In the social production of their existence, men inevitably enter into definite relations, which are independent of their will, namely relations of production appropriate to a given stage in the development of their material forces of production. The totality of these relations of production constitutes the economic structure of society, the real foundation on which arises a legal and political superstructure and to which correspond definite forms of social consciousness. The mode of production of material life conditions the general process of social, political and intellectual life. It is not the consciousness of men that determines their existence, but their social existence that determines their consciousness.[62]

This, one might conclude, inspires Nishida to often write in critical tones toward these kinds of apparently passive sentiments that are taken at face value. Marx appears to say that consciousness is a passive receptacle of the social conditions surrounding the subject. Nishida writes critically and honestly about the gap, the nothing, the space, the emptiness between entities which evokes the space between entities as the groundless ground of a non-substantialist ontological project.

> In order to say that a certain effect is born of the interaction of thing and thing, there must always be conditions; there must always be a situation. A thing, nevertheless, must be something independent, something fixed. But in that an independent thing is constituted in a double opposition, in an infinity of oppositions, change cannot even be conceived. This is because with the disappearance of thing interacting with thing, something like force is inconceivable. Force does not merely belong to a single thing, nor is it something divorced from the thing. To negate external causality is of necessity nothing other than to lapse into subjectivism or idealism. What sort of thing, then, is "condition"? The true condition, gives rise to a certain event that depends on its conditions, or what is

called a situation, is the world of things, rather it is something called the world
. . . a thing is within the situation.[63]

PROPERTYLESSNESS IN MARX, OR NISHIDA'S GROUNDLESS GROUND

In the *Grundrisse* what appears as the "self-propelling content of capital" if read through Nishida, and a greater schematic of conditioned coproduction, otherwise referred to as interdependent origination, is an allusion to "intergenerational"/interdependent arising. How we use the land now builds "karma" for future generations, and it is crucial to remind ourselves that the word "Karma" literally means "action"; it is a form of yoga centering around the practice of good livelihood in work. Hence, a society that alienates labor power from value creates a self-negating form of work practice. Marx says in an important footnote: *"Labor becomes productive only by producing its own opposite."*[64]

Hence, the grounding of value produced in a capitalist society must be produced by labor power value which is expropriated away from those who actually produce it, and workers are cast into masochistic-antagonism as the normative social relations. A relation that turns inward and may reify masochistic-antagonism is a form of self-identity. The exchange of labor power rests in the propertylessness of the laborer that produces by producing its opposite. The dialectics of opposites, perhaps not the unity of opposites, but the morphology that occurs through the cause and effect of material conditions acting upon ontological substances that then produce opposite substances is encapsulated in the famous line from the *Communist Manifesto*: all that is solid melts into air.

In the famous line that opens the first volume of *Capital*, Marx says: the wealth of societies where capitalism prevails appears as an immense collection of commodities. Perhaps this should be read as the groundless ground of capital as accumulating value as labor power produces a value that circulates away from labor. As capital accumulates objects, labor loses objects. An analysis offered by Marx in his general law of uneven accumulation in *Capital* can be extended into an ontological principle of capitalist biopower, the lived ontology of labor as a tendency toward "propertylessness"—what this means is, labor is in a recurring tendency of losing ontological properties, the properties constitutive of humans being, into humans laboring in an estranging mode of production. Hence, Nishida turns to "human being" or *"Ningenteki Sonzai"* in 1938. There is something more that Nishida offers in his analysis that a Western reader of Marx might not have conceptualized. The "self-aware-determination of radical negativity"—or the self that observes the corporeal self, and reveals it as the avatar that it is, this goes back to a completely different history of metaphysics in the Asia. Nishida engages with this throughout his writings, all the way up to and including his final essay *Nothingness and the Religious Worldview* an essay that can be interpreted as a global-perspective from which—the self is a projection of atman and brahman—atman is the soul within the corporeal body, and brahman is the "godhead"; or the view of the self, and the universal soul that extends to all life beyond the atomized individual soul within the singular corporeal body.

As Nishida explains in this last essay,

> Zen has nothing to do with mysticism, as many think. Kenshō, seeing one's nature, means to penetrate to the roots of one's own self. The self exists as the absolute's own self-negation. We exist as the many through the self-negation of the One. Therefore, the self has a radically self-contradictory existence. The very process of self-realization, in which the self-knows itself, is self-contradictory.[65]

If the land is the base, then the subsumption of the world market into private property/territorialized effect on the absolute sense of self in a general form, the material conditions that produce consciousness in neo-liberal capitalism are formed on the basis of territorializing land into ground rent; therefore, the kenshō described by Nishida *must* create itself as a radically self-contradictory existence as antithetical to this absolutizing One-ness with this base.

Hence, the last lines in Nishida's last essay:

"The state reflects the corruption of the pure land in this world."

Mu No Jikakuteki Gentei (The Self-Aware Determination of Radical Negativity)

Nishida's work on self-negating selfhood provides a dialectic with nothingness and self. Self is an avatar, an empty form, and before that is the nothingness, out of nothingness is the self, not vice versa. Self is the projection out from the nothingness that vanishes when one tries to locate "it"—that nothing, that gap, the silence is what pulls thought forward. A theme of antagonistic tendencies within capitalism, exploitation and alienation, class conflict can produce a sense that the subject of history undergoes mechanized flattening into merely ideological projections. The future becomes a discourse of fantasy projection rather than the realization of actual antagonistic tendencies occurring now. Thus, what is true in practice, what works, what constitutes labor, what constitutes a functioning set of ideological fantasies constitute the moment when the abstract and fantasy dimensions of ideology find a focalization point and attain a plenitude of historical relations invested in reality.

> *The self that sees the bird—rather than "I" see the bird. Mu no jikakuteki gentei (the self-aware determination of radical negativity). If consciousness can be understood as a concrete result from a prior nothingness, then there are no givens of intuition and of representation. Is how Nishida writes about the self later on in his career a description of the symptomatic way that this antagonism is left unresolved as the subject finds itself fluttering like a bird in the midst of market forces?*
>
> *The market value is always different, is always below or above this average value of a commodity. Market value equates itself with real value by means of its constant oscillations, never by means of an equation with real value as if the latter were a third party, but rather by means of constant nonequation of itself (as Hegel would say, not by way of abstract identity, but by constant negation of the negation, i.e. of itself as negation of real value).*[66]

To understand consciousness as a way in which conditions are understood cannot be understood if you extract labor from its relation to value, and material conditions are so intricately differential that it would be foolish to view labor power as an autotelic principle, a wheel that turns itself. Consciousness is labor power in its material conditions, related to capital, value, production, the instruments of production, place (implacement/basho), and labor power is not the essence (or Aristotlean "substance") of human existence. Labor power can be a force or valiance for human life to exist throughout human history, and yet, if we take Nishida's views on force seriously, there is always a gap between subjects that can tear apart the force that appears to bond entity A to entity B, as if there is a merely mono-causal and mono-effectual relation between two (or more) entities. "Production in general is an abstraction," then "production also is not only a particular production. Rather, it is always a certain social body, a social subject, which is active in a greater or sparser totality of branches of production."[67]

Consciousness is an effect of social relations rather than a concrete substantive fact. "The scientifically correct method (takes) the concrete as concrete because it is the concentration of many determinations, hence unity of the diverse."[68] Marx constructs a view of consciousness from the assertion that one cannot begin from concrete or real a priori givens of intuition and representation. His method is uniquely Vedic in that it takes the concrete as a result (the self that sees the bird—no jikakuteki gentei)—self-knowledge as a determinate horizon that is produced. The internal cognitive perception is only possible through this prior determination, that is internal qua external—both inside and outside the substantial form of the body. Subject (shukan) as a cognitive, epistemological, phenomenological subject that is given to exist prior to cognition, knowing, and experience is that which aspires to transcend beyond its corporeal finitude. Cognition would be impossible without some semblance of prior active intuition, however, selfhood can only temporarily become fully fixed on one situated point. Selfhood is a prior nothingness upon which its corporeal form dances as if merely an avatar.

If the self truly identifies with objective reality as objective then that form of clinging keeps the self stuck in samsara. Once the illusion is identified as the illusion that it is, then the self is freed. In other words, truth is an illusion we have forgotten is an illusion, remembering that truth is an illusion is a key to breaking the cycle of rebirth and reaching nirvana (transcendence of the desires of the flesh—and also, the literal word for when the funeral pyre is extinguished after the corporeal form has been cremated).

In combining Nishida with Marx, there is a sense that Nishida's work is much more than simply a phenomenology. It is in philosophy, morality, religion, governance that we see the result of the conditioning of human beings. Marx's materialism asserts that the conditions of production determine the concrete character of human life. In Nishidan words, this would be "active intuition" the act of doing, making, producing, and creating is what creates the self, creates the history necessary to produce a subject. In doing this, one gets an expansive view of Marxist "production," it is not merely someone in a factory, but production includes all aspects of material conditions, aesthetic and ideological production as well as the production of, and amplification of, the body itself—"Nature becomes one of the organs of his own activity, annexes his own organs, adding stature to his own body."[69]

Nishida Kitarō begins his 1938 essay "Human Being" by saying that human history begins with the process of production. Humans emerge as tool-making beings that can produce and reproduce their own basic needs. What this does is open up a clearing in time and space that allows for the logos to emerge, and to put this in terms that Marx might have used, necessities could be reproduced with briefer turnover times.

In saying this, humans are both creative and an integral part of the creative process that allows for production to occur; without human beings there would be no tools, without tools there would be no human being. Tools allow for the contemplative qualities of human beings and yet with tools there is a subjective aspect with which the tools can be used. Tools are not merely ready-made, tools are "there" (inherited and developed from prior generations of human beings), but man is not bound by merely the objective usefulness of that tool. A hammer can be used to hammer a nail, or it can be used as a weapon to destroy life, or as an object that enhances aesthetic reflection, a painting of a hammer is a use for the hammer beyond its mere utility in hammering and it would be a different sense of logos. History emerges as humans become tool-making animals, which allows for the conditions of appreciable material progress to occur, and this event was not a clumsy political accident but set in motion of technical inertia upon a political plane.

Even with the development of human beings as tool-making and tool-using creatures, man is cast into the world into a dialectic of freedom and necessity. Humans are always free to do whatever, and yet, survival depends upon the necessity of providing food, clothing, and shelter for survival. If man fades too far onto one side of the dialectic, say, becoming totally and absolutely free, this would mean a line of flight from necessity—and necessity requires work. To grow food, to make clothing, to build homes require that labor power is utilized in some way. Yet, if human beings are completely obsessed only with the necessity of producing basic needs then human beings would squash the faculty of human logos (reason) by objectifying it in pure utility of labor power. Humans must exercise some freedom to develop poiesis or the creative activity by which human beings bring something into existence that has not existed before.

Nishida's hypothesis is that poiesis develops prior to logos—"*logos emerges from poiesis.*"[70] Or, to put it in the words that Marx utilized in *The German Ideology*:

> Humans must be in a position to live in order to be able to "make history" . . . but life involves before everything else eating and drinking, housing, clothing, and various other things. The first historical act is thus the production of the means to satisfy these needs, the production of material life itself.[71]

THE "TERRITORIALIZING" OF LAND

Privatizing, or more accurately, the "territorializing" of land traps in wealth, labor power is penned in as if human livestock, in the sense that capital hopes the stock-value, the market value of labor power will increase over time. Locked into territorial battles that waste most of the resources that human life and animal life rely upon. Marx himself says that land and labor power are the "original sources of all wealth."[72] The base of the economy is labor power **and** the available use of land, with the superstructures of law, the state, private property being the ideological "ethos" built atop that reflect and reproduce the social order at the base.

Karma Yoga spans back to some of the earliest forms of Hindu practice and it entails a sense of developing a meaningful purpose to the work one conducts during the course of a lifetime. Karma, translated from Sanskrit, means something close to "action," and in parallel to a sentiment expressed by Marx, the world we inherit from previous generations is circumscribed by conditions not of our choosing. Past actions impact the current moment. The missing link in these discussions, as karma is somehow understood in capitalist appropriations of new-age spiritualism to mean something like sitting still and fixating upon the present moment, when in fact, Karma has to do with how past "power" and actions flow into the development of future merit. The past is a "continuity of discontinuity" to appropriate from Nishida Kitarō's usage of the concept "soku."

We do not necessarily understand the future qua the past, the future as an extension of the qualities of the past, but as open to the possibility of "satori," an instant, unexpected awakening that strikes without prior notification. The future is something nobody expects, nobody can expect it, because it has not yet happened. Troubling as it may sound the future is completely contingent. This means that there is absolutely no guarantee of the enhanced productive capacity of workers leading to increased accumulations of commodities, nor would that telos be desirable in the context of ecological exigencies the likes of which require a trans-valuation of that primitively capitalistic sense of problem-solving.

Stockpiling more commodities without mindfulness of the effect on the environment is to remain in the grip of samsara. If our karmic work is transferred into future generations and we are held within the cycle of rebirth until we learn our lessons, then souls are reincarnated again and again until all the necessary lessons are learned, and the karmic actions we set into motion now are connected to the consequences of those actions we will inherit when our "atman," our souls are reborn again, and again, and again. We are also amidst the inertia of past actions as well, inertia that can and must shift. "Now" is not only now. Now is a factor of conditioned coproduction with what was prior and effects what will occur next.

CARE TOWARD THE LAND

To be clear, there is no evidence to indicate that Marx ever seriously engaged with Dōgen (1200–1253), the founder of Sōtō Zen. He had no knowledge of Chan Buddhism either, and as far as is known, very little Buddhist philosophy circulated through Europe when Marx was alive, except the research done by colleagues of his such as Karl Köppen. There is deep ecology and Marxist green ecology today. Activists inspired by people like Murray Bookchin[73] and the deep ecology movement, such as Jason Moore,[74] are inspired to form critiques of capitalism, not as a world economy, but as a world ecology. Instead of the world economy, we should look at capitalism as a world ecology, where three entwined processes were fundamental to the formation of this disastrous ecology. First is primitive accumulation, a range of processes where humans became dependent upon the "cash nexus" for their survival, going to the marketplace, and earning a wage became necessary to pay the purchase price to obtain commodities like food, clothing, and shelter. Peasants were forced off the land in centuries-long processes of "proletarianization" that occurred where land was privatized and workers were forced into a status of precariousness in relation to the land. The third process is the way in which the forces of production turned nature into something solely for the use of capital accumulation.

Marx already caught glimpses of capital moving toward this view of nature as a standing reserve solely for its own use as a source of capital accumulation. In the third volume of *Capital*, he writes:

> To what circumstances does the manufacture in the present case (owning a waterfall) owe his surplus profit . . .? In the first instance, to a natural force, the motive force of waterpower which is provided by nature itself and is not itself the product of labor, unlike the coal that transforms water into steam, which has value and must be paid an equivalent, i.e., cost something. It is a natural agent of production, and no labor goes into creating it. But this is not all. The manufacturer who operates with the steam-engine also applies natural forces which cost him nothing but which makes labor more productive, and . . . increase surplus value and hence profit.[75]

Perhaps the deepening of the communist project is necessary through meditating on the words of Dōgen who says: "Mountains and waters right now are the actualization of the ancient buddha way."[76] The line may seem odd, but our connection to one another is grounded in our connection to the land. Dōgen understood that when he wrote something that may seem odd out of context: "Mountains walking is just like humans walking"[77] and, "If walking stops, buddha ancestors do not appear. If walking ends, buddha dharma cannot reach the present."[78] Labor power is based upon the metabolism of nature, and nature that is metabolized by labor is also changed by that process.

UTOPIA, PURE LAND, AND GROUND RENT

Pure land is here, immanent in the world, heaven on earth. Communism is the "real movement" rather than an ideal forced upon a reality where it does not fit. It is fair to say that land-rent troubled Marx deeply, and obviously pure land in most forms of Buddhist thought is figurative and literal, and as Marx points out correctly in *The German Ideology* that the use of land as private property is what forces subjects to be egoist, then it would be fair to say that the rent of land reveals an egoist appropriation of nature and to metabolism of nature that then changes "human nature" or at least forms of the epistemological-historical a priori from which the subjective basis of human nature appears as if it were objective.

TRINITY FORMULA: RENT, LABOR, AND MONEY

The state is a transcendent apparatus of capture that incorporates everything into its form of interiority through three primary mechanisms. Marx called rent, labor, and money the "trinity formula."[79]

In the third volume of *Capital*, Marx writes that "Capital is not a thing, it is a definite social relation of production pertaining to a particular historical social formation, which simply takes the form of a thing and gives this thing a specific social character."[80] In capitalism specific revenues:

> Profit, ground-rent and wages, they actually are so in the sense that capital for the capitalist is a perpetual pumping machine for surplus labor, land for the landowner a permanent magnet for attracting a part of the surplus-value pumped out by capital and finally labor the constantly self-renewing condition and means for the worker to obtain a part of the value he has produced and hence a portion of the social product measured by this portion of value.[81]

And therefore, workers in communism must be the owner of their own personal labor power and this can only happen through the freedom in the economic realm of life that consists in the fact that humanity and the social relations of producers must regulate their interchange with nature rationally by bringing it under common control instead of being ruled by some blind power (i.e., the vacuous motives of capital).[82]

NOTES

1. Kobayashi Toshiaki. *Nishida Kitarō no yūutsu*. Iwanami Shoten: Tokyo, 2003. Pg. 207.
2. William Haver. *Ontology of Production: Three Essays*. Duke University Press, 2012. Pg. 11.
3. Michel Foucault. *Nietzsche, Freud, Marx*. 1967.
4. Nishida Kitarō. *Last Writings: Nothingness and the Religious Worldview*. Pg. 123.
5. Nishitani Keiji, *Nishida Kitaro*. Pg. 30.
6. Ibid.
7. Ibid.

8. *1844 Manuscripts, Private Property and Communism.*
9. *Principles of Communism.*
10. Marx. *Capital Volume 3*, specifically chapters on credit and currency, chapters 25–32.
11. Slavoj Zizek. Hegel on the Wired Brain, Like a Thief in Plain Sight, and most of Zizek's work after the 2008 financial collapse focuses on the acceleration of wealth inequality, all of which is concealed from the public "in plain sight" as novel forms of ideology paint a harmonious face of "liberal-pluralist-diversity-identity-politics" on the brutal violence of coercion that underlies the system of wealth accumulation, as cultures are a way for capital to solicit evermore perverse desires as a way to dig out new markets, perhaps in the subconscious desires of the consumers themselves.
12. David Harvey. *Anti-Capitalist Chronicles*, chapter 13 "Production and Realization" in particular, published in 2020.
13. Red Pine. *The Heart Sutra: The Womb of Buddhas.* Counterpoint Press: Berkeley. Probably the best book length analysis of the Heart Sutra.
14. Nishida Kitarō. "The Standpoint of Active Intuition." In *Ontology of Production: Three Essays*. Translated by William Haver. Duke University Press, 2012. Pg. 67.
15. Pierre Lavelle. "The Political Thought of Nishida Kitarō." *Monumenta Nipponica* 49, no. 2 (Summer 1994). Pg. 139–165.
16. Nishida Kitarō. *Nothingness and the Religious Worldview.* Translated by David A. Dilworth. Pg. 123.
17. Ibid. Pg. 68.
18. Nishida Kitarō. "The Standpoint of Active Intuition." Pg. 68.
19. Ibid. Pg. 81.
20. Ibid. Pg. 81.
21. Ibid. Pg. 82.
22. Ibid. Pg. 85.
23. Ibid. Pg. 84.
24. Ibid. Pg. 64.
25. Ibid. Pg. 65.
26. Ibid. Pg. 64–65.
27. Ibid. Pg. 79.
28. Ibid. Pg. 88.
29. Ibid. Pg. 79.
30. *Grundrisse.* Pg. 690–715 in the Penguin Edition is the "Fragment on Machines."
31. Ibid. Pg. 83.
32. Karl Marx. *Capital Volume 1.* Postface to the second edition of Capital, translated by Ben Fowkes. Pg. 102.
33. Nishida Kitarō. "The Standpoint of Active Intuition." Pg. 83.
34. *NKZ Volume 13.* Pg. 294–295.
35. Nishida Kitarō. "The Standpoint of Active Intuition." Pg. 80.
36. Ibid.
37. *NKZ Volume 13.* Pg. 294–295.

38. Karl Marx. *Capital Volume 1*. Pg. 177.
39. E.M. Forster, *A Passage to India*. Pg. 5.
40. Louis Althusser. *On the Reproduction of Capitalism*. Pg. 29.
41. Karl Marx. *Grundrisse*. Pg. 298.
42. Karl Marx. *Capital Volume 1*. Translated by Ben Fowkes. Pg. 798.
43. Ibid.
44. *History of Madness, Birth of the Clinic, Discipline and Punish*, and then later on in his career phobias about the sexual revolutions of the seventies lurking he wrote about the potential for perversions to be cast into this category as all sorts of "dead weight" leisure time activities were being criminalized—monitored, so forth, most likely because these were activities outside of the matrices of what capital would constitute as "productive-labor-power"—Michel Foucault spent his entire career researching subjects in the Industrial Reserve Army of labor power as Marx would have put it. In ontological terms: that which exists but is unrepresented as a political subject, except in the eyes of capital perhaps as a spectral nothingness (das Nichts) to be transformed into Something, a finished productive body. Zen meditation in the lotus position would be the paramount of a docile body, potential inscription into war.
45. Marx. *Capital Volume 1*. Chapter 25—The General Law of Capitalist Accumulation. "The Nomadic Population." Pg. 818–821. Translated by Ben Fowkes.
46. Ibid. Pg. 818, italics are my own, as a way to make it clear that the nomad is cast about according to where the market pushes or pulls the nomad and not "free," capital placates its needs by deterritorializing labor and therefore there is always a nomadic population on its fringes.
47. Not that the label "nomad" is so homogenous, it is a fluid signifier with many fragments within and external to it, in that the proletariat, or the petit bourgeois, or even the bourgeois if they are not careful can fall into the precarity of menial work on the fringes of society, so this "diseased group" often is utilized as a phobia inducing, paranoia inducing cluster of precarious labor power to keep the working class loyal to capital.
48. Marx definitely has in mind a literal mobilization of labor power as a "light infantry" that moves from territory to territory to do menial work. Gilles Deleuze and Felix Guattari in emphasizing the nomadology as the war machine may also insinuate a virtual-figure of the "nomad" that factors into building an ideal-image of the war machine, along with actual material nomadic populations.
49. Ibid. Pg. 818, obviously this phobia-mongering of diseased "gypsies" and "nomads" was a fundamental component of the "Make Germany Great Again" propaganda of Nazism as fallout from the Great Depression. Capitalist accumulation both needs the nomad as "soldiers of industry and as tenants" as Marx writes, but also as a phobia inducing way to mobilize "national-oneness"—which clearly scapegoats the nomads that are produced by the very mechanisms of capitalist accumulation that rely upon nomadic labor-power.
50. Karl Marx and Frederick Engels. *Collected Works Volume 46: Marx and Engels 1880–1883*. Pg. 214. Letter #120. Marx to Engels. March 1, 1882.
51. Simplicius. *Commentary on Aristotle's Physics*. Pg. 562. lines 3–6.
52. Matsuo Bashō, 1644–1694, inventor of the famous haiku form of poetry.

53. Nishida Kitarō. *The Logic of Place/Basho en Mu*. 1926. Pg. 415.
54. John Krummel and Shigenori Nagatomo. *Place and Dialectic: Two Essays by Nishida Kitaro*. Pg. 29.
55. Nishida Kitarō. *The Logic of Place/Basho en Mu*. Pg. 416.
56. Miki Kiyoshi. *The Study of the Human*. 1936.
57. George Lukacs. *History and Class Consciousness*. 1920.
58. *Grundrisse*. Pg. 105.
59. Lenin. *Oeuvres, Vol. XXII*. Pg. 328. December 1915–July 1916. Editions Sociales: Paris, 1960.
60. *German Ideology*. Pg. 369.
61. Nishida Kitarō. *Nishida Kitaro zenshu (Collected Works of Nishida Kitaro)*. Vol. 3. Iwanami Shoten: Tokyo, 2003. Pg. 426–427.
62. Karl Marx. *A Contribution to a Critique of Political Economy*. 1859.
63. Nishida Kitarō. "The Standpoint of Active Intuition." Pg. 71.
64. Karl Marx. *Grundrisse*. Pg. 305.
65. Nishida. *Nothingness and the Religious Worldview*. Pg. 108.
66. *Grundrisse*. Pg. 137.
67. Marx. *Grundrisse*. Pg. 86–88.
68. *Grundrisse*. Pg. 101.
69. *Capital*. Pg. 285.
70. Nishida Kitarō. *Ontology of Production: Three Essays*. Translated by William Haver. Pg. 151.
71. Marx. *The German Ideology*. Pg. 47.
72. Ibid. Pg. 507.
73. Murray Bookchin. *The Ecology of Freedom*. AK Press, 2005.
74. Jason Moore. *Anthropocene or Capitalocene? Nature, History, and the Crisis of Capitalism*. AK Press: San Francisco, 2017.
75. Marx. *Capital Volume 3*. Pg. 782.
76. *Moon in a Dewdrop: Writings of Zen Master Dōgen*. Edited by Kazuaki Tanahashi. "Mountains and Waters Sutra." Pg. 97. North Point Press: San Francisco, 1987.
77. Ibid.
78. Ibid. Pg. 98.
79. Marx. *Capital Volume 2*, chapter 48, "The Trinity Formation."
80. Marx. *Capital Volume 3*, chapter 48, "The Trinity Formation." Pg. 953.
81. Ibid. Pg. 960–961.
82. Deleuze and Guattari have a useful diagram on Pg. 443–444 of *A Thousand Plateaus*.

Acknowledgments

Marx after the Kyoto School: Utopia and the Pure Land took shape gradually, and I would be remiss without thanking the many people who formed the intellectual history of this text. Sadly, many of the people whose work informed these texts are now across the threshold of the dharma into another life. I also realize in writing these acknowledgments that, in a way, this book has been created as an expression of "philia"—the support of collegial friendship which forms the basis of philosophy.

Thank you to William Haver for showing me what it means to carefully read with a committed eye and for introducing me to Nishida Kitarō. Sincere gratitude to the late Ben Agger, editor of *Fast Capitalism*, for supporting my work at a time when I was unsure if anyone would ever give me a chance to publish. Sincere gratitude to the late Gerry Coulter who published my work in the *International Journal of Baudrillard Studies* with the kind words "this is a groundbreaking work." Rest in peace to William Spanos whose books *The Errant Art of Moby Dick* and *America's Shadow* inspired me more than he ever knew by showing me how to read against the grain to see how power gets down to our capillaries. Thank you to my undergraduate professors at SUNY Fredonia whose courses were formative events in my intellectual development.

Bill Martin, whose work on ethical Marxism, and a brief stop off for coffee at the 2012 SPEP Conference in Rochester, gave me encouragement to pursue these lines of thought on the cusp of Marx and Buddhism. Immense thanks to Gene Grabiner; after teaching *Capital* for decades, you were kind enough to give me your course notes. A treasure beyond quantification by any cash-nexus.

Thank you to Donald Weiss whose many lunches, breakfasts, coffee breaks, and book *The Specter of Capitalism* served as a much-needed counterpoint my positions. As Nietzsche said, every philosopher needs a jousting partner. Unfortunately for me it is difficult to disagree with such a robust and free-thinker. Your humor and wit kept me optimistic in a field that has become radioactive towards freedom. Keith Faulkner, thank you for pursuing patient, careful readings as a point of inspiration in a parallel realm through the Graduate Center for Advanced Studies, one of the rare places where rigorous thought is occurring.

Thank you to Jaden Adams and Mohammed Salemy who created a culture of inventive radical thought that inspired so many bright minds at the New Centre for Social Research and Practice. They gave me the chance to hear Nick Land on bitcoin and take a course with Nick Srnicek and sit in on lectures on Marx given by Ray Brassier. These were transformative experiences with brilliant minds whose influences cannot be understated.

Many thanks to those who attended and organized the Why Kyoto School Today? Conference at King's College in March 2019. Allowing me to present my work when it was at an extremely rough stage gave me a boost in confidence to stick with what was a vague idea of a book at that time. I was humbled to have the chance to observe the work of Michiko Yusa, Jason Wirth, Bret Davis, Brian Schroeder, and too many others to list. Thanks especially to John Maraldo who gave much-needed compassionate encouragement after my paper presentation and whose work in the area of Japanese philosophy has been deeply inspiring as an example of a committed scholar. Although he may not wish to be mentioned, I want to thank John Krummel whose constructive criticisms at the twelfth hour saved the life of this book. Thank you Dennis Stromback for putting together a panel at the APA Conference in 2021 on behalf of the International Association of Japanese Philosophy where I presented segments from this work. The feedback from that session was very helpful.

Thank you to a friend who influenced this book through conversations over Indian lunches about satsang meditation, films, and the satori moments only obtainable on the closest thing to the "pure land" on earth, the golf course. Even though we are two paths diverging in the yellow woods, spatially and politically, I wish to express gratitude for having a great friend. Namaste, Larry Castellani.

Bibliography

Adorno, Theodor. *Negative Dialectics*. New York, Continuum Press, 1973.
———. *Against Epistemology*. Cambridge, MIT Press, 1983.
———. *Kierkegaard: Construction of the Aesthetic*. Minneapolis, University of Minnesota Press, 1989.
———. *Notes to Literature*. New York, Columbia, 1992.
———. *Aesthetic Theory*. Minneapolis, University of Minnesota Press, 1997.
———. *Critical Models: Interventions and Catchwords*. New York, Columbia University Press, 2005.
Adorno, Theodor; and Horkheimer, Max. *Dialectic of Enlightenment*. New York, Continuum, 1972.
Aitken, Robert. *The Gateless Barrier: The Wu-Men Kuan (Mumonkan)*. San Francisco, North Pointe Press, 1990.
Althusser, Louis. *Lenin and Philosophy and Other Essays*. London, Monthly Review Press, 1971.
———. *The Future Lasts Forever: A Memoir*. New York, The New Press, 1993.
———. *Machiavelli and Us*. London, Verso, 2000.
———. *For Marx*. London, Verso, 2005.
———. *On the Reproduction of Capitalism: Ideology and Ideological State Apparatuses*. London, Verso, 2014.
Althusser, Louis; and Balibar, Etienne. *Reading Capital*. London, Verso, 2009.
Appadurai, Arjun. *Modernity at Large*. Minneapolis, University of Minnesota Press, 1996.
Arrighi, Giovanni. *The Long Twentieth Century*. London, Verso, 1999.
Augustine, John Morris; and Seisaku, Yamamoto. *The Philosophy of Nishitani Keiji 1900–1990: Lectures on Religion and Modernity*. Lewiston, NY, Edwin Mellen Press, 2011.
Badiou, Alain. *Ethics: An Essay on the Understanding of Evil*. London, Verso, 2001.
———. *Saint Paul: The Foundations of Universalism*. Stanford, Stanford University Press, 2003.

———. *Being and Event (L'etre et l'evénement)*. New York, Continuum, 2005.
———. *Logics of Worlds: Being and Event 2.(logique la monde: l'etre et l'evénement II)*. New York, Continuum, 2006.
———. *Theoretical Writings*. London, Continuum, 2006.
Bakunin, Mikhail. *God and the State*. Saint Louis, Dialectics, 2013.
Balibar, Etienne. *We, the People of Europe?* Princeton, NJ, Princeton University Press, 2004.
Bastani, Aaron. *Fully Automated Luxury Communism*. London, Verso, 2020.
Bataille, Georges. *Visions of Excess: Selected Writings, 1927–1939*. Minneapolis, University of Minnesota, 1985.
———. *Erotism: Death and Sensuality*. San Francisco, City Lights, 1986.
———. *Tears of Eros*. San Francisco, City Lights, 1989.
———. *The Accursed Share Volume 1: An Essay on General Economy*. New York, Zone Books, 1991.
———. *The Accursed Share Volumes 2 & 3*. New York, Zone Books, 1991.
———. *Theory of Religion*. New York, Zone Books, 1992.
———. *The Sacred Conspiracy: The Internal Papers of the Secret Society of Acéphale and Lectures to the College of Sociology*. London, Atlas Press, 2017.
Baudrillard, Jean. *The Mirror of Production*. Saint Louis, Telos Press, 1975.
———. *In the Shadows of the Silent Majorities*. New York, Semiotext(e), 1983.
———. *Simulacra and Simulation*. Ann Arbor, University of Michigan Press, 2000.
———. *The Spirit of Terrorism*. New York, Verso, 2002.
Bell, Daniel. *The Cultural Contradictions of Capitalism*. New York, Basic Books, 1976.
Benoit, Hubert. *Zen and the Psychology of Transformation: The Supreme Doctrine*. New York, Pantheon Books, 1955.
Berlin, Isaiah. *Karl Marx: His Life and Environment*. New York, Oxford University Press, 1959.
Bey, Hakim. *Immediatism*. Oakland, AK Press, 1994.
Bhikkhu, Bodhi. *In the Buddha's Words: An Anthology of Discourses from the Pali Canon*. Boston, Wisdom Publications, 2005.
Bookchin, Murray. *The Ecology of Freedom: The Emergence and Dissolution of Hierarchy*. Oakland, AK Press, 2005.
Bottomore, Tom. *A Dictionary of Marxist Thought*. Oxford, Blackwell Publishing, 2006.
Brannigan, Michael C. *The Pulse of Wisdom: The Philosophies of India, China, and Japan*. Los Angeles, Wadsworth Publishing, 1995.
Butler, Judith. *Subjects of Desire: Hegelian Reflections in Twentieth-Century France*. New York, Columbia University Press, 1987.
———. *Psychic Life of Power: Theories in Subjection*. Stanford, Stanford University, 1997.
Butler, Judith; Laclau, Ernesto; and Žižek, Slavoj. *Contingency, Hegemony, and Universality*. London, Verso, 2000.
Carter, Robert E. *The Nothingness beyond God: An Introduction to the Philosophy of Nishida Kitarō*. St. Paul, MN, Paragon House, 1997.

Chan, Wing-Tsit. *A Sourcebook in Chinese Philosophy*. Princeton, Princeton University Press, 1963.
Chibber, Vivek. *Postcolonial Theory and the Specter of Capital*. New York, Verso, 2013.
Confucius. *Analects*. London, Oxford University Press, 2008.
Coward, Harold. *Derrida and Indian Philosophy*. Albany, SUNY Press, 1990.
Curley, Melissa Anne-Marie. *Pure Land, Real World: Modern Buddhism, Japanese Leftists, and the Utopian Imagination*. Honolulu, University of Hawaii Press, 2017.
D'Amico, Robert. *Marx and Philosophy of Culture*. Gainesville, University of Florida Press, 1981.
Davis, Bret; Schroeder, Brian; and Wirth, Jason, eds. *Japanese and Continental Philosophy: Conversations with the Kyoto School*. Bloomington, Indiana University Press, 2011.
Debord, Guy. *The Society of the Spectacle*. New York, Zone Books, 1995.
Deleuze, Gilles; and Guattari, Felix. *Anti-Oedipus: Capitalism and Schizophrenia Volume 1*. Minneapolis, University of Minnesota Press, 1972.
———. *A Thousand Plateaus: Capitalism and Schizophrenia Volume 2*. Minneapolis, University of Minnesota Press, 1980.
Derfler, Leslie. *Paul Lafargue and the Founding of French Marxism, 1842–1882*. Cambridge, Harvard University Press, 1991.
Derrida, Jacques. *Aporias*. Stanford, Stanford University Press, 1993.
———. *Specters of Marx*. New York, Routledge, 1994.
———. *The Gift of Death*. Chicago, University of Chicago Press, 1995.
———. *Acts of Religion*. New York, Routledge, 2002.
Dilworth, David A.; Vigliemo, Valdo A.; and Zavala, Agustin Jacinto, eds. *Sourcebook for Modern Japanese Philosophy: Selected Documents*. Westport, CT, Greenwood Press, 1998.
Dōgen. *Moon in a Dewdrop: Writings of Zen Master Dōgen*. San Francisco, North Pointe Press, 1985.
———. *Shōbōgenzō*. Annotated by Mizuno Yaoko. Tokyo, Iwanami, 2000.
Dousinzas, Costas; and Žižek, Slavoj. *The Idea of Communism*. New York, Verso, 2010.
Eagleton, Terry. *Ideology: An Introduction*. New York, Verso, 1994.
Engels, Friedrich. *The Origin of the Family, Private Property, and the State*. New York, International Publishers, 1971.
———. *The Peasant War in Germany*. New York, International Publishers, 1971.
———. *The Principles of Communism*. New York, Pattern Books, 2020.
———. *Socialism: Utopian and Scientific*. Monee, IL, Radical Reprints, 2021.
Forgacs, David trans. *The Antonio Gramsci Reader*. New York, New York University Press, 2000.
Franck, Frederick, ed. *The Buddha Eye: An Anthology of the Kyoto School*. New York, Crossroad, 1982.
Fraser, Nancy; and Honneth, Axel. *Redistribution or Recognition?: A Political-Philosophical Exchange*. New York, Verso, 2003.

Garfield, Jay L. *The Fundamental Wisdom of the Middle Way: Nāgārjuna's Mūlamadhyamakakārikā*. Oxford, Oxford University Press, 1995.

Goto-Jones, Christopher. *Re-Politicizing the Kyoto School as Philosophy*. London, Routledge, 2008.

Graeber, David. *Fragments of an Anarchist Anthropology*. Chicago, Prickly Paradigm Press, 2004.

———. *Debt: The First 5,000 Years*. Brooklyn, Melville House Publishing, 2014.

———. *The Utopia of Rules: On Technology, Stupidity, and the Secret Joys of Bureaucracy*. Brooklyn, Melville House, 2016.

Habermas, Jürgen. *Communication and the Evolution of Society*. Boston, Beacon Press, 1979.

———. *Theory of Communicative Action volumes 1 & 2*. Boston, Beacon, 1982.

———. *Moral Consciousness and Communicative Action*. Cambridge, MIT Press, 1999.

Habjan, Jernej; and Whyte, Jessica. *(Mis)Readings of Marx in Continental Philosophy*. New York, Palgrave, 2014.

Harootunian, Harry. *Marx After Marx: History and Time in the Expansion of Capitalism*. New York, Columbia University Press, 2017.

Harvey, David. *Limits of Capital*. New York, Verso, 2006.

———. *Anti-Capitalist Chronicles*. London, Pluto Press, 2020.

Haver, William. *Ontology of Production: Three Essays by Nishida Kitarō*. Durham, NC, Duke University Press, 2012.

Hegel, Georg Wilhelm. *Philosophy of Right*. London, Oxford University Press, 1967.

———. *Science of Logic*. London, Allen and Unwin Ltd, 1969.

———. *Phenomenology of Spirit*. London, Oxford University Press, 1977.

———. *Introduction to the Philosophy of History*. Indianapolis, Hackett Publishing, 1988.

———. *Lectures on the Philosophy of Religion*. Los Angeles, University of California Press, 1988.

———. *The Encyclopedia Logic*. Indianapolis, Hackett Publishing, 1991.

Heine, Steven. *Zen Skin, Zen Marrow: Will the Real Zen Buddhism Please Stand Up?* New York, Oxford University Press, 2008.

Heisig, James W.; Kasulis, Thomas; and Maraldo, John C. eds. *Japanese Philosophy: A Sourcebook*. Honolulu, University of Hawaii Press, 2011.

Heller, Agnes. *Theory of Need in Marx*. New York, St. Martin's Press, 1976.

———. *A Radical Philosophy*. New York, Basil Blackwell Inc., 1978.

Herrigel, Eugene. *Zen in the Art of Archery*. New York, Pantheon Books, 1953.

Hōnen. *Complete Works of Hōnen Shōnin*. Kyoto, Heiraku-ji Shoten, 1974.

Horkheimer, Max. *The Eclipse of Reason*. New York, Seabury Press, 1947.

———. *Critical Theory: Selected Essays*. New York, Herder and Herder, 1972.

Hua-Ching, Ni. *Tao: The Subtle Universal Law and the Integral Way of Life*. Santa Monica, CA, Seven Star Publishers, 1998 (8th printing).

Huai-Chin, Master Nan. *The Diamond Sutra Explained*. Florham Park, NJ, Primordia Publishers, 2004.

Inazo, Nitobé. *Bushido: The Soul of Japan*. Tokyo, Merchant Books, 1908.

James, C.L.R. *The Black Jacobins: Toussaint L'Ouverture and the San Domingo Revolution*. New York, Vintage, 1963.
Jameson, Frederic. *Postmodernism, or the Cultural Logic of Late Capitalism*. Durham, Duke University Press, 1992.
———. *The Cultural Turn: Selected Writings on the Postmodern, 1983–1998*. New York, Verso, 1998.
Johnson, J.W. *Utopian Literature: A Selection*. New York, McGraw Hill, 1968.
Jun'ichirō Tanizaki. *In Praise of Shadows*. New York, Harper & Row, 1967.
Kaltenmark, Max. *Lao Tzu and Taoism*. Stanford, Stanford University Press, 1965.
Kawashima, Ken; Schäfer, Fabian; and Stolz, Robert. *Tosaka Jun: A Critical Reader*. Ithaca, Cornell University Press, 2013.
Klossowski, Pierre. *Living Currency*. New York, Bloomsbury Academic, 2018.
Kojeve, Alexandre. *Introduction to the Reading of Hegel*. New York, Basic Books, 1969.
Laclau, Ernesto. *On Populist Reason*. New York, Verso, 2005.
———. *Politics and Ideology in Marxist Theory: Capitalism, Fascism, Populism*. New York, Verso, 2011.
Laclau, Ernesto; and Mouffe, Chantal. *Hegemony and the Socialist Strategy: Towards a Radical Democratic Politics*. New York, Verso, 2014.
Lafargue, Paul. *The Right to be Lazy*. San Francisco, Radical Reprints, 2020.
Lao Tzu. *Tao te Ching: The Definitive Edition*. New York, Penguin Publishers, 2001.
Lauer, Quentin. *Hegel's Concept of God*. Albany, SUNY Press, 1982.
Lawrence, Cecile; and Churn, Natalie. *Movements in Time: Revolution, Social Justice, and Times of Change*. New York, Cambridge Scholars University Press, 2012.
Lazzarato, Maurizio. *The Making of the Indebted Man*. Los Angeles, Semiotext(e), 2011.
Lenin, Vladimir. *Materialism and Empirio-Criticism*. New York, International Publishers, 1927.
———. *What is to be Done?: The Burning Questions of Our Movement*. Moscow, International Publishers, 1984.
———. *Imperialism: The Highest Stage of Capitalism*. New York, International Publishers, 2004.
———. *State and Revolution*. Mansfield Center, CT, Martino Publishing, 2011.
Lopez, Donald eds., *Buddhism in Practice*. Princeton, Princeton University Press, 1995.
Lukács, Georgy. *The Ontology of Social Being Part 2: Marx*. New York, Merlin Press, 1978.
Lyotard, Jean-Francois. *The Postmodern Condition*. Minneapolis, University of Minnesota Press, 1984.
———. *Just-Gaming*. Minneapolis, University of Minnesota Press, 1985.
———. *The Differend: Phrases in Dispute*. Minneapolis, University of Minnesota Press, 1988.
———. *Peregrinations: Law, Form, Event*. New York, Columbia University Press, 1988.
———. *Inhuman*. Stanford, Stanford University Press, 1988.

———. *Heidegger and "the Jews"*. Minneapolis, University of Minnesota Press, 1990.
———. *Phenomenology*. Albany, SUNY Press, 1991.
———. *Libidinal Economy*. Indianapolis, Indiana University Press, 1993.
———. *Lessons on the Analytic of the Sublime*. Stanford, Stanford University Press, 1994.
Machiguchi Tetsuo. *Empire Metaphysics: Miki Kiyoshi's Philosophy of History*. Tokyo, Sakuhinsha Press, 2004.
Major Works of Karl Marx. *Capital, Volume 1*. Translated by Ben Fowkes. New York, Vintage Books, 1977.
———. *Capital Volume 2*. Translated by David Fernbach. New York, Penguin Publishing, 1978.
———. *Capital Volume 3*. Translated by David Fernbach. New York, Penguin Publishing, 1981.
———. *Theories of Surplus Value, Volumes 1–3*. Moscow, Progress Publishers, 1954.
———. *Grundrisse*. Translated by Martin Nicolaus. New York, Penguin Publishing, 1973.
Maraldo, John C. *Japanese Philosophy in the Making Part 1: Crossing Paths with Nishida*. Nagoya, Japan, Chikosudō Publications, 2017.
———. *Japanese Philosophy in the Making Part 2: Borderline Interrogations*. Nagoya, Japan, Chikosudō Publications, 2019.
Marcuse, Herbert. *Reason and Revolution: Hegel and the Rise of Social Theory*. Boston, Beacon Press, 1960.
———. *One-Dimensional Man: Studies in the Ideology of Advanced Industrial Society*. Boston, Beacon Press, 1964.
———. *Eros and Civilization: A Philosophical Inquiry into Freud*. Boston, Beacon Press, 1967.
———. *Negations: Essays in Critical Theory*. Boston, Beacon Press, 1968.
———. *An Essay on Liberation*. Boston, Beacon Press, 1969.
———. *Five Lectures*. Boston, Beacon Press, 1970.
———. *Studies in Critical Philosophy*. Boston, Beacon Press, 1972.
Martin, Bill. *Ethical Marxism: The Categorical Imperative of Liberation*. Chicago, Open Court Press, 2008.
Marx, Karl; and Engels, Friedrich. *Collected Works: 1835–1895 (Volumes 1–50)*. New York, International Publishers, 1975–2004.
Moore, Jason, ed. *Anthropocene or Capitalocene?: Nature, History and the Crisis of Capitalism*. Oakland, PM Press; Kairos Books, 2016.
Mouffe, Chantal. *The Return of the Political*. New York, Verso, 2005.
Murthy, Viren; Schäfer, Fabian; and Ward, Max. *Confronting Capital and Empire: Rethinking Kyoto School Philosophy*. Boston, Brill Publishing, 2017.
Nagao, Gadjin M. *The Foundational Standpoint of Mādhyamika Philosophy*. Albany, SUNY Press, 1989.
Nāgārjuna, Ācārya. *Elegant Sayings*. Berkeley, Dharma Publishing, 1977.
———. *The Precious Garland: An Epistle to a King*. Boston, Wisdom Publications, 1997.

Nancy, Jean-Luc. *The Inoperative Community*. Minneapolis, University of Minnesota Press, 1991.
Negri, Antonio. *Marx Beyond Marx*. Brooklyn, Autonomedia, 1991.
———. *Insurgencies: Constituent Power and the Modern State*. Minneapolis, University of Minnesota Press, 1999.
———. *Empire*. Cambridge, MA, Harvard University Press, 2000.
———. *Savage Anomaly*. Minneapolis, University of Minnesota Press, 2003.
———. *Time for Revolution*. New York, Continuum, 2003.
———. *Multitude*. New York, Penguin Press, 2004.
———. *Political Descartes: Reason, Ideology, and the Bourgeois Project*. London, Verso, 2007.
———. *Commonwealth*. Cambridge, MA, Belknap Press, 2009.
Negri, Antonio; and Guattari, Felix. *Communists Like Us*. New York, Semiotext(e), 1990.
Nishida, Kitarō. *Zenshū (Collected Works)*. *Multiple volumes*. Tokyo, Iwanami shoten, 1947–2002.
———. *Tetsugaku ronshū (Philosophical essays)*. Volumes 1–3. Ed. Ueda Shizuteru. Tokyo, Iwanami shoten, 1989.
———. *An Inquiry into the Good*. Translated by Masao Abe and Chrisopher Ives, London, Yale University Press, 1990 (1921).
———. *Intelligibility and the Philosophy of Nothingness: Three Philosophical Essays*. Translated by Robert Schinzinger. New York, Pantianos Classics, 1958.
———. *Last Writings: Nothingness and the Religious Worldview*. Translated by David Dilworth. Honolulu, University of Hawaii Press, 1987 (1945).
———. *Place and Dialectic: Two Essays by Nishida Kitarō*. *"Basho" (1926–27) and "Logic and Life" (1936–37)*. Translated by John Krummel. London, Oxford University Press, 2012.
Nishitani, Keiji. *Religion and Nothingness*. Translated by Jan Van Bragt. Los Angeles, University of California Press, 1982.
———. *Collected Writings of Nishitani Keiji*. Tokyo, Sōbunsha, 1986–1995.
———. *The Self-Overcoming of Nihilism*. Translated by Graham Parkes and Setsuko Aihara. Albany, SUNY Press, 1990.
———. *Nishida Kitarō*. Translated by Yamamoto Seisaku and James Heisig. Los Angeles, University of California Press, 1991.
Padmasambhava. *The Tibetan Book of the Dead*. New York, Penguin Books, 2005.
Pine, Red. *The Zen Teachings of the Bodhidharma*. San Francisco, North Pointe Press, 1987.
———. *The Diamond Sutra: The Perfection of Wisdom*. Berkeley, Counter Point Press, 2001.
———. *The Heart Sutra: The Womb of Buddhas*. Berkeley, Counter Point Press, 2004.
Proudhon, P.J. *What is Property?* New York, Dover Publishers, 1970.
Rahula, Walpole. *What the Buddha Taught*. New York, Grove Press, 1959.
Ranciére, Jacques. *The Ignorant Schoolmaster*. Stanford, Stanford University Press, 1991.

———. *On the Shores of Politics*. New York, Verso, 1995.
———. *Disagreement: Politics and Philosophy*. Minneapolis, University of Minnesota Press, 2004.
———. *Hatred of Democracy*. New York, Verso, 2005.
———. *The Emancipated Spectator*. New York, Verso, 2011.
———. *Aisthesis: Scenes from the Aesthetic Regime of Art*. New York, Verso, 2013.
Robinson, Cedric. *Black Marxism: The Making of the Black Radical Tradition*. Chapel Hill & London, University of North Carolina Press, 1983.
Ryan, Michael. *Marxism and Deconstruction: A Critical Articulation*. Baltimore, Johns Hopkins University Press, 1982.
Saint-Simon, Henri. *Social Organization, The Science of Man*. New York, Harper and Row, 1952.
Sargeant, William transl. *The Bhagavad-Gita*. Albany, SUNY Press, 1984.
Schmitt, Carl. *Political Theology: Four Chapters on the Concept of Sovereignty*. Cambridge, MIT Press, 1985.
———. *Political Romanticism*. Cambridge, MIT Press, 1986.
———. *The Crisis of Parliamentary Democracy*. Cambridge, MIT Press, 1988.
———. *The Concept of the Political*. Chicago, University of Chicago Press, 1996.
———. *Land and Sea*. New York, Telos Press, 2015.
———. *The Nomos of the Earth: In the International Law of the Jus Publicum Europaeum*. New York, Telos Press, 2018.
———. *The Tyranny of Values and Other Texts*. New York, Telos Press, 2018.
Shinran. *The Complete Works of Shinran*. Kyoto, Jōdo Shinshū Hongwanji-ha, 1997.
Stcherbatsky, Th. *Buddhist Logic volumes 1 & 2*. New York, Dover Press, 1962.
Suzuki, D.T. *Zen Buddhism*. Garden City, NY, Anchor Books, 1956.
———. *The Training of the Zen Buddhist Monk*. Tokyo, Globe Press Books, 1994 (1934).
Tanabe, Hajime. *The Complete Works of Tanabe Hajime*. Tokyo, Chikuma Shobō, 1963-64.
Tatsuya, Higaki. *Nishida Kitarō's Philosophy of Life*. Milan, Mimesis International, 2020.
Thompson, E.P. *The Making of the English Working Class*. London, Vintage Books, 1963.
Thompson, Ernie. *The Discovery of the Materialist Conception of History in the Writings of the Young Karl Marx*. Lewiston, New York, Edwin Mellen Press. 2004.
Tien Tam, Dharma Master Thich. *Pure Land Buddhism: Dialogues with the Ancient Masters*. New York, Sutra Translation Committee of Canada and the United States, 1992.
———. *Horizontal Escape: Pure Land Buddhism in Theory and Practice*. New York, Sutra Translation Committee of Canada and the United States, 1994.
Tosaka, Jun. *The Complete Works of Tosaka Jun*. Tokyo, Keisō Shobō, 1966–67.
Vattimo, Gianni. *The End of Modernity: Nihilism and Hermeneutics in Postmodern Culture*. Baltimore, Johns Hopkins University Press, 1985.
———. *The Transparent Society*. Baltimore, Polity Press, 1992.

———. *The Adventure of Difference: Philosophy after Nietzsche and Heidegger.* Baltimore, Johns Hopkins University Press, 1993.
———. *Belief.* Stanford, Stanford University Press, 1996.
———. *Beyond Interpretation: The Meaning of Hermeneutics for Philosophy.* Stanford, Stanford University, 1997.
Vattimo, Gianni; and Zabala, Santiago. *Hermeneutic Communism: From Heidegger to Marx.* New York, Columbia University Press, 2011.
Virno, Paolo. *A Grammar of the Multitude: For an Analysis of Contemporary Forms of Life.* New York, Semiotext(e), 2004.
Vološinov, V.N. *Marxism and the Philosophy of Language.* Cambridge, Harvard University Press, 1986.
Walker, Gavin. *The Sublime Perversion of Capital: Marxist Theory and the Politics of History in Modern Japan.* Durham, NC, Duke University Press, 2016.
———. *The Red Years: Theory, Politics, and Aesthetics in the Japanese '68.* New York, Verso, 2020.
Watsuji, Tetsuro. *The Complete Works of Watsuji Tetsuro.* Tokyo, Iwanami Shoten, 1961–63.
Weiss, Donald. *The Specter of Capitalism and the Promise of a Classless Society.* London, Humanities Press International, 1993.
Williams, Raymond. *The Country and the City.* New York, Oxford University Press, 1975.
Wirth, Tetsuzen Jason M.; Schroeder, Shūdō Brian; and Davis, Kanpū Bret W. *Engaging Dōgen's Zen: The Philosophy of Practice as Awakening.* Somerville, MA, Wisdom Publications, 2016.
Yamamoto, Tsunetomo. *Hagakure: The Secret Wisdom of the Samaurai.* Tokyo, Tuttle Publishing, 2014.
Yusa, Michiko. *Zen and Philosophy: An Intellectual Biography of Nishida Kitarō.* Honolulu, University of Hawaii Press, 2002.
Zedong, Mao. *Ghost of Confucius, Fond Dream of the New Tsar.* Peking, Foreign Language Press, 1974.
Žižek, Slavoj. *The Sublime Object of Ideology.* New York, Verso, 1989.
———. *For They Know Not What They Do: Enjoyment as a Political Factor.* New York, Verso, 1991.
———. *Enjoy Your Symptom: Jacques Lacan in Hollywood and Out.* New York, Routledge, 1992.
———. *Mapping Ideology.* New York, Verso, 1994.
———. *Indivisible Remainder: On Schelling and Related Matters.* New York, Verso, 1996.
———. *Ticklish Subject: The Absent Center of Political Ontology.* New York, Verso, 1999.
———. *The Fragile Absolute: or, why is the Christian Legacy is Worth Fighting For?* New York, Verso, 2000.
———. *Welcome to the Desert of the Real.* New York, Verso, 2002.
———. *The Puppet and the Dwarf: The Perverse Core of Christianity.* Cambridge, MA, MIT Press, 2003.

———. *Parallax View.* Cambridge, MA, MIT Press, 2006.
———. *Violence: Six Sideways Reflections.* New York, Picador, 2008.
———. *In Defense of Lost Causes.* New York, Verso, 2008.
———. *Living in the End Times.* New York, Verso, 2010.
———. *Less Than Nothing; Hegel and the Shadows of Dialectical Materialism.* New York, Verso 2013.
———. *Absolute Recoil: Towards a New Foundation of Dialectical Materialism.* New York, Verso, 2015.
———. *Incontinence of the Void: Economico-Philosophical Spandrels.* Cambridge, MA, MIT Press, 2017.
———. *Like a Thief in Broad Daylight: Power in the Era of Post-Human Capitalism.* New York, Seven Stories Press, 2018.
———. *The Relevance of the Communist Manifesto.* New York, Polity, 2019.
———. *Hegel on the Wired Brain.* London, Bloomsbury Academic Publishing, 2020.
Žižek, Slavoj; Hamza, Agon; and Ruda, Frank. *Reading Marx.* Cambridge, UK, Polity Press, 2018.
Žižek, Slavoj; Santner, Eric; and Reinhard, Kenneth. *The Neighbor: Three Inquiries into Political Theology.* Chicago, University of Chicago Press, 2005.

Index

alienation and estrangement, xxi, 15, 65–67, 83–84, 108–32, 151–52, 164, 211–16; *entäußerung* "externalizing", 65–67; estrangement "entfremdung", 126, 149, 172
Arhat, 20–21, 64
Aristotle: "humans are the animals (zoë) that speak (logos)", 96; "metaphysics and the four causes", 85–87; *Nicomachean Ethics*, 153
automatic factory, 95–97, 107, 143–44
Avīci (lowest hell), 64

basho (place), xx, 3, 40, 60, 164–69, 177, 188, 190–200, 203
bodhisattva, xxii, 7–8, 15, 20–21, 22–31, 64, 116–17

Chan Buddhism (Heart, Diamond, and Lotus Sutras), 31, 116–17
conditioned co-production (*pratītyasamutpāda*), ix, 14, 29, 39–73, 164, 188, 215–20; general intellect, 107–8
constant and variable capital, 90–95

Dhammapada, 25, 78
Dōgen, xix, xxi, 56–57, 220–21; Shōbōgenzō, xix, 56

dukkha, xi, 7–12, 18, 35, 121, 127, 147, 190–91

eightfold path (Marxist interpretation), 21–31

falling rate of profit, 73–100, 123, 143, 176, 205–6; the Okishio Theorem, 93–95
four yogas, 2–5, 23, 215; bhakti, 23; Buddha and "sitting yoga" of meditation, 2–5, 9, 53, 193; Jnana, 6; karma, 26, 95, 219; Marx and meditation, 2–3; raja, 23; "yoking", 125

general intellect, 33–34, 62, 96, 150, 189, 198; conditioned co-production (*pratītyasamutpāda*), 107–8
general law of accumulation, 43, 111, 118, 204–5, 215

Hegel, Georg Wilhelm: family and "terra firma", 175–76, 187; Marx differentiates his work from Hegel, 25, 32; "spirit is a bone", 68
Hindu philosophy, *see* "yogas"; ānanda, 12–16; awakening under the bodhi tree, 3, 12–14; the four sights,

3–12; four stages of life, 18–20; Siddhartha's early life, 6

industrial reserve army of labor, 10–11, 27, 141, 205

jiko, 58, 111, 173, 191; mujunteki jikodoitsu ("contradictory self-identity"), 67–69
Jun'ichirō Tanizaki's *In Praise of Shadows*, 59

karma, xi, 2, 10, 17–23, 26, 43–44, 87, 95, 197, 215–22
kenosis, 41–45, 177–79
kenshō, 22, 29, 45, 60, 175, 216; *The Gateless Barrier*, Lin Chi (Rinzai) school, 53–58, 209–10
kleshas, 16–19, 84
kōan, 29, 53–58, 66–69, 175, 209

Mahayana, xi, xxii, 4–7, 17, 20, 30, 53, 177
Marx, Karl (cited throughout the text)
Miki Kiyoshi: (junsuina shūkyō) pure phenomena of religious experience, xx; kyōdōshughi ("cooperativism"), x, 101–3
mu, 55–58, 67, 146, 183–222

nihilism, 43–48, 117, 165, 204
Nishida Kitarō: *Expressive Activity* ("Hyōgen Sayō"), 45, 48–49, 66; Fichte's *Tathandlung*, 68; *Human Being* ("Ningenteki sonzai"), 65–67, 215; *Inquiry into the Good* ("Zen no kenkyu"), xix, 56–58, 63, 167, 186; *Intelligibility and the Philosophy of Nothingness*, ix, 32–33, 57, 60, 111, 123–24, 166–67; *Nothingness and the Religious Worldview* ("Bashoteki ronri to shukyoteki sekaikan"), 58, 65, 129, 177, 184, 216; *Standpoint of Active Intuition* ("Kōiteki chokkan no tachiba"), 40–41, 53, 65–66, 85, 129, 183, 186, 192, 195–99, 208, 218

Nishitani Keiji: the great doubt and the great death, 43–48, 213; *Religion and Nothingness*, 46

pervasion, 39–73, 96, 117, 156, 157, 164
poiesis, xv, 32–34, 89, 124, 166, 183, 198, 210, 211, 219
property and ontology, viii, xiv–xvii, 15, 18, 24, 79, 82, 85, 101–61, 162–225; circulation, 10, 19, 106, 122–39, 144, 146, 177, 187, 204–5; modes of production, 10–11, 19, 88, 92, 114, 120–22, 129–31, 139–40, 168, 200–1, 214–15; reproduction, 6–16, 23; simple reproduction, 89–90, 94, 99; social reproduction, 6, 24, 73–74, 90–92, 118
pure land, 12, 20, 31, 63, 111, 128, 155, 161, 166, 173–74, 177–78, 183–222; Hōnen and Shinran, xxi–xxiii

real-subsumption, 96, 123, 134, 144–46, 155

samsara, xi, 4–5, 10–18, 19, 39–72, 84–85, 108, 164, 218, 220
Schmitt, Carl: Blut and Boden (blood and soil, fascist ethos), 176
Shinran: influence on Nishida Kitarō, 55; *Jōdo Shinshū* influence on Miki Kiyoshi, xix
soku, 31, 220
Sōtō zen, 210, 220–22

tanha, 12, 15, 121, 127, 213
Tao te Ching, xii, 5; Nishida and "three types of power" described in Tao te Ching, 173–75; Tao and sitting yoga, 193, 194
Tathagātha, 55
Tathandlung, 68
Theravada, xi, 4–5, 7, 12, 20, 117

Zettai Mu, 183, 191, 200–10

www.ingramcontent.com/pod-product-compliance
Lightning Source LLC
Chambersburg PA
CBHW062130300426
44115CB00012BA/1871